LETHAL DOSES

THE STORY BEHIND 'THE GODFATHER OF FENTANYL'

JOHN MADINGER

WILDBLUE
PRESS

WildBluePress.com

LETHAL DOSES

I will accept any rules that you feel necessary to your freedom. I am free, no matter what rules surround me. If I find them tolerable, I tolerate them; if I find them too obnoxious, I break them. I am free because I know that I alone am morally responsible for everything I do.

~ **Robert A. Heinlein**, *The Moon is a Harsh Mistress*

Amen.

~ **George Erik Marquardt**

Every good quality has its bad side, and nothing that is good can come into the world without directly producing a corresponding evil. This is a painful fact.

~ **Carl Jung**

DEDICATED

To the memories of Jimmy Birdsong, Warren Henderson, Troy Leathers, Jim Puckett, and Lonnie Wright, agents of the Oklahoma Bureau of Narcotics and Dangerous Drugs, who chased Erik Marquardt by the light of the moon.

Rest in peace, friends.

PRELUDE

*"We don't know yet who's putting this stuff out there,
but whoever he is, he's an ice-cold son of a bitch."*

~ DEA Agent on fentanyl, 1991

Days Inn, Effingham, Illinois, May 7, 1991

"You can call us anything you want, but what we are is a
couple of goddamn killers."

Erik Marquardt never sugared the pill. Joe Martier did
not dispute his partner's verdict. The proof of their guilt had
covered the front pages of newspapers across America when
their first batch of poison exploded three months earlier onto
the streets of New York.

Within hours, police cars were circling through
neighborhoods in the Bronx, across the river in New Jersey,
and as far away as Hartford, Connecticut—loudspeakers
warning of "toxic heroin" as addicts collapsed in the street
and ambulances wailed toward overwhelmed emergency
rooms.

Narcan, the almost miraculous antidote to narcotic
poisonings, saved hundreds of lives that first weekend, but
not all of them. Thirteen people died in the first three days,
and four others in the week that followed. Within a month,
fentanyl would kill eleven more in Philadelphia: six of them
dead in a 24-hour period.

These unfortunates were only the first of hundreds who would follow over the next two years.

Their deaths brought tremendous pressure on police up and down the Eastern Seaboard to stop the people behind the poisonings before more died. But no one was looking for the killers in a bar in Effingham, Illinois.

"It's murder, is what it is," Marquardt, known to his friends as "Squeak," told Martier. "I mean, it's not first degree maybe, or anything like that, but we know statistically that a certain number of people are going to die."

Martier didn't argue the point; Squeak had said something similar several times before, warning everyone in their tight circle about the lethality of the white powder he produced in his Wichita lab. When handling something as deadly as this stuff, there was absolutely no room for error, Squeak had cautioned.

But drug trafficking has always been a chain leading from the source to the consumer, one with multiple opportunities for lapses or slip-ups or even malice. With fentanyl, any of these—however trivial—could be fatal. They already had been.

Effingham, roughly halfway between Marquardt's Wichita and Martier's Pittsburgh, bills itself as the "Crossroads of America," and lies at the junction of two major interstate highways. Traffic on I-57 goes north and south, and I-70 stretches east to west, meeting at Effingham to give travelers a choice, as crossroads always do. Continue ahead on the same path? Turn around and go back? Change course to the left or right?

The two men at the table—in that instant the only fentanyl traffickers in the United States—paused for a moment at that fateful junction. February's bodies, dozens of them, lay very visibly in the road behind. More death gathered in the darkness before them, and they both knew it.

A couple of goddamn killers came to the crossroads.

And forged on ahead.

PART I

Erik—Fortunes in Formulas

CHAPTER 1

1405 I Street NW, Washington, D.C., Thirteen years earlier

A freezing rain drove all but the hardiest of the dealers from Franklin Square on the morning of January 17, 1978. It was already the worst winter that many District of Columbia residents could remember, and the heroin sellers who usually claimed the benches in Benjamin Franklin's long shadow had moved to warmer, drier accommodations. On that frigid Tuesday morning, one platoon in America's War on Drugs gave up, at least for a day, and went into winter quarters.

Fifty yards away, across icy 14th Street, the war went on in a 12-story glass cube with a panoramic view of the park, Franklin's statue, and the now-empty benches. The irony wasn't lost on the people filing into the headquarters of the Drug Enforcement Administration shortly before 9:00 a.m. The weather had done what they couldn't, shutting down the drug traffic a stone's throw from the single largest concentration of narcs on the planet.

But everybody on both sides of 14th Street knew the dealers would be back in the park tomorrow.

On the fourth floor, eighteen trainees straggled into a classroom and settled into the places marked for each of them with a blue nameplate and the DEA seal. Those students—a mix of city, county, and state police officers from all over the country, plus two from the U.S. Army—

had just finished their first week at the DEA's academy. They would be there for nine more weeks, suffering like the instructors, the dealers across the street, and everybody else in the city, through Washington's winter from hell.

This class, P-19, had a few bosses—sergeants and lieutenants who were training for command positions in police narcotic units—but most were "street agents," like the three from the Oklahoma Bureau of Narcotics and Dangerous Drugs Control, the first from their agency to go through the course.

The program was the prestigious National Drug Enforcement Officers Academy where DEA provided almost exactly the same rigorous training it gave its own new agents, including firearms, defensive tactics, and physical fitness. All of the trainees were moving gingerly, feeling the effects of their workout in the gym the afternoon before.

The Tuesday agenda was a mix of law and background on the controlled substances that were at the heart of the country's drug statutes. These sessions laid the groundwork for all of the courses to follow, and the DEA took them seriously, using attorneys to teach the criminal law and procedure sections, and its resident expert to lecture on drugs and pharmacology. That man was DEA Special Agent John Maher.

Maher was a former Marine who had fought in the Pacific in World War II, then enlisted in the country's War on Drugs in 1956. Joining the Treasury Department's Bureau of Narcotics, he chased Mafia dope dealers on the East Coast, and learned the narcotics business from top to bottom.

Over the years, Maher had become the DEA's authority on controlled substances and his expertise was such that he consulted frequently with the pharmaceutical and other industries regulated by the DEA.

An Irish street cop with a gift for storytelling, Maher had a reservoir of tales from the drug wars over twenty years' deep. Though he had to present some of the driest material in the DEA's training programs, he livened it up with a broad smile, good war stories, and with his Man of Many Secrets persona.

Early in every class, other instructors "accidentally" disclosed that Maher was the only living person outside the Coca-Cola Company to view Coke's famously top-secret formula, which was then kept in a safe deposit box in an Atlanta bank vault.

Though pressed hard by the students, Maher—who unconvincingly denied the rumor—refused to divulge any of Coke's corporate confidences, saying no, he would not disclose anything about the formula to a bunch of cops or to anyone else, for that matter.

"What would you do with it, anyway?" he asked, reasonably enough, with a grin. "Make your own and compete with Coke? Good luck on that." There were all sorts of practical problems with that scenario, he pointed out. You'd have to re-create the entire Coca-Cola production and distribution network, and do it on a global scale. There was advertising and marketing to consider. "What's your slogan going to be? 'We've got the formula. Ours is the same as Coke'? Hell, Coke's already used 'It's the real thing.'"

When he got tired of answering the same old questions, Maher—who had been through this performance in classes P-1 through P-18 over the years—changed the subject to the topic for the day: Opiates and Opioids.

For narcotic agents in America and around the world, this traditionally meant heroin. The day before, Maher had covered heroin, the morphine that births it, and the opium that is the mother of both. He'd talked about the pharmacology of the drug, the cultivation of the opium poppy and the ways opium was gathered and processed, the history and myths of a drug and the evolution of a trade that stretches around the world and back into the mists of time.

Wars had been fought over opium and heroin; were still being fought, for that matter. Enormous fortunes were won and lost; governments were being built and based on the drug even as he spoke. There was power in the poppy: destructive force and wonderful healing benefits. People and tribes and entire countries had clashed for centuries to possess the poppy and to keep others from possessing it, and the conflicts continued to that very moment and into that very room.

After all, everyone in the building owed their jobs to America's War on Drugs and its commitment to keeping the fruit of the poppy away from addicts like those across the street in Franklin Square.

Maher finished up his talk about heroin and turned to its chemical family, the other substances that chemists have pulled from the opium poppy, *Papaver somniferum*. All of these compounds, like heroin and morphine, have the same effects on people: suppressing coughs, killing pain, depressing the central nervous system and, to some degree, the same side effects: euphoria, constipation, and of course, addiction.

These opiates may be less powerful or, in some cases, more powerful than heroin, but a major difference between them is that most of them have medical uses, and are available at pharmacies on a doctor's prescription.

The same is true for the opioids: drugs that are chemically similar but do not come from the opium poppy at all. Chemists make drugs like meperidine, fentanyl, and methadone in the laboratory, synthesizing them from organic chemicals. These, too, Maher said, were used in medicine, and methadone, of course, is widely used in addict maintenance and treatment programs across the United States.

"Then there are some others, drugs you get from thebaine, the Bentley compounds, things DEA says I'm not even supposed to talk about. So I won't," Maher said, reverting for the moment to his Man of Many Secrets mode.

Of course, the trainees wanted to know *why* the DEA didn't want to talk about these drugs, but Maher had the answer for that question, too. "Because they're locked up safe inside Pandora's Box right now," he said. "And all the junkies are happy with heroin or whatever they can get from the quacks or on a script. But when the wrong people ever decide to play Pandora and lift the lid off the box, we'll have a very big problem."

This very big problem started almost inconceivably small, Maher said…a problem measured not in kilos or pounds, or even ounces or grams, but in millionths of a gram. The DEA estimated that in 1978, American addicts would consume four tons of pure heroin valued at eight billion dollars. That was a lot of dope, and the agents in that room and all the others in America like them, did their best to seize as much of it as they could before it went into someone's arm.

It was possible, Maher said, to manufacture a synthetic narcotic so powerful that you could replace all eight thousand pounds of pure heroin with less than three pounds of powder. If you had the right chemicals, the right equipment, the right laboratory, and the right chemist, you could fit the equivalent of the annual American heroin supply in your car's glove compartment. With room left over for maps and a flashlight.

Such a scenario went beyond theory; chemists had already produced compounds that were thousands of times more powerful than morphine or heroin. These substances had no value in human medicine since the difference between an effective dose and a lethal one was so infinitely small as to be non-existent. You could use some of them on animals, though…big ones like elephants and rhinos, whose massive bodies could absorb the equivalent of hundreds of injections of morphine in one stunning jolt.

Maher was willing to talk about one of these super drugs, Etorphine, one of the Bentley compounds that veterinarians also knew as M-99. With 1,500 - 3,000 times the strength of morphine, an infinitesimally small quantity could be loaded into one of those tranquilizer darts you see on wild animal television shows and fired from a safe distance at an unsuspecting elephant. Within minutes, the powerful narcotic would act exactly like a good shot of heroin on a human. Breathing would become shallow, the central nervous system would slow, and it would be bedtime for the animal.

If the dosage had been calculated precisely to fit the animal's weight, the effects would wear off as its body metabolized the drug. If not, one of two things would happen: either the animal would wander on along, a little tipsy, maybe—or it would drop down, dead as a hammer.

Etorphine is dangerous for elephants. How dangerous is it for humans? Every single dose is shipped in a package with an emergency antidote injection kit in case of accidental human ingestion.

"And that's where we are with these things and people. If somebody puts the fentanyl analogues or Etorphine or some of the thebaine drugs on the street, we'll have a lot of dead junkies," Maher said. "Hundreds of them, maybe thousands."

There is really no reliably safe way to dilute or "cut" such a drug the way the street dealers do heroin or cocaine.

Across the street in Franklin Square on balmier days, the dealers on the benches hawked packets of heroin cut to 10 percent or less in purity. Occasionally a customer would get a bag with better than average contents, the product of a sloppy cut or some mix-up along the lengthy distribution chain from the opium field to that bench on 14th Street—a "hot shot."

The lucky junkie who got one and survived the experience got one hell of a rush, and maybe woke up on a gurney at George Washington University Medical Center's E.R. He or she usually headed straight back out to the square, looking for whoever had sold that last bag, avidly seeking out another just like it.

The unlucky recipient of a hot shot also got a hell of a rush and a trip on a gurney, only that ride went directly to the D.C. morgue.

With these drugs, every last bag would be a potential hot shot. It would be like playing Russian Roulette with five of the six revolver chambers loaded, Maher said, although he and most of the trainees had been on the street long enough to know plenty of junkies who would like those odds enough to test them.

Was it possible for these exotic and deadly substances to be manufactured outside of some major chemical company? Could some speed cook turn away from making run-of-the-mill methamphetamine and go to one of these super narcotics for the much-greater profits?

Again, Maher went back to theory. Chemists in university laboratories or corporate research facilities had made the original discoveries. Those places had the resources and the equipment, not to mention the talent. You didn't normally see that combination in a clandestine lab somewhere out in rural America.

Only a week before, police just outside the District in Prince George's County, Maryland, had seized a PCP laboratory and $70,000 worth of the drug. It made the news because the chemist set up the lab in a Chevrolet camper van: a foreshadowing of the RV that started the fictional careers of Walter White and Jesse Pinkman in *Breaking Bad. That* was much more like the usual setting and skillset on the clandestine side.

Still, sooner or later, there was likely to be somebody out there who would figure it all out, who could put all the pieces together.

But what would he look like, this hypothetical mystery alchemist, this conjurer of substances so lethal that the mighty DEA did not even want them mentioned? And with this question, the smile vanished and jovial, friendly Johnny Maher, everybody's genial Irish uncle, turned stone-cold serious.

This person they were talking about now was not your ordinary drug trafficker or even clandestine lab operator. This was an altogether different and exceptionally dangerous character. For starters, Maher said, such a man would be extremely intelligent, someone who had learned the always-hazardous processes necessary to make an illegal substance, but who also understood the chemical principles at the molecular level. He would be an especially talented chemist, someone who had mastered the techniques, knew his way around the laboratory, and could tell when a problem was developing before things turned fatal.

And giving the man his due, Maher conceded, he would also have to be very brave, because he was smart enough to know that he would be working with substances so lethal that the margin for error would be measured in thousandths, even millionths of a gram.

"If he makes a mistake, he'll only find out when the devil calls him to breakfast in Hell," Maher concluded.

* * *

By an amazing coincidence, that very man was expecting breakfast at almost exactly the same moment 1,241 miles away…not in Hell, exactly, but in a small blue farmhouse outside tiny Beggs, Oklahoma. A girl was supposed to be bringing a favorite, biscuits and gravy, so when George Erik

Marquardt, who almost everyone called "Squeak," heard the knock at the front door, he went to answer it.

He wore an army jacket over a flannel shirt, stinking of chemicals. A respirator covered his face and he carried a separation funnel, absently forgetting to put it down when he heard the knock.

The girl with his biscuits and gravy was not at the door when he opened it, however. Two agents of the Oklahoma Bureau of Narcotics, also wearing respirators, pulled him out of the house and onto the front step in the frosty January morning.

"Is that you, Mel?" Marquardt asked, peering through the fogged faceplate of his mask.

"Yeah, Squeak. Got a warrant," Agent Melvin Sires said as he turned Marquardt around to be handcuffed.

Squeak gave the funnel to the second agent, Warren Henderson, and put his hands behind his back. With that small gesture, although nobody could know it at the time, the key had just been put into the lock of Pandora's Box. When the key turned and the box opened, John Maher's worst fears would be realized, the horror would be released, and hundreds of Americans would be dead.

And a poison called fentanyl would be in the land.

CHAPTER 2

Milwaukee, Wisconsin, April 22, 1965

This was a weird one, and the Milwaukee police officer who stopped the car wasn't sure exactly what he had. He'd first noticed the banged-up ten-year-old Chevrolet when it rolled through a red light. The car had two different non-matching license plates, neither of which belonged on that vehicle, but it was the driver who held the patrolman's attention.

He was a 19-year-old resident of Waukesha, about fifteen miles further west. "Wearing boots, but no shoes or stockings, trousers which were torn and ragged, without any underwear, being unshaven and unkempt," the driver apologized politely and said he could produce no driver's license because he'd never gotten one. He explained that he had bought the car that same day for $65 and didn't have any money left over to register it, so he'd taken a couple of plates from neighbors' cars and mounted them up.

His name, he said, was George Marquardt, and he was sorry for having inconvenienced the officer.

The bemused patrolman wasn't quite sure what to make of this unusual character but told him not to worry, he was no trouble, and transported him in handcuffs to a holding cell in the Third District police station.

It got weirder at the initial court appearance the next morning where Marquardt, seemingly very open and obliging, told the judge that although he was a "nuclear instrument technician," he wasn't employed at the moment (a lie), but was "keenly interested in physics and, specifically, isotopes, and in contact with several rather distinguished scientists and centers in the country for physics and isotope work."

This seemed improbable, given the circumstances of the crime and the arrest, not to mention Marquardt's curious appearance. The judge, perplexed by the sharply contrasting images presented in court, decided that a mental evaluation was in order and referred Marquardt—still in custody—to the Milwaukee County General Hospital.

"That was certainly ironic, though obviously very welcome," Marquardt laughed many years later. "Considering the fact that I knew that particular hospital far better than my own high school and had keys that fit almost every door in the building."

He didn't share this information with the judge (or the fact that he'd looted Milwaukee General's pharmacy for narcotics for more than a year), but comfortably ensconced in familiar surroundings, Marquardt settled in for his interview with the court's psychiatrist.

Dr. William Feierstein was immediately taken with his new patient, and while the consensus at the court was that the defendant was "delusional," a couple of phone calls to Marquette University, where Marquardt had been employed, verified his story "in every respect."

Marquette faculty members described him as "a very brilliant boy with a keen insight into science, and an almost intuitive approach to many complex scientific problems."

Dr. Feierstein reported that his patient was "very cooperative, oriented, and considered this somewhat of a learning experience." The doctor didn't know—and Marquardt didn't feel obliged to tell him—that he'd already had extensive "learning experience" with psychiatrists in the past.

"They had sent me to one previously, after an incident at school, so I had the benefit of almost three years of modern psychiatry," he said. "I was learning to be a manipulator, to get what I wanted from people. And if you're going to do that, you can't do much better than to have a few years of Freudian analysis. One can learn a great deal from a classically trained psychiatrist. They can be very useful."

Dr. Feierstein was certainly helpful and prepared a report for the court with a suggestion that "the present charge, if followed through, would be extremely detrimental in the long run, and it is hoped that it could be at least laid aside for the time being."

The judge adopted the doctor's recommendation, fined Marquardt $100 for the driver's license and traffic violation, gave him a stern talking-to, and set him free.

Already wise beyond his nineteen years to the arcane but threatening ways of court-appointed psychiatrists, judges, and other liberty-infringing authority figures, Marquardt hadn't been completely forthcoming in his contacts with both Dr. Feierstein and the judge. In fact, with the wool firmly pulled over their eyes, they were blissfully unaware that the offbeat character who had just passed through their lives and out the courthouse door was already a career criminal who broke bad at age twelve.

They surely wouldn't have been so quick to "lay aside" their charges if they had known, as he went to retrieve his $65 car, that he was driving up to Madison, where he did in fact have a job as a laboratory assistant at the University of Wisconsin. Marquardt hadn't shared that information because his employment was a cover for an ongoing scheme to pillage scientific equipment from the UW and a half dozen other major Midwestern universities.

The judge would have been even more surprised to hear that his defendant was already the biggest narcotics trafficker in Milwaukee, and probably all of Wisconsin.

And Dr. Feierstein would have undoubtedly changed his opinion about the "extremely brilliant boy…who with proper supervision and some direction could be an extremely useful individual," if someone could have told him that George Erik Marquardt would someday kill more people than any criminal in American history.

* * *

Waukesha, Wisconsin, 1946 - 1951

On what might fairly be called the first morning of the Baby Boom generation, George and Bunny Marquardt welcomed a baby boy into their young family. "Right down the road down here at Waukesha Memorial Hospital. January 30th, 1946, 11 minutes after 2:00 in the morning. Born dead. I was blue. They had to get some life back into me, so I was told," Erik said much later.

His father had been born in South Dakota, then relocated years before with most of his family to Waukesha, where he went to school and now held a solid white-collar job as a draftsman at Alloy Products, Inc., a Waukesha manufacturing company that produced stainless steel pressure vessels, tanks, and other equipment for the food, packing, and chemical industries.

Mostly, it supported "America's Dairyland," Wisconsin's famous milk, butter, and cheese producers. However, during World War II, the company—like the rest of America's manufacturing sector—turned to producing materials for national defense. The *Waukesha Freeman* proudly reported that, "From 1944 to the war's end, Alloy Products made aviator's supply equipment and oxygen tanks for every American plane that flew in the war."

The senior Marquardt, an essential war worker, did not serve in the military, but volunteered in Waukesha's Civil Defense Corps and became a reserve patrolman with the Waukesha Police Department. He carried Auxiliary Police badge #1 and worked at least one shift every week throughout the war and into the 1950s.

George married Bunny Spillman on September 23, 1944, at her parents' home in Waukesha. A Waukesha native, Bunny worked at Waukesha Motor Company, a manufacturer of truck and tractor engines, and lived with her parents in their family home at 504 East Main Street. After the birth of her son sixteen months later, she left her job to be a full-time homemaker and mother, and the little family moved into the house at 500 East Main.

This was the world that welcomed George Erik Marquardt, the first child—and first grandchild—in the family. Called Erik almost from the beginning, his family recognized very early that this was an exceptional child who developed very quickly and showed signs of both advanced social skills and intelligence. He was talking in complete sentences at one, reading children's books while conversing brightly with grown-ups at two, and asking perceptive, even penetrating questions at three.

Many of these questions were about science—usually electricity—which captivated him. "He loved electricity as a toddler and, for safety, Dad built him a circuit board to play with. He was able to wire the doorbell from the time he could barely reach the thing," his sister, Gini, recalled, and this fascination would continue through his school years, leading him into other areas of science.

"I wanted to know the answers, so I asked the adults around me who were supposed to have them," Erik said. "Sometimes they actually did."

Enchanted by this curious and articulate child who seemed to immediately grasp not just their explanations, but the concepts behind them, his family answered his questions and indulged his interests, even as they expanded far beyond those of a normal two- or three-year-old.

"They brought me things of various sorts, books and glassware. I started engaging sometime in the early grades, fooling around with chemistry. I could get chemicals from the local chemical supply houses or bulk chemicals like benzene, and common acids and things like that on the spot from the pharmacies."

He didn't burn the house down, and he was learning on his own. "I began to prepare, again working from a laboratory manual, the simple inorganic compounds and, as supplies and finances permitted, organic compounds. Chemistry sets, I had several, the big models. Chemistry was a popular hobby, just one part of the growing-up-in-America experience, like an electric train.

"I found chemistry fascinating, but I was conservative about it, as I had this idea that if I could find it described someplace in the literature, that would tell me I could do this. I essentially worked my way step by step through these things, looked at the illustrations and developed a vocabulary from the things that I read."

He wasn't just a bookworm. Gini said, "He was always able to go out and play in the neighborhood and find friends. He liked to sing, and laughed and sang often, and he was always surrounded by family and friends. Just a normal, happy American kid."

The happy part of that childhood experience came to a crashing halt with a medical emergency, one that was both life-threatening and life-changing.

"I had a strangulated hernia operation when I was four years old. Just about killed me. And what can you say? The whole thing was kind of traumatic," Erik said.

This was no small thing. The surgery carried an estimated mortality rate of 1.45 percent for children under six, which would have been frightening enough for Erik's parents, but the doctors managed to make it worse. They advised Bunny and George not to tell Erik anything about the procedure, and then told them that no parental visits would be allowed during his hospitalization, which would last ten days to two weeks.

This was a normal and accepted practice in the United States prior to 1960. "I think the assumption was that children that little wouldn't remember," Gini said.

His sister, Mary said, "He remembered 'til the day he died, and he was bitter. He felt like they abandoned him. At the time, he must have thought they had left him."

The impact of abandonment on this cheerful, inquisitive, and highly intelligent child was utterly shattering as his parents dropped him off at Waukesha Memorial Hospital without telling him why, said goodbye, and vanished completely from his life for two weeks of imprisonment in a hell of pain, strangers with knives and needles, isolation, terror, and loneliness.

He remembered, admitting the trauma. "You get sick, they haul you off to the hospital, and you don't know what the hell's happening, it might be all kinds of dreadful things. Parents disappear, and all of a sudden, you're in a bed with a white sheet and somebody sticks this or that. The whole thing was very confusing and unnerving."

Traumatic though it might have been, he absorbed two very important and lasting lessons. The first was that adults had the power. They had absolute control over the lives of children, and could wield it in ways that not only *seemed* arbitrary and capricious to a four-year-old, but actually were. Contrary to little kids' expectations, adults might not know the right thing, and might not do it even if they did. Children needed to be able to trust their grown-ups, especially their parents above all. After the hospital, Erik no longer did.

The second lesson was more subtle, though no less powerful, and he carried it with him for the rest of his life. He said he eventually forgave his parents and believed they hadn't intended to inflict this pain on him. But forgiving was not forgetting, and he always remembered that in making their catastrophic decision, they had relied on the advice of medical experts—educated, credentialed men—trusting the professionals who "knew best."

If these people were as smart as their diplomas and licenses alleged, he wondered, why did they get this advice so badly wrong when it was clearly obvious to even a four-year-old boy? Henceforth and forever after, possession of a PhD or an M.D. or any other credential meant less than nothing to Erik Marquardt.

Segen's Medical Dictionary tells us that Freudian analysis is a process "in which the patient and psychiatrist identify traumatic events and experiences that occurred in the patient's childhood, and which have been repressed in adult life."

Fear of abandonment, not to mention actual abandonment itself, are deeply traumatizing for children. But Erik, who was exposed to this analysis in childhood and at various times as an adult, scorned the idea that youthful experiences like his hernia operation were either repressed or the reason for his "breaking bad."

It's hard to argue, however, that this event did not change his life or alter its direction. His mother certainly thought so, blaming herself for the whole fiasco—and for the results.

* * *

Fifteen years later, Dr. Feierstein commented on his patient's relationship with his parents, and the intentional distance Erik had injected into the relationship.

"He denies any friction within the family and states that he would probably receive help from them, either voluntarily or if requested, but in some distorted point of view he feels that this help would, in a sense, produce obligations or restrictions which would be basically inimical to his philosophy."

Although Dr. Feierstein did not describe this philosophy in his report, Erik left plenty of clues in his behavior.

He didn't have a driver's license, and never got one because he knew how to drive, he didn't need to be validated by obtaining certification from the state.

He took the two license plates because he didn't have the money to register the car legally and knew cars without tags drew police attention. Then he immediately attracted some of that attention by rolling through a red light.

When caught, he confessed to everything and didn't contest the charges, accepting responsibility and the consequences. As his sister Gini said, "[It was] like George Washington cutting down the cherry tree. He did it, but he wouldn't lie about it."

The doctor called attention to Erik's "distorted point of view" that accepting any help from his parents would "produce obligations or restrictions." He would accept financial help from his parents when the police arrested him on a much more serious charge less than a year later, but that would be the last time he would be in the Marquardt home or part of his family's life. No obligations or restrictions, no further ties that bound.

The happy, laughing, singing Erik, the adored heart and center of the Marquardt family, had gone away and never came home again.

Bunny Marquardt grieved the loss of her only son for the rest of her life.

CHAPTER 3

Thursday, September 6, 1951, Waukesha, Wisconsin

School was always going to be a challenge for Erik, but he and everyone around him had high hopes on his first day of kindergarten at White Rock Elementary School.

Waukesha and the rest of the United States entered the 1950s on the cusp of a new era. It would become known as the "Baby Boom," a period of unprecedented growth and societal change as America adjusted to its new position as Earth's newest superpower and leader of the Atomic Age.

Education became a central focus in American lives as millions of discharged servicemen married and took advantage of the GI Bill to go to college, and young parents sought out good schools for their children. From kindergartens to the Ivy League, the American educational establishment made the same sometimes-wrenching adjustments, coping with the sudden swell of students at all levels and their parents' almost unanimous belief that the path to future success and happiness led through a schoolhouse door.

Erik's first teacher was Joy Schumann, a recent graduate of the University of Wisconsin, where she had majored in child development. Graduating only three months before, this was her first year in White Rock's only kindergarten classroom.

Nothing in her training had prepared her for a student like Erik Marquardt. He had many questions. Unfortunately, Joy Schumann didn't have any of the answers that mattered.

"When he started school, he was bright and inquisitive, but questions about electricity and atoms were not something a kindergarten teacher could deal with," Gini recalled.

Besides being a source of immense frustration to the five-year-old, this was a problem for everyone else. In kindergartens all across America, teachers faced an unprecedented increase in enrollment as the first wave of Baby Boomers hit the kindergartens that September.

Other Waukesha schools opened new kindergarten rooms to handle the overflow—almost a third more children than usual. At White Rock, they just increased the class size, which meant Miss Schumann had over thirty kindergarteners in a room that had previously held fewer than twenty. Her time for dealing with questions about Ohm's Law and x-rays would have been severely limited, even if she had known the answers that might have satisfied her curious pupil.

Even if the overwhelmed teacher had been able to answer the questions, Miss Schumann quickly discovered that they only led to another, and then the next. She was barely coping with her other charges and focused on preparing her kindergarteners for their next step: promotion to first grade.

The five- and six-year-old children in her class did not need to understand Newton's Third Law of Motion, or the first two laws, either. What they needed, the Waukesha school board told Miss Schumann, was to navigate the pages of *Fun with Dick and Jane* and *Go Away Spot*, the school's New Basic Reader books, to be able to count and color inside the lines, and to hit a couple of other important benchmarks.

One of these standards that the school thought particularly critical proved to be beyond his ability—so in the spring of 1952, Erik Marquardt failed kindergarten.

She couldn't recommend his promotion, the harried Miss Schumann told Erik's parents near the end of a trying school year. He hadn't checked her required boxes. It didn't matter that Erik was doing basic math, had moved far beyond Dick and Jane's various adventures, and was reading the school's textbooks for sixth graders and other advanced material. He had fallen behind, the teacher said; unlike his classmates moving on, he was completely unable to skip. He should be held back until he had mastered this vital kindergarten skill.

"At that time, there was a strong belief in the link between physical and cognitive development," teacher Gini Marquardt recalled. "Skipping was one measure, and he failed."

"It wasn't that I couldn't skip," Squeak shrugged. "I just didn't want to. I completely failed to see the point of it, and nobody could explain to me why it was so important. Still don't. How many adults—any people, really—do you see skipping on their way to work or picking up some groceries?"

As for Miss Schumann's suggestion that he repeat kindergarten, "My parents refused that," he said, and on he went to another year of struggle in first grade.

Gini described the situation facing her parents in the late 1950s: "He was an outlier, and he didn't fit academically. When you have children who are that far outside the norm, who don't 'fit,' teachers have a hard time dealing with that. So school was incredibly painful for him."

At White Rock Elementary School, battle lines were being drawn. On one side, Wisconsin's—and America's—educational establishment labored to adapt to the changing expectations of the World War II and Great Depression generation, and their flood of Baby Boom children. On the other side was a bright, gifted kid who mostly wanted to find a place where he and his talents would fit in. Both combatants used all the weapons at hand, although the outcome of any such mismatched conflict was foreordained. Initially, Erik didn't appear to be fighting at all. "He was never badly behaved at school. He was charming and polite, and never talked back to his teachers or challenged them. Always well-behaved," Gini said. "He was tall, always bigger than other kids in his class, but he never bullied anyone, tried to be kind."

Through first and second grades, he put his head down and tried to find ways to adapt, but there were signs this wasn't working. "Our mother went to school one day and was in the corridor outside the second-grade classroom when she overheard the teacher saying, 'Well, we don't want to hear what Erik has to say, do we, class?'"

While the remark outraged his mother, who let the teacher know it, Erik shrugged it off. It was just another bad part of going to school, and he was used to all the bad parts by then. Everything about school was a struggle.

Gini cited Dr. Phillip A. Perrone, a professor in the Department of Counseling Psychology at the University of Wisconsin-Madison, who described the experience of being gifted and talented in a regular classroom as "trying to listen to everyone talk in very slow motion."

That's how he remembered it; Erik said long afterward that solitary confinement at Leavenworth Penitentiary was tough, but not as bad as school days in Waukesha.

"School was absolute torture, but even then, he tried *so* hard to be polite and respectful. He was that little kid who didn't misbehave in class," Gini said. But those accumulating stresses and strains could not continue building before someone—teachers, parents, or Erik himself—cracked. And after four years, at age eleven, he did.

"The fire in the wastebasket was absolutely a call for help kind of thing," Gini said.

Erik had an explanation. "During a period of time in fifth grade, I experienced a lot of problems at school. Basically, they wanted me to do this and do that. 'No, I'm not interested and I don't want to play.' Then, of course, they ramp up the pressure and I become more defiant. Finally, 'Well, I'll tell you what, I'm going to light this place up.'"

As fires go, it wasn't much: a tiny blaze in a metal trash can that was quickly extinguished without causing any damage or injuries. It got everybody's attention, though, and the fire alarm that sent White Rock's children and teachers scrambling outside into the cold March morning focused 100 percent of that attention onto the fifth grader who'd started the fire but wouldn't lie about it, and readily confessed that he had lit the match.

Now there were meetings, intense discussions with parents and counselors, and an educational establishment that saw a perfect opportunity to shed its non-conforming problem child. Wisconsin had a place for youngsters like this in April 1957, and everybody in Waukesha—especially boys like Erik—knew it very well.

The Wisconsin Industrial School for Boys had opened its doors as the State Reform School in 1860, a place for "the victims of unfortunate marriages, quarreling, drinking, thieving, slothful parents," as well as indigent orphans and others who "are merely bright, intelligent boys with an extra amount of spirit and mischievousness."

All but one of the buildings at the school are gone today, but in 1957 they sat ominously close to the Marquardt residence, barely a mile from White Rock Elementary—a forbidding, silent, but very visible caution to every boy in Waukesha thinking about misbehaving.

The Industrial School got plenty of experience over the next century with "bright, intelligent boys with an extra amount of spirit and mischievousness." It had some practice with arsonists, too; one of its earliest inmates had burned down the first building on the site in 1866.

The faculty at White Rock Elementary thought the Industrial School would be perfectly capable of dealing with an eleven-year-old firebug acting out his frustrations with matches and school trash cans.

It was, of course, a solution appealing only to the educators, and this effort to remove Erik from his home threatened to tear the family apart. Gini said, "Considering that home was the only place that felt safe for him, it seems obvious now that it would have been a horrible idea," but the pressure on his parents was intense.

They felt the sting of guilt, too. "Our pastor was able to connect them with a counselor, and Erik was allowed to stay in the home, but they worked really hard to blame the school failures on our parents, which created a lot of stress."

The incident and its aftermath widened the growing fissure between Erik and his parents. The arrival of sisters Gini and Mary over the next two years, and the need to care for infants and toddlers, opened it even further.

Erik sat in limbo while the adults around him decided his fate. Someone—Erik believed it was his father—suggested allowing him to move to the South Dakota farm to continue his education there. This proposal was something the school officials, teachers, and above all, Erik himself, enthusiastically supported. "My father at one point told me this would happen."

It was an alluring vision, one he held onto for the rest of his life, saying much later that all of the conflict with school and teachers could have been avoided "by simply shipping me off to live with relatives on the South Dakota prairie. I probably would have sat out there and done the things one does around a little prairie town, and then vanished into obscurity."

Gini, however, scoffed at the idea that he would have been contented for long in the simplicity of farm living, and thought Erik was dreaming. "No question that he would have been happier on the farm, but I don't think it would have changed the future outcomes much. I think the chemistry was something he just had to do."

It was not to be. "My mother's family fought it hard, so it did not come to pass," Erik said, and this latest struggle—a conflict among people who uniformly cared about the child and wanted to do "what was right" by him—firmly convinced him that only liberation from all the adult authority figures in his life would give him the freedom he craved.

There was no formal declaration of independence in the style of unhappy adolescents everywhere—no running away, no self-harm or suicide attempts. He didn't turn to recreational drugs, which were almost unheard of in 1958 Wisconsin anyway, or to petty juvenile crimes like vandalism or shoplifting. There was no more open conflict with teachers or trash can fires at school.

Erik just quietly went away.

The rift between the boy and his parents had grown into a gulf, and though he stayed part of the family, he spent less and less time in the home. Both of his sisters remember him fondly, admitting that they weren't close at the time due to the age difference, but also to his deliberate absences.

Gini said, "He was twelve years older than us, and so by the time Mary and I were born, there was an overlap when we were toddlers, and we have no memory of it. There was a bond there because Erik really was very, very nice to his little sisters; he was a great brother and he liked babies. But Mary and I don't have a whole lot of memory of him being there…little spots here and there. Him crawling in the window in the middle of the night. That made an impression."

"That didn't seem unusual," Mary said. "It was life with Erik."

CHAPTER 4

Dry Wood Lake Township, South Dakota, Summer 1958

Erik's ancestors came to the New World in 1864, a Prussian family of seven that arrived in New York amid the cataclysm of America's Civil War. The Marquardts joined hundreds of thousands of immigrants settling in the Upper Midwest, and many moved again in the years after the war as part of the swelling migration that populated Laura Ingalls Wilder's Great Plains.

Grandfather George Frank, a World War I Navy veteran, found love on those plains and married May Olson of Sisseton, South Dakota in 1920. They stayed long enough to welcome a son—Erik's father, George Wallace—before moving to Wisconsin.

Like her new husband, May had been born in America, but her parents, Sigfrid and Johanna were Swedish immigrants who had settled in Dry Wood Lake Township near Sisseton, where they joined earlier settlers scratching out a living on this bleak and lonely remnant of the American frontier.

Even in 1957 this was rough country with its vast skies and endless, empty rolling prairie, blazing hot in summer and bitterly cold with deadly blizzards and deep snow in winter. It was still the place that Karl Rølvaag wrote about in his epic 1924 novel, *Giants in the Earth*. "Here was the endless prairie, so rich in its blessings of fertility, but also full of a great loneliness—a form of freedom which curiously affected the minds of strangers, especially those to whom the Lord had given a sad heart."

It was that "form of freedom" that called to Erik, and he loved the 320-acre farm like no other place he had ever been or ever would be again. He began traveling with his parents to the farm almost as soon as he could walk. The family enjoyed vacations there that began after the school year ended, and eventually stretched into most of the summer months, an annual adventure that ended in his own version of heaven.

In 1958, the Olson property lay at the end of a gravel road that stretched west over a low rise toward Dry Wood Lake. It was a poor place, not very prosperous as the topsoil was only four inches deep and solid rock below and hadn't much advanced from fifty or a hundred years before. Now it barely supported a shrinking but still-extended family that raised a crop of wheat, alfalfa, or flax each year, and an assortment of animals—mostly sheep and a few cows.

The house, which was old, unpainted, and beaten into exhaustion by seventy years of South Dakota summers and winters, offered almost no amenities. Water came from a creaky pump in the yard, and any electrification went for lighting and a radio. The farm kitchen had water from a well but no refrigeration, no television, no indoor plumbing.

Two horses pulled farm wagons and carried small children around the property, but great-uncle Evald Olson also had an elderly red Allis Chalmers tractor and a Ford Model A short-bed pickup truck, practically the only evidence of modernity on the place. Erik learned to use the tractor and all its farm implements, and though barely able to see over the Model A's dashboard, he learned how to drive there, bouncing over dirt roads and farm fields, even taking the aging truck on errands as far as Sisseton, about eight miles away on public roads.

"Nobody ever bothered with anything like a driver's license, and I was far from the only boy in the area driving a farm truck," he recalled. "It was a matter of necessity, practicality. The farmers needed labor, and that always included everyone in the family pulling their share of the load. Boys needed to grow up fast, and part of that was learning to drive. I don't recall anyone ever looking twice at me or any other kid behind the wheel. If getting the job done meant breaking the law, then the law got broken, because not getting the job done might mean starving or the family losing the farm, which was worse."

Society's rules did not much matter on the Olson farm, or on the prairie around it where survival took precedence. Within a decade, America would be orbiting spacecraft and preparing to land a man on the moon, but the Olson farm was a throwback, an 1890s island in an America plunging toward the 21st century through the wild excesses of the Sixties, an unwinnable and divisive Asian war, nuclear terror, and into the Information Age.

On a farm outside Sisseton, South Dakota, none of this mattered, and life promised to go on as it had on the prairie for a hundred years. All of that suited Erik, who grew to love it.

Gini remembered, "I'm not sure if it's genetic or what, but the open sky in South Dakota, there was just a sense of freedom. He could run around in the fields. There was a dog, and he would sneak out at night and use the dog as a pillow and just look at the stars. It was less structured, fewer expectations, an escape."

In what would become a recurring pattern in his life, Erik found opportunities as well as freedom in South Dakota. Some of those opportunities were illegal.

A 1954 federal statute banned the interstate shipment of fireworks into any of the thirty-three states where the law barred them. Fireworks had been prohibited in Wisconsin but demand—especially among teen and pre-teen boys— was ever fierce. If one had access to fireworks stocks in another state, such as South Dakota, where they were legal and readily available, and a ticket on the Milwaukee Road to Wisconsin, one could exploit another law—that of supply and demand—to purchase an inventory, ship the explosive cargo by train, tack on a substantial profit margin, and retail the goods to a horde of eager adolescents in Waukesha.

Aware of Wisconsin's ban and the federal law, but untroubled by either, Erik exploited both to the fullest. "There was never any problem getting inventory or finding customers, and after a couple of trips I had a regular clientele."

He thought he could keep this up for as long as he wanted, but there was a huge obstacle in that path—a source of incredible stress and frustration that would strain his family to the breaking point. This was the unjust and unreasonable edict that required Wisconsin boys to attend school to age sixteen. The law meant that his time on the farm would be limited to summers. This curbed his earning potential, but also kept him away from the place he loved and in a place he despised.

Selling illegal fireworks shaded just on the wrong side of the law, which was one reason for keeping his involvement—and the profits—a secret. He'd also learned another reason early on. Secrets should especially be kept from parents who taxed kids' earnings, legal or illegal.

"If you had a paper route or some such, they knew exactly how much you made, and they were likely to have you put some or all of it into a 'college fund' or something like that, whether you planned to go to college or not. I didn't let anybody know how I was making my money or how much I had."

This wouldn't be the biggest secret he kept from his parents. Although the gap between them had grown, even Erik admitted that they had tried to do their best to put him onto a sustainable path for the future. "They had both grown up in the Depression and hadn't always had an easy time of it when they were younger. So, they wanted what every parent of that era wanted: for their offspring to have a better life than they had."

Both—but especially his mother—recognized his intelligence early and tried to encourage his interests, though without any clear understanding of where it was all headed. "I'm sure they expected me to go to college and become an academic. They even expressed that at various times. I never had any interest in that path."

What did interest him was nuclear physics and electricity, and his parents gave him support and space to explore both. His mother encouraged him to read, and he had picked it up fast, reading children's books early and more adult fare by the time he hit grade school.

"I learned to read from the Graybar [electrical equipment] Catalog, among other things," he said.

By fourth and fifth grade, he was consuming college chemistry and physics texts. His reading interests didn't necessarily coincide with the school's curriculum, but they fortified him in his explorations. Those mostly took place in the family basement, which had been turned over to the youngster and quickly filled with all manner of scientific equipment and supplies.

He created an appropriately dark and spooky place, a secret underground lair with cold concrete walls and stone floors lit by bare electric bulbs. Wooden tables piled with glassware and humming electrical equipment filled the space that Erik appropriated over time; everything was scrounged from all over the Milwaukee suburb and, eventually, even the larger city itself.

He had high-voltage power supplies, scintillation counters and signal generators, oscilloscopes, vacuum pumps, and transformers—45,000-, 60,000-, and even 90,000-volt castoffs rescued from some business or warehouse. Much of it was war surplus material, or equipment made obsolete as America's technology revolution spun up in the 1950s.

He lugged everything down into the cellar, where it blew every fuse in the house until Erik bypassed the electrical panel by going outside to the pole and tapping directly to the main.

Most of the stuff in the basement was dangerous; some of it was deadly. He had equipment that could throw electrical arcs across a couple of feet, and radioactive material that today would be stored in locked vaults under armed guard. There were also chemicals far more volatile and toxic than anything in the Christmas chemistry sets given to American boys throughout the 1950s and 60s. "It was like Frankenstein's laboratory down there," he remembered.

One of his keenest interests for years was x-rays, and he collected and stored several x-ray machines and their radioactive elements downstairs in his underground den. "These were the days when shoe stores used to x-ray your feet to fit you for shoes," Erik said. "Some of them had fairly powerful equipment before the government decided, rightly so, that this wasn't a very good idea, or very safe."

In July 1959, Wisconsin banned the use of these x-ray devices to fit shoes, making use and possession of the fluoroscopes a crime. Waukesha's shoe stores had to get rid of their x-ray machines, which no one else wanted, and were illegal to possess anyway. Erik purchased them for as little as a quarter, or just picked them up curbside when their owners abandoned them. Down in the basement, he stripped out the radioactive material and incorporated it into a much more powerful—and illegal and completely unregulated— machine of his own creation which he used to x-ray his home, mapping out the knob and tube electrical system, plumbing, and every other detail.

As the scientific gear in the basement expanded, raised more questions, and created more opportunities for experimentation, his need for equipment and supplies grew beyond what could be scrounged, begged, or borrowed around Waukesha. There were only so many shoe stores in town, and after all their x-ray machines had been moved to the Marquardt basement, he had to go further afield to find more, leaving home to get it.

Almost all kids are looking for some independence at that age and a little older, but for a host of reasons—some legal, some financial, some cultural—most can't acquire much liberty, or do much with whatever they get. Determined not to be one of those kids, Erik embarked early on an uncompromising lifelong pursuit of freedom and never looked back.

CHAPTER 5

Waukesha, Wisconsin, 1958

Freedom. No kid in American history ever craved it more, sought it harder, or schemed for it more intently. Erik Marquardt fought for his independence every day of his seventy-three years, which is beyond ironic since he spent more than half that time behind stone walls, iron bars, and razor wire fencing.

In his first decade, however, freedom lay as far away as South Dakota and nearby, only feet from the family home.

This wasn't a wealthy household, a family living in privileged circumstances. Their block of East Main was a slightly seedy mix of older houses, small garages, neighborhood bars, and taverns sandwiched between the Soo Line's railroad tracks, a Standard Oil storage facility, and "a large and very dirty foundry," as Gini Marquardt described it. "I still have family furniture missing the finish from bad air quality. It took the paint off the teachers' cars at White Rock once, and the foundry had to pay to have the cars painted."

Directly across Main Street, Tony Pucci's bar was the "friendly neighborhood saloon," and a popular hangout for the trainmen working at the Soo Line's roundhouse next door.

Railroads were a key part of life at the time, not just on Waukesha's Main Street but on America's. Only yards from the front porch of the Marquardt home, Soo Line trains rumbled past, freight cars pulled by steam locomotives. Three blocks south, easy walking or biking distance for an eight-year-old, the tracks of the Chicago & Northwestern paralleled Main Street, and across the Fox River and a couple of blocks north, the rails of the Milwaukee Road drove westward toward Minnesota, the Dakotas, and on to the Pacific Ocean.

Gini remembered the experience of living next door to a trainyard: "The roundhouse was probably four houses away from ours, and the switching yards were endlessly fascinating. Nothing was more awesome, even then, than watching the big steam engines go by. We were a porch-sitting family, and after supper on summer nights, would sit and watch the trains and cars go past. It was even better in the steam days when Erik was young, but the entertainment value is still good."

The allure of the rails captivated the eight-year-old boy watching intently by the side of the tracks for two reasons. First, unlike the new diesel locomotives that growled quietly along without revealing the secrets of their power, steam engines wore their technology on the outside, presenting a noisy, busy whirlwind of spinning iron wheels, thrusting drive rods, pumping valves, hissing steam, the chuffing of the exhaust as it escaped the funnel, and the mournful, three-tone shriek of its steam whistle. For someone obsessed with discovering how things worked and why, steam engines created almost an infinity of interesting questions. He thought they were marvelous.

About 365,000 miles of railroad track crisscrossed the nation in 1955, a vast web of steel that spanned the continent, and touched almost every city and town in the country. In the years before the Interstate Highway system was completed, while air travel was something of a novelty, railroads tied the country together as they had for over a hundred years. And, as Erik learned, almost every foot of those tracks connected to the same rails that ran past the Marquardt house.

One could, he learned, board a train in Waukesha and go almost literally anywhere, and as far as your imagination would take you. The horizons were as endless as the possibilities, and the rails leading away from Waukesha sang an irresistible siren's song of freedom.

There were a couple of obstacles in the path of this seductive vision. Parents had understandable reservations about watching their not-yet-nine-year-old son vanish aboard a passing freight bound for Bakersfield, Biloxi, or even Beloit. The need to be in school for nine months each year was an obvious constraint, and he quickly learned of another—one that would bedevil him for the next sixty years.

There were, he discovered, laws.

He learned this in a roundabout fashion at what should have been a time of joy and satisfaction as the window onto freedom opened wide enough for the child to see the promise beyond. Gini described how it happened: the formation of a pattern that repeated for the rest of his life. "His intelligence set him apart, but he could always talk to people of any age, and lived the life of any child of his time. Social skills were probably a second great talent."

Using these advanced social skills, the little kid standing at the side of the tracks made friends with the trainmen working in the switchyard and on the trains rumbling past.

Not long after they got used to him asking his questions, he started trying to cadge a ride in the cab of the mighty locomotives. Before long, he was riding the engines to neighboring towns—and once or twice, as far as Milwaukee before hopping down and catching another train full of friendly railroad men back to Waukesha. The engineers, brakemen, firemen, and conductors enjoyed this little seeker's company, and would sit with him and answer his questions as their trains rolled through the Wisconsin's countryside and smoking cities.

But there was a hitch.

"They could only take him so far, as they wouldn't take a kid across the state line," Gini said. There were laws.

He knew the chemistry and the physics, understood the science behind the huffing black behemoths, could explain in detail how coal and water and steel and flame could be harnessed to move a hundred freight cars from Waukesha to Kenosha. He understood the mechanics of the engines, and all of their interconnected systems from the cowcatcher to the caboose. But although the rails stretched south toward Chicago, an invisible barrier—a legal one—stood between him and the freedom in the distance.

By probing and feeling around the edges of this unfair and arbitrary prohibition, he discovered that like most laws, this one had exceptions—loopholes you could exploit if you knew the system. Those grimy but sociable Soo Line trainmen might not be willing to transport their little passenger past that invisible legal barrier at Kenosha, but there were plenty of railroad employees who would gladly do so. These people would take you anywhere you wanted to go, and do it in the comfort and style of a Pullman car rather than a noisy locomotive or a smelly, smoky caboose.

All you needed was a ticket. And for that, all you needed was money.

"Money was a key to freedom. If you had it, you could do what you wanted, when you wanted. But you damn sure couldn't let anybody know you did have it, or where you'd gotten it."

Erik turned to what he knew, solving—at least temporarily—his money troubles with some basic basement chemistry. He wasn't making drugs yet; that would come later. Instead, he produced a substance much more popular in Waukesha, Wisconsin.

And in the fall of 1958, Erik Marquardt, age twelve, broke bad.

CHAPTER 6

Waukesha, Wisconsin, 1958

A family member suggested the scheme.

Erik's maiden aunt, who lived in the house next door, had never married but had a long-term live-in boyfriend. An uncle in all but name, he was the first to suggest a sure-fire moneymaking proposition.

It was illegal, but not the kind of crime anybody except the U.S. Treasury Department got very excited about. Since the nearest Treasury agent was some distance away in Milwaukee, the road seemed clear.

Do you think you could make up some alcohol down there in that basement? Uncle Hank wanted to know. Because if you can, as bootleggers had been proving since the founding of the Republic, there's money in moonshine.

Erik thought he could. The chemistry of this new enterprise held much of the appeal, but he turned out to have a knack for the business end, too. He started with a helpful manual that included detailed instructions in layman's language, exactly what the beginning bootlegger needed to know. *Fortunes in Formulas for the Home, Farm and Workshop*, a 1939 "how to" guide for home chemists, taught techniques for the manufacture of everything from crayons to carbonated pineapple champagne.

There wasn't much demand in Waukesha for pineapple champagne, but the book provided detailed advice for distilling beverage alcohol, and helpfully included directions for using a wide variety of raw materials, not just the usual corn, barley, wheat, and rye.

Erik made batches with fruit, carrots, sweet potatoes, and even artichokes and bananas. This experience would be quite useful years later for prison distilleries where inmates have to make do with whatever is handy.

He did some experimenting, tried different processes, and took considerable pride in the results: a kick-ass product that created heavy demand among his growing customer base.

"The formulas all require sugar, of course. I settled on Br'er Rabbit Molasses, which has plenty of sugar. It came in a bottle with a green label. Distilling it down was no problem. I generally didn't put out anything that was more than 150 proof—75 percent alcohol. I usually put it back in the same bottles and sold it as 'Green Bunny.' People got a big kick out of that. Busted out laughing, some of them, but they bought it. Most of my clientele was kids from school, but I warmed a lot of ice fishing huts, too."

He had competition. "My aunt's boyfriend, who was a regular customer and something of a connoisseur, told me there were seventeen other stills operating between our house and the courthouse downtown. I learned fairly quickly that I had to have a better product. Mine was distinctive, and I took time to do the chemistry right."

A twelve-ounce bottle of the molasses sold in grocery stores for a quarter at the time, and after emptying it, distilling it, and refilling the bottle with 150 proof alcohol, he resold the Green Bunny for a dollar. Since he was stealing power from the pole outside and had begged, borrowed, or stolen all of the distilling equipment the seventy-five cents over his cost was pure profit.

Fortunes in Formulas offered helpful hints on making beer, ale, and other beverages that his uncle said would also be popular. But for various reasons, some having to do with hard-to-explain odors escaping from the basement, Erik decided to stick with his Green Bunny.

"I worked a couple of deals with the grocery stores in the neighborhood, and they let me buy cases of Br'er Rabbit at a discount. That increased my profit margin. I applied the funds to a variety of projects. Some of the stores actually ran out of Br'er Rabbit for their regular customers a couple of times."

He would continue to sell Green Bunny, a reliable moneymaker, for five years, though the project became more of a hobby and favor to friends and loyal customers as the neighborhood changed and people moved away from bootleg liquor. In that period, Erik developed some new interests, and made some friends that had nothing to do with chemistry or science, though they proved conclusively that the boy was growing up.

He discovered his most passionate interest—aside from science—early on. He was still struggling at school, fighting back with truancy and a sort of passive-aggressive resistance that drove his teachers in junior high and high school crazy. "I was interested in old technology, history, the Civil War. World War I. Laboratory manuals. Nobody else in my class was reading those. I was a perfectly normal kid…for 1906."

It irritated his teachers to see this kid sitting in the back, reading a book and "not participating," and a few of them called him out on it. They generally only tried this once, because Erik had read the material from the course texts, memorized it, and his response could be just as snarky and sarcastic as the question. This, of course, annoyed the teachers even more. He spent time on benches outside the principal's office, and ditched school altogether more often.

Erik did push harder, challenging authority before that would become much more fashionable later in the Sixties. The school fought back by requiring psychiatric evaluation. "I had the courtesy of what you would consider three-plus years of Neo-Freudian analysis from a board-certified psychiatrist, which I thought was extremely valuable because it's something you couldn't obtain at any price now. They simply don't spend that much time with an individual patient. It's 'Here, take two of these and six of these and go about your business.'

"So I was able to understand myself and other people in my interaction with them far better. And the hostility and contempt vanished and was replaced by, 'Oh, this is just another problem.' I was equipped with the tools necessary to avoid conformists, and to go about managing my own life."

This worked out much better than he expected, as the doctor was quite sympathetic. He loaned Erik textbooks, encouraged his hobby, and even obtained glassware for him. Best of all, the doctor frequently signed slips excusing his patient from school, giving Erik a license to travel widely and explore commercial opportunities, so he rode the rails of the Chicago and Northwestern, and the Milwaukee Road…trains that took him all over southern Wisconsin and as far away as Illinois.

He needed this distance because he'd discovered a new and consuming passion, another one that set him distinctly apart from his generation. He became a fan of, and almost obsessed with, classical music. And that brought him to another obsession of teenage boys: girls. Or in Erik's case, women.

Fascinated by the classical composers, he piped their music into the basement via a shortwave radio tuned to stations in Berlin, Moscow, and Prague and with vinyl discs purchased with moonshine money. He soon acquired a substantial collection, and Green Bunny production carried on in style to the strains of Wagner, Beethoven, Mozart, and Brahms.

Canned music had its limits, though; he wanted to hear it live. Milwaukee had its own orchestra, and the Chicago

Symphony had its winter season in town, which brought world-class musicians and conductors to within tuba distance of Waukesha. The weekend concerts didn't interfere with school or any of his ongoing extracurricular activities, so he started attending, marveling alone in the darkness at the beautiful Pabst Theater where he was surrounded by like-minded strangers, absorbing an experience that he found more miraculous than chemistry.

It was classical music that introduced him to women, and the overture took place in the hallowed halls of a '50s and '60s shrine: the record store. Scouting albums one day in a music store on Prospect Avenue in Milwaukee, an older woman "made some caustic but accurate remarks about my female companion," who was shopping for rock and roll. Erik and the woman, Madeline, struck up a conversation, and she invited him to the Chicago Symphony's performance that weekend in the Windy City.

There were some conditions. He'd have to dress and act the part of a lady's escort, which meant formal attire. He solved that problem by stealing his uncle's tuxedo and having it altered by a local tailor and showing up at the train station in Milwaukee, half expecting it to all be a gag. It wasn't, and the Chicago trip was the beginning of a relationship that took the two of them to Chicago, and on to concerts as far away as Cleveland.

"My version of perfection? An evening in Cleveland at the Severance, that golden stairway, George Szell conducting, Madeline, the moon over the lake. Rules? They never existed."

CHAPTER 7

Madison, Wisconsin, May 10, 1959

It was a dark and stormy night on the University of Wisconsin's campus. Outside the Memorial Union's Great Hall, lightning flashed, and thunder cracked as inside, a thousand people gathered to hear from one of America's greatest scientists.

J. Robert Oppenheimer spoke for an hour and a half about physics, his philosophy of life, and its relationship to his approach to science in a presentation called, "The Tree of Knowledge."

"The world is full of new and beautiful knowledge. We need it," Oppenheimer told his audience, but cautioned that "knowledge for knowledge's sake and knowledge for the sake of exploitation are in conflict." He called for "effort, study, and above all, love," and warned his listeners that "civilization rests on our power to tell each other about things."

Most of Oppenheimer's message was lost on the thirteen-year-old listening raptly in the audience. Erik Marquardt had come to hear about radiation, x-rays, and nuclear physics, and when the time came for questions, he was one of the first to the microphone. He was intensely interested in "knowledge for knowledge's sake," so he asked about radioactive isotopes in a way that impressed the distinguished physicist, who wanted to meet the boy behind the penetrating questions.

After he was invited backstage after the lecture, the sixth grader and the father of America's atomic bomb spoke privately for two more hours. Erik was the only attendee so privileged.

"Only about physics, not the philosophical discussion that the rest heard," Erik recalled.

In their hours together, Oppenheimer was most taken with Erik's approach to physics, one that did not contemplate scientific problems from the same perspective—the analytical method used by Oppenheimer and other physicists. This was an untrained youth, someone without any formal grounding in the mathematics and physical sciences that Oppenheimer's peers used in nuclear physics. But the kid "got it," grasping and understanding the concepts, and was able to intuitively visualize solutions that Oppenheimer and others would arrive at only by working through problems using mathematics.

That intuitiveness wasn't unheard of; Oppenheimer knew other people who had the same ability. According to physicist Freeman Dyson, Richard Feynman, a colleague on the Manhattan Project, had the ability to solve complex physics problems "out of his head without ever writing down the equations. He had a physical picture of the way things happen, and the picture gave him the solutions directly with a minimum of calculation. It was no wonder that people who had spent their lives solving equations were baffled by him. Their minds were analytical; his was pictorial."

This non-analytical, "pictorial" approach came naturally to Erik, who understood Oppenheimer's admonition that evening that acquisition of knowledge required effort and study—but he rarely followed it. Instead, he found himself capable of solving problems as Nobel Prize-winner Feynman did, by "grasping ideas as entities rather than arriving at them by rational steps."

John Duncan, an agent with the Oklahoma Bureau of Narcotics who interviewed Marquardt much later said, "He told me one time that he visualized that he was a single point in the center of a molecular structure, and could actually intuitively see how molecules combined. He was a hundred percent serious about that."

His peers and employers noticed this ability very early, his first employer, Marquette University, describing him as "a very brilliant boy with a keen insight into science and *an almost intuitive approach* to many complex scientific problems."

Other interviewers recalled asking about a chemical process or method, and seeing him "turn within himself" to work it out, visualizing the steps and the elements needed to achieve the result.

"That's very unusual," Dr. Donna Nelson, University of Oklahoma chemistry professor, and past president of the American Chemical Society said. "This isn't how science is normally done. There are very few people who have the kind of intuitive grasp of the subject matter that it enables them to solve problems without working through the usual steps."

He was constantly experimenting, testing himself to see whether his vision was correct. What would happen if you tried this reaction under pressure or in a vacuum? What would you get if you tried this reagent instead of the one described in the literature? Yield and purity. Could you get more of your desired end product, or a better one, if you changed this step or that one?

Because he had this special ability, he frequently got the results he expected.

Like many people with unusual gifts, Erik thought everyone else saw things the same way he did, although Robert Oppenheimer had at least suggested that this wasn't so. He was a keen admirer of the giants of 19th and early 20th century German science, and others who did pure chemistry before the Second World War, and he modeled himself on these men, mimicking their pursuit of knowledge for knowledge's sake.

"I, as a youngster had, and still have, enormous respect for the old gentlemen, the pre-WW2 folk. You see this in my admiration for Gordon Alles [credited with the development of amphetamine sulfate and MDA-Ecstasy] and [LSD inventor Albert] Hoffman, and contempt for the retreads like [psychopharmacologist Alexander] Shulgin. The Farben crew, people like Carl Bosch, Fritz Haber, and Walter Reppe, were the gods that reside on Mount Olympus. Such men will stand alone and above, their achievements never to be equaled. No one else is even close."

That admiration extended beyond these men's skills in a laboratory to their philosophy. Carl Bosch, a Nobel Prize winner and possibly the greatest chemical engineer in history, made one of the most significant contributions ever to humankind with his development of the industrial production of ammonia and nitrogen fertilizers. Because of Bosch's work, every country in the world could obtain ammonia from hydrogen and nitrogen out of the air, giving it the means to fertilize the crops to feed its population. Half of all the people on the planet today depend on Bosch's process for their food base.

But also thanks to Bosch, every country in the world could make explosives from ammonia and nitrogen, and countries like Bosch's Germany would need that capability in a couple of years as it joined others in the First World War.

The contents of Pandora's Box didn't particularly concern Erik or Bosch; just the means by which the box could be opened.

Erik had similar respect for another seeker of "knowledge for knowledge's sake," whose too-brief career saw him lift Pandora's lid twice.

Albert Niemann began his career in science as a pharmacist's apprentice before attending George August

University of Göttingen (German: Georg-August_ Universität Göttingen). Here, he studied under a giant of German science, Friedrich Wöhler, who obtained some leaves from the Peruvian coca plant and gave them to his graduate student to analyze.

Niemann's research, published in 1860, won him his PhD. Like Friedrich Sertürner, another German chemist who had pulled the first alkaloid, morphine, from the opium poppy fifty years before, Niemann had successfully isolated the alkaloid from the plant material, and he named it "cocaine," adding the -ine suffix that accompanies all of the alkaloids.

The new Herr Doktor Niemann then went back to work on two common chemicals, ethylene and sulfur dichloride. He found that when mixed together, they produced a clear or sometimes yellowish-brown liquid: bis (2-chloroethyl) sulfide. It was nasty stuff, having a rather pungent odor described as resembling horseradish or mustard.

Niemann also noticed that "even traces brought into contact with the skin, while painless at first, result in a reddening of the skin after several hours, and in the following days produce blisters which fester and heal slowly and with great difficulty, leaving behind significant scarring."

Called "sulfur mustard" for the smell, the noxious new compound didn't seem to have any obvious uses or value and Niemann didn't get much time to discover what other properties this sulfur mustard might possess, or what uses his cocaine might be put to, as he sickened and died of a mysterious lung ailment at age twenty-six in 1860. He was therefore unaware that his two creations would cause untold suffering as others put both to bad use in the future.

Cocaine, at least, would soon find some beneficial and truly marvelous uses as a local anesthetic, especially in eye surgery, where doctors and patients considered it almost miraculous.

Sulfur mustard, on the other hand, had no industrial or pharmaceutical value whatsoever, but that didn't stop some other German scientists from finally finding a use for it. In 1916, Germany was at war, and they put it into artillery shells and fired them across the trenches, where they exploded into yellowish-brown clouds. Soldiers called it "mustard gas."

Niemann's two discoveries raise an ethical question about the chemist and the chemistry, one that may have different answers in other times.

If he had known about the application of his discoveries, that cocaine would be transformed into a thing called 'crack' that would ravage entire cities, ruin countless lives, and create a generation of stunted and suffering infants, would Niemann still have pressed on with his experiments with coca leaves?

If someone had told him that sulfur mustard would be weaponized and used to kill and cripple tens of thousands of his fellow men, would he have continued his research into ethylene and sulfur dichloride?

The answer would probably have been "yes," because Niemann and the other German, French, and English chemists of the period were interested in "pure" research, the "knowledge for knowledge's sake" that Oppenheimer spoke about. They wanted the answers to questions about how chemicals would react with each other.

There were no questions about morality or right and wrong. For these 19th century scientists, the giants that Erik emulated, nothing existed but the chemistry.

In Erik's view, Niemann did his science out of "abstract curiosity" rather than an attempt to exploit a discovery. "This I understand: one does science for whatever satisfactions it gives one—really fun! Who knows (or cares) if it will make a better world? Once upon a time, this was trumpeted to be the ideal model for scientific discovery. I still like it."

Had he lived, Niemann would have no doubt been pleased that his discovery finally found some medical and commercial value. As a trained pharmacist, he would have certainly been gratified to hear that cocaine had such wondrous effects as an anesthetic, and undoubtedly disheartened at the sad application of sulfur mustard as a weapon. But good news or bad, ultimately, he still would have fiddled with those chemicals.

That same principle applied to another of those old scientists that Squeak deeply admired. Dr. Fritz Haber was a Nobel Prize winner, and partnered with Carl Bosch in the Haber-Bosch process to obtain ammonia from hydrogen and nitrogen from the atmosphere. Haber was a chemist's chemist, and the ultimate believer in a scientist's moral neutrality. He practiced what he preached.

Though the Haber-Bosch process was a tremendous boon to mankind, Haber is also known for a far darker achievement. Perhaps no chemist in history has lifted a more horrific lid than he, the Father of Chemical Warfare.

"Death is death," he said, defending his weaponized chemical creations. In Haber's view, you're just as dead whether it comes by explosives or poison gas.

Applying this philosophy, the patriotic German worked enthusiastically throughout World War I to provide his country with the best chemical weapons possible.

But Haber had one more contribution plucked from under Pandora's lid.

After Germany's defeat, his institute produced a cyanide-based pesticide called Zyklon-A. Enormously valuable to humanity, it was extremely effective in the elimination of insect- and rodent-borne disease that killed millions around the world every year.

As with Niemann's sulfur mustard, someone else found another, far less beneficial use for that chemical by modifying it slightly and calling it "Zyklon-B."

Millions would discover, including Haber's own Jewish relatives, that Zyklon-B was the gas the SS used at Auschwitz.

CHAPTER 8

Washington, D.C., 1950

Early in 1950, the United States Senate formed a Special Committee to Investigate Organized Crime in Interstate Commerce. Thirty million Americans tuned into the televised hearings to watch major organized crime figures Frank Costello and Albert Anastasia, mob moll Virginia Hill, and others answer questions—or evade them—about various rackets in the United States.

In one session devoted to the drug business, Committee Counsel David Shivitz questioned Samuel Levine, a Group Supervisor of the Federal Bureau of Narcotics (FBN), about heroin trafficking by a group of New York mobsters infamously known as "Murder Incorporated."

The "close-knit syndicate" of Jewish and Italian American gangsters was described in the hearing as "a gang of men who ruthlessly ordered murders on a wholesale scale," and were reportedly responsible for 400 to 1,000 murders between 1929 and 1941, mostly in New York and New Jersey.

During his testimony, Levine told the committee that many of the men in Murder Inc. were also involved in the heroin trade. One of them was Emanuel "Mendy" Weiss, considered by FBN to be one of the biggest heroin traffickers in the world. Levine testified that Weiss had set up "during the latter part of 1939...a clandestine laboratory in which morphine was adulterated and later distributed in the illicit traffic."

Shivitz wanted to know more.

Mr. SHIVITZ: And this clandestine laboratory you referred to in which morphine was adulterated and distributed, what sort of a laboratory was that? Is that a complex thing?

Mr. LEVINE: That is a complex thing, set up by these dope peddlers, with competent chemists, so that they can adulterate and convert the morphine to heroin,(sic) the heroin being the much more desired product in the city.

Mr. SHIVITZ: It takes a great deal of capital investment and technical skill to set up a laboratory of that sort?

Mr. LEVINE: It does.

There were those who would beg to differ. Ten years later, someone would do the same thing on a budget of less than twenty dollars in an abandoned morgue in Waukesha, Wisconsin.

Erik Marquardt was fourteen years old at the time.

* * *

Resthaven Hospital Morgue, Waukesha, Wisconsin, 1960-1961

The Marquardts thought quite highly of their family doctor. The Waukesha general practitioner had an office a few blocks away from the family home, and had been treating them for years. He became closer to Erik after George Marquardt had a heart attack.

Gini described the event, a milestone in their family's life: "Erik helped with shoveling coal into the old stoker for the furnace and shoveling snow. We lived on a corner and with our grandparents next door, too, so there was a lot to shovel. One evening they were shoveling, and Dad had chest pains. Mom was at a movie and Erik insisted he go in the house. Mary and I were kept in the dining room while Erik called the doctor, who came over and called the ambulance, and they came to take Dad to the hospital with a heart attack."

Erik's call and the physician's prompt attention saved George Marquardt's life, making the doctor something of a hero in the Marquardt family, so, when the doctor, who knew about Erik's abilities with chemistry and physics, asked for a favor, Erik was intrigued and receptive.

By 1960, the doctor, who had been seeing patients in Waukesha for over three decades, was probably one of the city's best-known citizens and the most prominent of the local physicians, but he also had a secret, one he shared with many American medical doctors at the time.

Drug addiction was far more common and a major problem within the medical profession where health care professionals had much easier access to narcotics than those in the general public. Charles Winnick, a prominent drug researcher at the time, reported that "the incidence of opiate addiction among physicians has been estimated…as being about one addict among every 100 physicians, in contrast to a rate of one in 3,000 in the general population."

In England, where heroin was still used in medicine, the addiction rate was even higher. Doctors accounted for 17 percent of the country's known addicts.

In the United States, because it had been banned from medical practice by the Anti-Heroin Act of 1924, those addicted medical men had access to other narcotics like morphine, codeine, meperidine, and methadone that were used in their practices. But if they wanted heroin, they'd have to get it like everybody else: from a dealer on the street. There weren't many of those in Wisconsin in 1960, and none at all in little Waukesha.

But maybe there was an alternative. Could Erik actually make some heroin? The doctor asked his young patient if it was possible.

Erik thought it was an interesting challenge, and went to the literature to find out. He discovered in his reading that he needed to start by synthesizing morphine, a process first developed by German pharmacist Friedrich Sertürner in 1804. He'd need some things, he told his patron: glassware and equipment and chemicals, but nothing too exotic or expensive. Twenty bucks should do it.

He also needed some raw material to work with. This meant, as it had for over a hundred and fifty years, opium.

The doctor thought he knew where to get some, going to a friend at Hoehle's Drug, a downtown Waukesha pharmacy about four blocks from the Marquardt home. The store owner let the two of them poke around the basement, where they found an old bottle of what used to be an opium preparation, once a gum or maybe a liquid, now dry and desiccated after years of sitting on a shelf in the cellar.

"They never threw anything away," Erik said. "There was stuff down there from before the drugs were even regulated. This weighed a little under two pounds. Hard as a rock and shiny. It looked like a large brown marble. I could knock myself out with it if I hit myself on the head. I'd guess it was at least fifty years old. Maybe more.

"I had to break the bottle to get it out, and I busted it up with a hammer in a bag to get it down into reasonable size pieces."

Now he had the raw materials, and he had the literature: a description of the extraction method dating back to the turn of the 20th Century.

"I wanted to use the same process that they'd used back when the synthesis was first done." (English chemist C.R. Alder Wright first acetylated morphine in 1874, but Bayer chemists Heinrich Dresser and Felix Hoffmann generally get the credit for the discovery in 1897 because

Bayer, the maker of aspirin, immediately patented it as diacetylmorphine and marketed it with the trade name "heroin," a cough suppressant and pain killer.)

There are two stages in the process for getting heroin out of opium. Sertürner's first step, the extraction of morphine from opium, is more complex than the second stage—Bayer's conversion of morphine to heroin. It takes longer, too; 30 – 36 hours of watched pots and bubbling kettles.

He had no problem getting the chemicals, but this left a major problem. "The basement was entirely unsuitable for this type of chemistry. Aside from the fact that my parents had access to the space, I needed a place with running water, ventilation, and electricity," Erik said.

And privacy.

The doctor thought he had the perfect place, one with everything required.

There aren't a lot of places much quieter and more private than the morgue.

Two blocks south, and easily visible from the Marquardt home where it stood at the top of a small hill, Resthaven began life as a luxury hotel, opening in 1909 to serve wealthy health-seekers who'd come to Waukesha for its famous spring-fed "healing waters."

Financial difficulties forced the hotel to close until 1919, when the facility was sold to the federal government for use as a veterans' hospital. Operated by the U.S. Public Health Service, in the years following World War I, Resthaven's patients mostly consisted of veterans suffering from what was then known as "shellshock," now called Post-Traumatic Stress Disorder. After those patients moved on, Resthaven served tuberculosis patients before finally closing in October 1958.

Two years later, Resthaven sat almost empty—immense, silent, dark, spooky, abandoned by the living, rumored to be haunted by the tormented spirits of the shell-shocked veterans of World War I's trenches who had lived and sometimes died within its brick walls. It was the sort of place that people told ghost stories about, that small children ran past without looking too closely, and that most folks ignored or avoided.

Since it was conveniently close to home, Resthaven offered the privacy Erik required. The doctor, through his role as the city physician, had access to the old hospital laboratory and the morgue, which were still connected to city water and power. Nobody was using the lab, which had been stripped of much of its equipment, and the morgue was reserved for emergencies. The doctor gave the keys to his young co-conspirator.

The morgue didn't bother Erik, and he was photographed with a friend, both grinning broadly, as the two lay in separate drawers, obviously not intimidated by the possibility of haunts from the previous occupants.

Then he got down to work.

"It was uneventful. I isolated the morphine. That was, as I remember, a pretty decent yield, above ten percent. I finished with about three ounces of white [heroin] crystals. I gave these to the doctor. I believe he had something of a substance abuse problem, but that didn't keep him from being a very good doctor and a nice fellow," Erik said of the moment he first became a clandestine drug manufacturer and a narcotics trafficker.

His first adventure making narcotics also led to his first inadvertent experience with the effects of those drugs. "With both the morphine and the preparation of heroin itself, I got quite euphoric. Very pleasantly euphoric. Just kind of a dreamy sort of sensation that you wanted to feel this way all the time. You have no worries, no cares. And I understood why people became addicted to it. That was what the opium smoker sought. And the doctor, too, I suppose."

His sister, Mary, who'd always been protective of her brother, saw things less charitably and was more bitter about the whole episode. She said of the doctor, "If he wanted some heroin, he should have gotten his own instead of having basically a kid make it for him."

Three ounces of pure heroin would go a long way toward relieving that substance abuse problem, at least for a while…but as addicts everywhere know, it won't last forever. It won't even last long enough. Before long, the doctor came back to Erik to see if he could repeat the magic.

They were out of raw material, though, and another search of Hoehle's basement came up empty.

No more opium? This wasn't an insurmountable problem, Erik told the doctor. He'd been doing some reading, and there were some substitutes almost as good. "He got me some thebaine to mess around with. That proved to be a most interesting challenge, and I was able to produce some Dilaudid after a week or so." [1]

Now out of opium and thebaine, Erik went back to the literature, then said that if the doctor could get some codeine, Erik could convert that into morphine, and then to heroin. Codeine was, like morphine and thebaine, a Class A narcotic under federal law at the time, but state and federal authorities viewed some preparations—codeine cough syrups and Tylenol with codeine tablets—as lower risk and did not monitor them as closely.

The doctor could get all of the Tylenol with codeine tablets he wanted, and he provided these in bulk to Erik, who carted them off to the morgue. He returned with more heroin a week or two later, repeating the process for more than a year.

Each year from 1926 to 1967, the Bureau of Narcotics and its predecessor published an annual report titled *Traffic in Opium and other Dangerous Drugs*. Although it regularly described clandestine heroin laboratories seized overseas, only once in that 50-year period did the Bureau report a

---

1. Dilaudid (dihydromorphinone or hydromorphone), is derived from thebaine, and is estimated to be 2-8 times more powerful than morphine.

heroin lab in the United States. That one, which the Bureau said it had heard about but never located, was operated in 1939 by Mendy Weiss for Murder Incorporated.

Maybe some others went undetected, or maybe Erik had the only other one. There was no clandestine drug manufacturing taking place in the United States in the late 1950s; all of the morphine and heroin conversion laboratories in the world were in Turkey, Lebanon, Italy, Corsica, France, Mexico, and in the Golden Triangle of Southeast Asia. Any labs converting coca leaves into cocaine were located in South America, and all of the other drugs being abused at the time—mainly amphetamines and barbiturates—were available by prescription.

Erik's heroin lab in the Resthaven morgue fell on the cusp of the Sixties, when underground operations making LSD and other hallucinogens and methamphetamine would spring up like magic mushrooms all over the country. With the possible exception of Murder Incorporated's rumored 1939 venture, the Resthaven morgue was, in all likelihood, the very first clandestine drug manufacturing operation in American history.

If so, this would make Erik Marquardt the country's first clandestine chemist.

First or not, it would be excellent practice for the time when he operated the country's only fentanyl laboratory, making a narcotic fifty times more powerful than heroin.

And killing people by the score.

CHAPTER 9

Milwaukee, Wisconsin, 1961 – 1963

Erik learned a lot from his first foray into drug manufacturing. There was demand for his product. The processes hadn't been difficult to master and didn't cost much to do. Best of all, the whole thing went completely unnoticed by anyone in authority who might have objected to a kid making heroin in a federal hospital in Waukesha, Wisconsin.

His most important lesson might have been that although he loved science, and pursued it in a quest for what Robert Oppenheimer called "knowledge for knowledge's sake," his heroin left him with a new understanding. That same interest in chemistry could have practical uses. There might, indeed, be fortunes in formulas.

Within a year, a new friend confirmed this impression in a major way.

On one of his scrounging expeditions into Milwaukee, Erik paused for a few moments under the awning of an Eastside liquor store to escape a passing rain shower. The owner, a middle-aged black man named Frank, came outside to check on this gangly white boy, and when the kid politely asked for permission to hang out for a spell to stay dry, an amused Frank said it was fine by him.

Erik, always alert for an opportunity, made his pitch for booze. It was the beginning of a beautiful—and profitable— friendship.

The relationship started out over liquor. Erik was still moonshining, but some of his customers—mostly the underage drinkers—wanted store-bought liquor and were too young to purchase it. Erik had made a few connections nearer home, but Frank owned the place in Milwaukee and had no problem with supplying—through a discreet cutout—a bunch of kids in distant Waukesha.

Erik began including the liquor store on his regular rounds in Milwaukee, but their relationship flipped when the subject of narcotics came up and Erik became the supplier.

Milwaukee didn't have a lot of drug addicts in the early 1960s. The Federal Bureau of Narcotics kept statistics on the cases it made, and the number of addicts it knew about. In 1964, the FBN identified 132 "active addicts" living in the entire state of Wisconsin. Agents in the state made no heroin cases in Wisconsin that year, and exactly one for marijuana.

Clearly, no one was getting rich supplying an illegal market this puny—even if the feds were, as was highly probable, greatly undercounting the number of heroin users in the state.

But Wisconsin didn't need addicts of its own to have a market. It imported some from its next-door neighbors, where the problem was much worse. Both Chicago and Minneapolis-St. Paul had addiction rates quite a bit higher than Milwaukee's, and the addicts used the convenient rail links to enjoy Wisconsin's more lenient drug laws.

A man could make some serious money tapping into those markets if he had the supply, and Erik had found some buried treasure that solved that problem. By a fortunate coincidence, it was codeine, a drug he'd already had some experience with, and codeine was already a problem in Milwaukee.

In 1962, the Milwaukee Police Department reported that: "Consistent with its past reputation, Milwaukee continued to be relatively free of illegal narcotic traffic…

While 98 arrests for narcotic law violations were made, the quality of the heroin available illegally is so poor that the users refer to it as 'dust,' and addicts find it so difficult to obtain that they are resorting to the use of cough medicine containing codeine..."

Although they didn't know it, the vice cops were talking about Erik Marquardt and his partner, Frank.

Codeine came up in one of his earliest conversations with Frank who, like the vice squad, knew people who might be interested in getting some of this cheap heroin substitute. Erik thought he might have a connection.

On another of his foraging excursions, he'd explored the bowels of an old charity institution, the Milwaukee County General Hospital, the same place where he would be held for a psychiatric examination three years later. The place is long-gone now, replaced by a modern medical center, but in 1962 it was a massive edifice of cream brick containing miles of busy corridors and dozens of departments. Erik ditched school, dressed appropriately and looked like he belonged, then wandered unchallenged through the hallways and acquired a set of keys that allowed him access to the few areas that were actually locked and secure.

"They weren't very security conscious in those days. The pharmacy door was usually locked, but my key worked on it. They were supposed to keep the Class A narcotics—the good stuff—in a secure vault, but they never locked it in the daytime. People had to come and go. And they had the worst procedures for dealing with the expired narcotics. They were like Hoehle's, the drug store in Waukesha; they never threw anything away. Only this was on an industrial scale. It was just a matter of finding it."

Squeak uncovered this bounty in the vast, gloomy hospital basements. He was looking for any equipment or glassware that might have been stored and temporarily forgotten, but found something much better in the back of the cellar.

"There it was, stacked floor to ceiling in old cardboard boxes. I thought they were empty, but no. They had gallon jugs inside, the big ones that pharmacists could use to fill the individual prescription bottles. Robitussin AC cough syrup."

In pharmacists' language, "AC" means "with codeine," and as the Milwaukee Vice Squad pointed out, junkies sought "Robe" AC avidly in the 1950s and early 1960s, especially in states like Wisconsin where the drug laws allowed pharmacists to dispense these cough medications by having the patient sign for them in a book.

Minnesota required a doctor's prescription for codeine preparations, so addicts there took the train down to Madison or Milwaukee to hit a few drugstores and stock up. But getting Robe from a single source on the street was even better, and when Frank mentioned the demand for codeine, his new partner knew right away where to go for a supply that dispensed with all of the legal processes and the need to appear in a pharmacy.

For a junkie from Minneapolis or Chicago, snaring a gallon jug instead of a puny little four-ounce bottle was like a dream come true.

"The first junkie I sold it to, we got $250 for a jug and the cat was practically crying, he was so happy," Squeak remembered.

They couldn't sell too many of those big jars, though. Most of those junkie customers rode the afternoon run of the *Twin Cities Hiawatha,* the Milwaukee Road's signature train, the twice-daily passenger liner that made the trip from Chicago through Milwaukee to Minneapolis-St. Paul.

You can imagine eight or ten of those sketchy-looking characters scattered throughout "The Indian," as the train was known, each lovingly cradling his gallon jug of codeine cough syrup as he counted the minutes to Minneapolis. This picture was bound to cause even the dimmest of narcotic agents, vice squad dicks, or railroad bulls to get suspicious.

Much better to break the sales up into smaller quantities, parcel the Robe into four or eight-ounce bottles, charge a bit more, and send the still-satisfied customers on their way with something more easily concealed.

Fortunately, another storeroom at the hospital provided a virtually unlimited supply of empty bottles waiting to be used by their pharmacy. Erik intercepted them by the crateful and wheeled them to Frank's waiting truck on the street using the hospital's own hand cart.

With both their Robe and their bottling problem solved, Frank moved into a diner close by the Milwaukee Road's downtown station where he could operate from a table inside, open for business whenever the Indian was coming or going.

That business boomed. Drug trafficking, it seemed, was the most profitable scheme Erik had tried yet, especially since they weren't spending a single nickel to acquire their product.

There were plenty of very satisfied customers catching the *Hiawatha*, and the money was so good, Erik thought they should mine the hospital vein for all the treasure it held. Frank, being older, wiser, and vastly more experienced, applied the brakes.

"I had access to all manner of other narcotics over there. Their expired supplies, the vault when it was left open. I could get morphine, methadone, Dilaudid, really powerful stuff. It seemed reasonable to me to assume that if the junkies were willing to pay this much for cough medicine, they would certainly be willing to pay more for the really good shit. Frank said, 'Yes they would, but then we'd be having a bunch of dead junkies getting off the Indian up in Minneapolis, and all the heat will come back down on us.' That was a good lesson."

Dead people, even dead junkies, bring heat. It was an important message. Erik remembered it, and tried to impress its significance on his new crime partners eighteen years later when they began making and selling a narcotic much more powerful than Robitussin AC—and killing people by the score.

That one was called fentanyl.

* * *

Nothing good lasts forever, and the operation finally crashed when Illinois busted Frank on a load of purloined outboard motors. He hadn't stolen them himself, but was fencing the hot outboards when the police followed one back to the liquor store. That drew him a short stretch in an Illinois prison. He went to Vandalia without giving up his partner in the codeine business, who faded quietly out of sight.

Erik remembered Frank fondly, and the aftermath of the fencing bust. "His wife told me to lay low for a while. Good lady. She said there had been some loose talk about some 'young professor of dope' floating around from a former employee at the liquor store. Ah, shit. We had big plans. He was a damn good partner and a first-rate criminal."

Erik had learned a few things from his first real turn as a drug trafficker. It paid to pick your partners carefully. Loose talk and dead customers could get you in real trouble. And the really big one: Drug dealing pays and pays big.

After Robe, the "young professor of dope" would be in the drug business off and on—mostly on—for the rest of his life.

He still had access to all that hospital dope, but he didn't have a distribution and marketing system, a way to sell these products to customers without taking unnecessarily high risks.

That brought him to another important lesson he'd learned, though, that sometimes you have enough money, and at this point, he did. He was almost completely independent of his parents in Waukesha, with a key to Madeline's apartment in Milwaukee and enough cash for train and concert tickets. Madeline paid for other necessities; the basement laboratory couldn't hold any more equipment; and he used the gear in real labs now, anyway.

He'd gotten to be a very proficient sneak, and in his various explorations, he'd noticed an awful lot of valuable items that were unattended and not properly tied down or locked up. He had contacts that were looking for some of this stuff: electronic equipment, assorted gear and supplies, some with serial numbers, some completely unmarked, and he found he could almost steal to order.

It seemed to be lower risk than drugs, so he went into a new career, putting heroin and codeine on a back burner… not giving it up, just letting it simmer…while the Young Professor of Dope turned to thieving.

CHAPTER 10

Milwaukee, Wisconsin, 1963

Erik still had a year to go before high school graduation day, although at this point, he was limiting his attendance to science classes, and those only occasionally as the mood struck. Much to the chagrin of his parents, who were unaware of the extent of his truancy issue, he made no effort to apply anywhere for college admission. He spent most of his days scrounging on the streets of Milwaukee or at Marquette University, with evenings at Madeline's apartment, or closer to home in the chemistry labs at Waukesha's Carroll College, or the town library reading chemical literature.

In one of these ramblings, he found a commercial laboratory in downtown Milwaukee and met a congenial group of chemists who, like almost everyone else he encountered, were immediately charmed by the high school savant who shared their interests and could converse easily at their level—and far beyond. The business sat across a busy street from a Milwaukee fixture and "olfactory landmark," the Red Star Yeast complex.

Red Star, which had begun life as a distillery, was renowned in the city for the pungent aroma issuing from the building's vats and chimneys. Before turning to the key ingredient in leavened bread, the company had produced straight whiskey and such brands as Livingston Bourbon and National Rye Malt Gin. It was the latter that interested the men at the lab and their young protégé; that and the new LSD drug getting so much attention.

Erik took his first hard look at LSD in 1963 when it became the topic at one of the bull sessions with the men at the downtown Milwaukee commercial lab, and sparked by a piece in *Life Magazine*. The article at the center of the discussion, "Chemical Mind Changers," explored the role of science—and chemistry—in shaping human behavior, and suggested that the nervous system is electrochemical and "the chemical side of the matter is even more fundamental."

Erik was intrigued.

The article went on to describe "psycho-chemicals" or "chemical mind-changers," and identified some of these substances: cannabis, the peyote cactus and its mescaline, the psilocybin of magic mushrooms, and another drug the "amazing new compound, LSD-25."

LSD—d-lysergic acid diethylamide tartrate—wasn't actually "new." The substance had been accidentally discovered by chemists Arthur Stoll and Albert Hoffman of Basel, Switzerland, and patented by Sandoz Laboratories in 1944. Hoffman, who would come to call the drug "my problem child," became the first person to feel its effects when he ingested a tiny quantity by accident on the day of its discovery. "I experienced fantastic images of an extraordinary elasticity. They were associated with an intense kaleidoscopic play of colors…I lost all control of time; space and time became more and more disorganized, and I was overcome with fears that I was going crazy."

Erik was so intrigued that he quickly sought out Hoffman's patent for the substance. It had been first registered in the United States in March 1948, and would expire in exactly two years in 1965. That sparked a lively discussion at the Milwaukee lab.

"This was the summer of '63. I had a buddy at Red Star Yeast in downtown Milwaukee. It's a yeast place, they've got these huge fermentation vats. That comes in handy as part of the synthesis for the LSD precursors. All of us are sitting around, me and him and a bunch of chemists from one of the labs in Milwaukee, reading about LSD and they're saying, 'We can make this.' I said, 'Hell, yes we can, by the tank carload, over at Red Star.' Then they're asking, 'Do you think these beatnik kids are dumb enough to pay for it?' Well, that's the big question, isn't it?"

They thought the yeast factory was ideal because, as Dr. Hoffman explained in his patent, a key precursor of LSD is lysergic acid, (hence the street name for LSD that would become very popular in a couple of years) and lysergic acid is synthesized from ergot, a fungus that grows on the heads of rye plants.

Nobody in the United States had more experience with growing and processing fungi (or making intoxicants out of rye) than Red Star whose yeast, bubbling fragrantly in its vats across the street and on its way to bakeries, breweries, and kitchens across America was, of course, also a fungus.

This speculation around the lab water cooler never got past the talking stage, and no one ever went across the street to ask if they might borrow one of Red Star's vats. But Erik didn't give up on the interesting new substance. He learned that others were doing the same thing in the same period, notably Harvard psychologist Timothy Leary who actively promoted the use of psychedelic drugs, including psilocybin and LSD.

Erik filed Leary away for future reference, and also found a film the Army had made that pushed him further into LSD's orbit.

The movie was a short promotional film produced in 1960 for the Army's Chemical Corps called "The Confused Cat," showcasing its research on the military applications of psychoactive chemicals. As *Life Magazine* had said, the film showed a caged cat dosed with a very small amount of a chemical agent that isn't identified but is understood to be LSD.

Before the dose, the cat "reacted normally when confined with a mouse," attacking without any hesitation. But "when exposed to an extremely small amount of the agent, the cat's personality completely changed." Now a seemingly terrified feline leaps wildly around the cage to escape first one, then two bewildered but undoubtedly very relieved white mice.

"The Confused Cat" made a real impression, and Erik continued to research these psychoactive drugs throughout the rest of 1963 and into 1964 as he entered his senior year at Waukesha High School. It would be a momentous nine months that saw him produce—and consume—his first two hallucinogenic drugs, win a major science competition, and leave the halls of academia, at least as a student, forever.

* * *

Milwaukee, Wisconsin, 1964

By the time Erik entered his senior year at Waukesha High School, the teachers who knew him—and most of them did, at least by reputation—fell into one of two camps. Each group held firm beliefs about their young pupil. In one camp, teachers like Charles Miller, the science instructor in Erik's junior year, thought Erik's intelligence "wasn't much above average," basing his opinion on classroom performance, which was—as even Erik will concede—rather dismal.

Typically, Erik dismissed Miller's conclusion, chalking it up to jealousy. "Miller did not much like the idea of a student knowing more about chemistry than he did," which was probably true. Some of the teachers, Miller especially, threw down challenges and observed the results, and since Erik almost invariably failed to succeed or even try very hard, it was easy to doubt his intellectual ability.

Miller arranged for Erik to try college chemistry, although it sounds like he might have been laying a trap. "I made arrangements that if he thinks he's so goddamn smart, let's get him enrolled in a chemistry class at Carroll College."

Since Miller was essentially setting up a legitimate excuse to ditch school, Erik jumped at the opportunity, and the head of Carroll's chemistry department, Dr. Arthur Sunier, agreed to take the high schooler into his college freshman chemistry class.

It didn't go the way any of them planned. Erik quickly bored of the introductory chemistry lessons and, as his interest level waned, so did his attendance. He did enjoy his personal interactions with Dr. Sunier, who treated him like an adult. "He gave me a huge amount of glassware and all kinds of chemistry books. And more than that, he took me over to the library at Carroll, and showed me how to methodically search the literature of chemistry, showed me how to use the journals in the way a professional chemist does. That may have been the most important thing that ever happened to me."

Twelve months later, in his senior year, the truancy issue loomed even larger, but in his last semester, he encountered Richard Stolsmark, a teacher from the other camp. Stolsmark believed his pupil to be, as Dr. Feierstein would say a year later, "an extremely brilliant boy, if not a genius in his field."

With time running out on high school, Stolsmark thought he'd give Erik another chance to prove himself.

The Junior Academy of Science was Wisconsin's equivalent of a state science fair. It held local and regional competitions, and then a statewide final contest to evaluate student science projects. Stolsmark urged Erik to enter the regional competition at Marquette University in Milwaukee. He expected Erik to produce a project on X-rays. "He knew more about X-rays than anyone I ever met," Stolsmark told a reporter years later.

Erik surprised Stolsmark twice. First, he agreed to enter the competition, and second, he chose to do a project on the carbon-14 process used to date archaeological artifacts. "It was a passing interest of mine. I'd done a bit of reading on it," Erik said.

His entry finished second in the regional competition.

Almost thirty years later, Stolsmark described the aftermath to reporter Donald Williams of the *Wichita Eagle* newspaper. "On the trip back to Waukesha in Stolsmark's station wagon, amid a mixed group of six students, Erick [sic] reacted in a black, obscene fury... 'The language was characteristic,' Stolsmark said. 'He would say whatever it took to embarrass people.'"

Erik remembers being angry but denies being in a "rage," claiming he didn't care about "something that was largely meaningless," and asking, "Who will remember the winner of such a thing five years from now, much less fifty?"

He also had a practical reason for not taking the loss too seriously. "The top prize at the statewide contest, was, I believe, a $200 scholarship. Since I had utterly no interest nor any intention of attending college, this was worse than useless." The fact that he made $200 every few days selling codeine to visiting Minnesotans may have also played a part in his disdain for the prize.

Whatever the response, his "second place is first loser" attitude became irrelevant when the winner at Marquette was unable to attend the finals, so the region's first runner-up would go in her place. Erik went with a serious "I don't give a damn" attitude toward the competition, and it showed.

In most of these science fair events, the contestants spend months doing their experiments, then preparing elaborate displays to present their results. His seventeen competitors fit the standard mold. Erik and Mr. Stolsmark drove up to Wausau on May 1, 1964, with exactly nothing.

His presentation the next day consisted of him sitting across a table from the judges and lecturing them for thirty minutes on the theory of carbon-14 dating, a suggested new technique, and applications of the method in other fields. Erik remembered that "the entire thing was the judges. One of them was a nuclear chemist, very obviously. It was something like an oral defense of thesis, and basically what they just wanted to do is grill me on how much I actually knew about nuclear chemistry, and they did."

It must have been good because the judges awarded him the first-place prize, although he had to split the $200 scholarship with a kid from Sheboygan who had a much more conventional presentation on "The Therapeutic Uses of Bacteriophage in Epidermal Infection in Rats."

When they drove home to Waukesha the next day, Sunday, May 3, Stolsmark remembered his student's arrogant attitude, his estimation that his victory proved beyond any doubt that he didn't need schools or teachers to achieve knowledge or success.

"I'm quite certain that I was rather insufferable," Erik said. "I made it clear any number of times that I had learned absolutely nothing of any value at school, and everything I did learn had come as a result of my own efforts rather than theirs. I suspect they resented that attitude. Did I need those people? No, I did not."

Funny…Waukesha High School seems to have felt the same way. On Monday morning, he found out that the school didn't need Erik Marquardt, either: it expelled him on the same day he was driving to the contest in Wausau. The official reason was "chronic truancy."

The school did record his ranking in the senior class; his grades placed him 631st in a class of 670, with a grade point average of 1.08. The school's yearbook for that year, the "Megaphone," contains not a single mention of his name. He's not listed with the senior class or with the list of "Seniors not pictured," and not named in any clubs or organizations. It's almost as if he was never in school at all.

"I won the war. Of course, a lot of people were mad at me, and a lot of people are still mad. I was the resident rebel. Not a belligerent one. Didn't go around with my collar turned up or a switchblade knife or anything like that. But school didn't suit me, so I didn't do anything that I didn't want to do. And once I got mobile where I could travel around, and found out there were quite a number of alternatives in life besides some structured path, I saw no future for me there.

"I always had this feeling that…times were changing, and the way things had been done in the past, whether the employment pattern was congenial or acceptable to me would be much different than they were. It was going to be much different in the future."

He'd discovered the Sixties.

CHAPTER 11

Milwaukee, Wisconsin, 1964

School might have decided it could do without Erik Marquardt, but he was far from finished with school. In fact, he went straightaway to college. He had no high school diploma, but that credential, as usual, didn't mean much. What he did have was talent, and the ability to work in a chemistry lab. Universities, including several located conveniently nearby, were always looking for people like that.

Lab assistants and technicians resided at the very bottom of the academic hierarchy, then and now. They're the uncredited key to many discoveries, the people who perform routine tasks, who observe equipment, who fetch and carry. They're the bottle washers, the equipment monitors, the people who keep laboratories functioning day in and day out.

To do their work, lab assistants need access to the lab, sometimes at all hours of the day and night. The people who hire lab assistants trust them with this access. As a couple dozen universities from California to Virginia would discover over the next few years, trusting Erik Marquardt with that kind of access was a big, big mistake.

After Waukesha High School washed its hands of him, he took his first job at Marquette University in Milwaukee. This episode marked several major milestones in his life. His few months at Marquette and a short-term job at the

University of Wisconsin in Madison would lead to his first felony arrest, first extradition, first prison sentence, first marriage, first child, and first divorce. It marked the beginning of a vocation in what, until now, had been mostly a hobby. As he would tell a federal judge in a later sentencing, "I don't believe I've ever had an occupation other than drug manufacturing."

That occupation began at Marquette.

The experience at the university there, though fairly short, taught Erik valuable life lessons about theft, swindling, and drug making, and showed vulnerabilities in the many similar institutions he would pillage in the future. Perhaps the episode is most significant because these few months constituted some of the only legitimate employment he would ever hold. A half-century later, when he finally reached Social Security's retirement age, he didn't bother applying for benefits. He'd never worked enough quarters to qualify.

Erik hadn't forgotten about the confused cat, or the other information being published in the popular press—and especially the work of two former Harvard psychologists, Richard Alpert and Timothy Leary, who were avidly promoting the psychedelic drugs they themselves were using. Fully determined to see for himself what all the hype was about, he intended to produce these substances, all completely legal at the time. He just needed access to a laboratory.

Unsuspecting Marquette had everything he needed to create any or all of the substances the Harvard men described as "consciousness expanding," and useful for "unplugging the mind, for unshackling it from narrow inhibitions." Ostensibly working on various experiments for faculty and students, the new lab assistant impressed the university's staff not just with his obvious intelligence, but also with his extraordinary diligence. He'd moved from the family home in Waukesha and was living in a cheap rented space in town, though he spent days—and nights on end—in the chemistry lab on campus.

"I made a habit of sleeping in the laboratory, often under the workbenches, which the faculty mistook as dedication. They believed I was monitoring the experiments and whatnot."

He wasn't spending his nights and weekends supporting other peoples' chemistry. Instead, using Marquette's facilities, equipment, chemicals, and library, he set up a fully functional drug lab in the chemistry department. Only five weeks after leaving Waukesha High School, he produced his first batch of mescaline. Three weeks after that, he had LSD.

Psilocybin "took somewhat longer because I wanted to follow Hoffman's method for extracting psilocin and psilocybin from the biological source, and I discovered that the so-called 'magic mushrooms' were in rather short supply in Milwaukee, Wisconsin at the time. But I was able to find a synthetic route to both substances…the same one, I later learned, that Hoffman had employed."

He'd been high before, accidentally, back in Resthaven's morgue, but he would never become a regular drug user. Many of his associates, even close ones, say they never saw him use any of the drugs he made, but he readily admits that he did experiment with all three of the psychedelics before deciding that he liked psilocybin best, with another, dimethyltryptamine (DMT), close behind.

While he would make them again over the next twenty years, he learned very early on that this particular sideline of the clandestine business had one major drawback. When it came to the psychedelics, "There was no money in it. These substances were all legal at the time, and not impossible to acquire from commercial sources," he said.

Even LSD's most prominent advocate proved to be a difficult customer. "I sent a sample of my second or third batch, which I thought was rather excellent, and some psilocin to Timothy Leary in Millbrook, New York, something like the first hippie commune. He wanted more but thought I should give it to him without compensation. Some theory of his that LSD and the other psychoactive drugs should be free for everyone, I suppose. I declined."

He would encounter Leary's reluctance to pay for LSD throughout the rest of the Sixties, and it left him with a fervent hatred for another counterculture icon of the era. "Those goddamn hippies all wanted free drugs," he says bitterly, the offended outrage in his voice still strong more than fifty years later.

He did go back to the psychedelics from time to time, especially after discovering that "hippie girls," on the other hand, were more than happy to offer value in exchange for free acid. But after the Summer of Love and Orange Sunshine, he focused his drug manufacturing career on substances customers would clamor—and pay real money— for: methamphetamine, mostly, and later, the narcotic called fentanyl.

Since he was using Marquette's resources to make the drugs, his production costs were nil, but they weren't generating any revenue, either, which led to a scheme that did produce some income. He began stealing electronic equipment. He'd made contacts in other universities before going to Marquette, and made more after going to work at UW…representing himself, somewhat accurately, as a member of the faculty or at least on staff.

"Universities and industries were transitioning from vacuum tubes to transistors, and equipment made during and after World War II was becoming obsolete very rapidly." His true passion centered on this equipment; most of his drug manufacturing for the rest of his life was just a means to acquire electronic laboratory equipment.

His contacts in the local scientific community, at labs, colleges, industrial laboratories, and his new freedom allowed him to spend more time hanging out with these like-minded friends, using their equipment, sharing their space, and doing odd jobs and small favors. He gained a deserved reputation as a capable lab technician and a knowledgeable equipment service tech, which gave him access to the scientific instruments that especially interested him. Because Erik wasn't just interested in fixing these things up; he planned on stealing as many of them as he could.

His main targets were big universities with lots of people, buildings, and more stuff than they knew what to do with. "They were getting a lot of surplus equipment from the government, excess military hardware from World War II. More than they could put in the labs, so they stored it. Some of it they'd never use. This was all pre-solid state, pre-transistor, so it was big, heavy, solid gear. Some of it weighed a hundred pounds or more. I got to be pretty strong. But if it was too big, I'd find one of their carts and use that."

He dressed the part and knew how to talk and act like a technician or a student who was moving a piece of equipment for a project. He could empty whole storerooms, limited only by access to transportation and his own chutzpah.

"Northwestern, University of Chicago, Purdue, Argonne National Lab, and then I got down further south into Illinois. Most of the schools in the University of Wisconsin system. Hit all of them."

His M.O. was simple: gain trust from the unsuspecting mark, identify whatever he wanted to steal, boost it—preferably in a way that would hide the fact that anything had gone missing—and finally, locate a buyer at another university. Rinse, repeat.

* * *

Madison, Wisconsin, 1965

He picked up something else in his time in Madison; he met and married a young woman from Nebraska who was then a student at UW. They took out a marriage license on May 26, 1965, barely a month after Erik's arrest in Milwaukee. Married in a civil ceremony two days later, the young couple immediately departed for the West Coast for their honeymoon.

Unfortunately, the marriage was doomed from the start. For one thing, this was something of a shotgun wedding; his bride was two months pregnant, and Erik took responsibility and "did the right thing" by her. A bigger issue for the couple would be legal; Erik's scheme to loot UW's lab had unraveled and the boom was about to be lowered.

The scheme started to fall apart when he sold a "piece of radiology equipment" to a Chicago equipment company for $450.00. When the company tried to re-sell the instrument, valued at $2,475, to the University of Illinois, staff there did some checking and learned that it belonged to the University of Wisconsin, which didn't know it was gone.

An inventory turned up more missing items with a value of between $5,000 and $15,000, and UW made a formal complaint against its former employee, who had also now disappeared.

A bench warrant followed, and, with the help of his bride's parents, Madison police tracked the young couple to Los Angeles where they were staying at the Conrad Hilton Hotel. Local police arrested him on June 10, and he spent the next month in the Los Angeles County Jail before the Dane County sheriff himself arrived to extradite him back to Madison.

His bride also returned to Wisconsin and sought an annulment of their two-week-old marriage.

Erik entered a guilty plea, and Circuit Judge Edwin Wilkie agreed to a sentence of probation. He ordered Erik to repay the $450 he'd received for the stolen radiology equipment, then gave him a one- to four-year term with no additional jail time, and Erik walked out of the courtroom a free man.

As an aside, the judge ordered Erik to provide child support for the expected baby. That issue became moot, however, when the court granted the annulment request in October, and his ex-wife put the baby up for adoption.

Now on probation, but not especially burdened by any of these social or legal encumbrances, Erik carried on as before and moved closer to home.

For his next trick, he'd irradiate Milwaukee and rip off some nuns.

CHAPTER 12

Milwaukee, Wisconsin, 1966

The trouble began with a gift of pigs, and Sister Mary Emilius was puzzled. Alverno College, a Roman Catholic school with about 1,500 students located just west of downtown Milwaukee, had been training young women for seventy-five years, mostly for careers as nurses and teachers. The school's Department of Chemistry had limited expectations for its students; nobody anticipated that Alverno would produce world-class research scientists or Nobel Prize winning physicists. That wasn't the school's mission or its focus, but Sister Emilius, the department chair since 1957, did her best with what Alverno and her Order of Saint Francis provided.

Always looking for ways to stretch her limited budget, in January 1966 she posted announcements at nearby Marquette University and the University of Wisconsin-Milwaukee asking for lecturers. Both schools had graduate programs in chemistry and physics, and she wondered if students working toward their PhDs might like a little teaching experience, sharing some of their training with Alverno's young women.

Sister Emilius had been born right there in Milwaukee as Elizabeth Kramer, and she understood her mission. She'd been educated at Alverno, got her PhD in chemistry from St. Louis University, taught biology and mathematics at a Catholic girls' school in Chicago, then chemistry and biology back at Alverno. She was passionate about science, had been published in her field, and took pride in having received grants from the Atomic Energy Commission and the National Science Foundation for the purchase of "nuclear equipment for teaching" and other laboratory equipment, which had boosted Alverno's chemistry and physics programs at no cost to the school.

So, she was pleased when a tall, well-dressed, personable young man answered the inquiry she'd posted at Marquette, saying he'd heard she was looking for some help with physics classes. He was currently doing research at Marquette for the Atomic Energy Commission, the man said, working toward his doctorate, and looking for a change of pace. The idea of teaching a semester at Alverno appealed to him, and best of all, he didn't ask to be compensated in any way, implying that the AEC would take care of that for him.

"I thought that would make it less likely that she'd do a lot of checking, which was important," Erik said. That's because his approach to Alverno was part of a bigger, more elaborate scheme to con an unsuspecting victim out of some electronic equipment, including Erik's Holy of Holies: a mass spectrometer.

The scheme started at nearby Marquette, where Erik was working as a lab assistant and making hallucinogens when no one was looking. The school had received a contract from a Wisconsin company that made car wax, and was interested in learning about the effect of radiation on various compounds of its product. This was a project after Erik's own heart, combining the chemistry of the wax and the radiation applied to it.

The research, conducted in a laboratory on the upper floor of the building that housed Marquette's physics department, produced some radioactive waste, "car wax and other material used in the testing. Not highly radioactive, but hot enough to excite a Geiger counter."

The school—and the federal and state governments—had protocols for disposal of the waste, rules for dangerous materials that researchers were expected to follow to protect the public. But these "were somewhat cumbersome," so they went out the window. Literally, because Erik, voting for expedience, opened the lab window and dumped the stuff into the breeze and onto downtown Milwaukee. "Not possible today, but things were more relaxed in those days," he said.

The contract had an additional benefit, because his work at Marquette brought him into contact with a private research laboratory that was in the process of upgrading its equipment. This included a mass spectrometer, the instrument that became his obsession. He would be on a permanent quest for these instruments for the rest of his life.

He had been introduced to the mysteries of mass spectrometry during his short stint at the University of Wisconsin, and was awestruck by the machine and its potential. "I thought it was wonderful. Surely," he told a reporter years later, "the mind of man could not have conceived an instrument more wonderful than this."

Arthur Winter had written, in his book *Organic Chemistry I for Dummies,* that "Organic chemists can use a mass spectrometer to ionize—or 'smash'—a molecular compound in gaseous form, sort the fragments, and then identify the molecule fragments based on their molecular weights."

Keith Hollenbeak, who was employed at the Halliburton Company's lab in Duncan, Oklahoma, later analyzed Erik's drug samples using his company's mass spectrometer. Hollenbeak described the process to a Wichita reporter in 1993, comparing the procedure to "studying ancient architecture by putting a building on railroad tracks, smashing it to bits with a train, picking up the fragments and saying, 'This is part of a wall, this is part of a kitchen…'"

The research company planned on donating the mass spectrometer and other unwanted gear, but told the eager young lab assistant they could only give it to an institution, not an individual. If he could find a suitable recipient, the equipment could be his. Or at least temporarily in his hands, which he knew would be good enough.

This led the budding con man to Sister Mary Emilius.

The nun and the grad student had some things in common besides a love for science. He had worked at the Argonne National Laboratory near Chicago, home to America's cutting-edge nuclear physics research, and so had Sister Emilius, doing post-doctorate research there in the summers of 1964 and 1965. In fact, they had actually met, and they talked about mutual acquaintances, people at Argonne and Marquette.

Sister Emilius had dealt with AEC people before; they had given her that grant to purchase equipment and supplies for her program in 1961, and she felt confident working with this earnest young scientist, especially since he knew someone that might be interested in donating some equipment to her department, which was always in need of more.

"We had an agreement to split the donation, with half going to Alverno and half to me, after passing through Alverno's hands long enough to satisfy the donors. I only wanted the mass spectrometer, which Alverno had no need for at the time. So it was a match made in equipment heaven."

Blissfully unaware that she was now a key part in a fraud scheme, Sister Emilius sat in on the first lecture, and was satisfied that her new presenter knew his stuff and wasn't overly interested in his all-female audience. The always-protective sisters at Alverno had to be careful about things like that, but he seemed engaging and was clearly very knowledgeable, though some of the physics talk quickly went over the students' heads.

He gave four lectures on nuclear isotopes and radioactive fallout, leaving both the students and the science faculty generally pleased with the program and its presenter. Meanwhile, Erik carefully cultivated the research people, lining up the transfer to Alverno where, he assured them, he was now employed.

As always, he used the opportunity of being allowed inside an institution to case the place, looking for opportunities. He found the pickings at little Alverno College to be disappointingly slim. "Extremely limited laboratory resources. Enough to teach people the basics so they could go and teach as elementary and high school science teachers. Almost no electronic equipment, and most of that was obsolete. Certainly nothing worth stealing."

He couldn't walk away empty-handed, though, so he asked Sister Emilius if she might provide him with some lead bricks used in the storage and transportation of radioactive materials. Known in the business as "pigs," the bricks had no other real purpose and, thanks to her grant, Sister Emilius had more pigs than she needed. So she agreed to give him ten of the hundred-pound bricks, which were valued at about $30 each and that was the last time Sister Emilius saw Erik Marquardt.

Concerned when her young lecturer failed to appear for his next class, she tried contacting him without success. She tried again over at Marquette, and then wrote a letter to the Atomic Energy Commission, asking when she might expect her lecturer to return and gently chiding them about employing someone with so little responsibility for leaving her in the lurch.

Her letter drew a hot response from the AEC, followed shortly after by the FBI. Both wanted to know more about this supposed AEC employee who, they all assured Sister Emilius, was no such thing.

He was not a PhD student or a researcher at Marquette, either. In fact, he'd never graduated from high school, and was currently on probation for looting the laboratories at the University of Wisconsin in Madison, the FBI told the appalled nun. He'd been arrested again recently, trespassing at a facility doing highly classified government nuclear research at the University of Virginia, which explained why he hadn't made it to his scheduled lectures at Alverno.

Given his standard M.O., it seemed logical that he would have taken this opportunity to pillage yet another college's laboratory, and the FBI asked Sister Emilius to see if anything, especially electronic lab equipment, was missing. She checked; going through her limited inventory didn't take long, and she said everything was accounted for. Except, of course, for the pigs. Those were gone.

It wasn't a major theft, only three hundred dollars' worth of lead, and not normally a federal issue. But the feds took things like falsely claiming to be a government official seriously in 1966, and a grand jury indicted Erik in July for impersonating an AEC employee.

"I never actually told her I was employed by the AEC, although I certainly tried very hard to leave that impression. Apparently I succeeded," Erik said. "But they were very good lectures, and they didn't pay me for them."

The story made American newspapers from New York to Hawaii, and the tale of Erik's quirky crime caper highlighted Alverno's embarrassment for hiring a "high school dropout" to teach classes on nuclear physics.

The State of Wisconsin wasn't happy that the man it had given a second chance had blown it by getting arrested out of state, and then indicted by the federal government. Correctly figuring that Erik hadn't learned his lesson, the state moved immediately to revoke his probation and locked him up in the Waukesha County Jail pending that decision.

As crimes go, this one didn't amount to much; nobody came out a big loser. Alverno was out ten pigs it had no use for, anyway. The research company had transferred the equipment it had agreed to gift to the college, and Alverno had everything—though not the mass spectrometer, "which subsequently dropped out of sight along the way, a mysterious mass spectrometer disappearance," Erik said.

Nothing else was missing and, in the end, the biggest losers, as usual, were Erik's parents.

Although he didn't ask them to do so, they paid for his attorney with money they had been setting aside to buy a house in the suburbs, away from the grit of Grand Avenue's bars and railroad tracks.

His sister, Gini, recalled the family's disappointment: "Mom and Dad had bought a beautiful suburban lot to build a house so we wouldn't have stayed on Grand forever. But there was never any mortgage on the property to speak of, and so when money started to go to lawyers, they had to sell the lot to pay legal fees. The suburban dream disappeared, and we just stayed there."

As would become his pattern for all future encounters with the criminal justice system, Erik pleaded guilty to the federal impersonation charges in September. At his sentencing in October, U.S. District Judge Robert E. Tehan observed that Erik had impressed professionals with his scientific knowledge, and had been asked to help them do research. "But unfortunately, those who were interested in assisting you were soon disillusioned by your general irresponsibility and deceitfulness."

This was his first lecture from a federal judge, but it would be far from the last. Judge Tehan gave Erik a year and a day in prison but allowed the sentence to run concurrently with the four years Wisconsin had handed out for the UW oscilloscope caper.

By the time the federal gavel came down, Erik had been installed in the Wisconsin State Reformatory at Green Bay. Here, in his first real prison term, he began learning, as convicts put it, "how to jail."

These skills, too, would also come in handy in the future, as the now-twenty-year-old would spend over thirty of his next fifty years in prisons from one end of America to the other.

CHAPTER 13

Wisconsin, 1967 – 1970

The reformatory, which looked and felt a lot like the high-security prison it would later become, was only a temporary home for what would prove to be a two-year-and-ten-month stretch. "There wasn't a lot of reforming going on, as I recall. They held a race riot just after I arrived. I made it a point to avoid those if at all possible."

The Corrections Department, assessing him to be a lower security risk, moved him to Fox Lake, a modern medium-security facility, and then to the even more congenial minimum-security "camp" established a few years before as a pre-release center at the former U.S. Air Force Station at Williams Bay.

"That was easy time," Erik said of his stretch on the shores of Lake Geneva. "We could come and go, looking for employment and whatnot. The place had been an Air Force base and then abandoned; there were still quite a few unoccupied buildings. I was able to put together a nice little LSD manufacturing facility just off the correctional center's grounds. That was quite popular with my fellow residents. I used the time to perfect my processes so that by the time I was released, I'd mastered most of the hallucinogens that were in demand at the time."

Wisconsin released its unrehabilitated inmate in February 1969, and Erik returned home to Waukesha for a brief probationary period. That didn't go well, either; his last couple of months in the family home ended abruptly when he vanished, along with his father's cherished MGB sports car. The car broke down in Chicago. Unable to pay for repairs, Erik abandoned it in a local garage.

It seems clear that Wisconsin's attempts to reform this particular inmate had failed, and by the time he was released in February 1969, eighteen months after the Summer of Love, his prison time had perfectly prepared him to meet the skyrocketing demand for the psychedelic drugs that became a trademark of the Sixties.

The federal government had banned possession of LSD in 1968 and placed it in Schedule I of the Controlled Substance Act of 1970, along with other drugs not deemed to have any value in medicine. This change in legal status created a black market for acid which Sandoz, whose patent had expired in 1963, stopped producing in 1965. Demand for the drug after 1965 would have to be filled by clandestine manufacturers, and most of those, by 1969, were in California.

Maybe there was gold to be made in the Golden State.

* * *

California, 1969

There wasn't. Although he met a few interesting people and learned a lot, California proved more bust than boom.

Things were happening in sunny California when Erik arrived. LSD was big that spring. It might have been outlawed by the government, but in the Age of Aquarius, it was available everywhere in the City by the Bay.

Seeing the demand, Erik connected quickly, able to name-drop with the best of them.

He met singer Janis Joplin, fresh off her appearance on the Ed Sullivan Show and playing some venues in the Bay Area, including Filmore West. "Nice lady," he reminisced later, "but one of those individuals who attempts to burn the candle at both ends and the middle with the predictable result. I'm surprised she lived as long as she did."

Joplin died of a heroin overdose the following year.

He dated a girl from Joplin's entourage, the first of a number of "Suzies," the generic name he applied to girls and young women he met who were eager to make an exchange for LSD, DMT, mescaline, or psilocybin. "I don't believe I met three sober people in the whole time I was there."

That included members of the Grateful Dead, who had previously been supplied with LSD by "Acid King" Augustus Owsley "Bear" Stanley, the first person to mass-produce LSD from clandestine labs he operated in Denver, Colorado and Orinda and Richmond, California. Stanley, already a legend in the budding LSD business, was in the middle of a court case arising from the 1967 seizure of his Orinda lab, and would be off to prison for manufacturing LSD in 1970.

Erik's assessment of Stanley was that he was a "very, very intelligent cat, but did not know how to be a successful criminal. I think it was a product of his entering the business when it was still legal, and trying to behave the same way after the government stepped in and said 'no, you may not do that anymore.'

"I was driving down the coast to Los Angeles and picked up some hitchhikers. Hippie types and connected with the Dead, and before it was all over, I ended up getting offered Stanley's job. He was locked up and they needed a chemist. They had lost confidence in Stanley, but they had the means. They said, 'Look, we'll set you up.' They could provide everything I needed. I said, 'Well, I bring my own shop. I'm not real worried about that.'

"One of these characters was a scion of a high-powered official at the Union Oil Corporation.

He assured me that they could get me piles and piles of glassware, and a pilot plant if I liked. Whatever I wanted. We were going to make LSD by the ton. And so I was coming back east to get my affairs in order and move out there. California Suzy would've very much liked that, and anyway, this all sounded very fun, and I thought, *well, maybe there would be some real money in it this time through the Grateful Dead* connection."

* * *

Northern Illinois, 1970

It started out well enough. To pay for the travels and his projected return to California, Erik found temporary employment at a Midwest university which he had not previously plundered of its electronic equipment...by this time, a shrinking pool of candidates.

Northern Illinois University, located in DeKalb, sixty-five miles due west of Chicago, needed lab assistants and Erik needed a lab. So this match, like the Alverno one, had apparently been made in heaven.

He had modified his M.O. at this point. Where previously he had worked in a lab long enough to identify the electronic equipment he wanted, then absconded with it, now he added a twist that would characterize most of his future career at colleges. From here on out, he went looking for a suitable place to set up a working laboratory, stole or conned chemicals and supplies, and then manufactured saleable hallucinogens for sale on campus. Only then would he disappear along with the equipment he wanted.

This process took a little longer, resulting in a few months of semi-legitimate employment and a W-2 form, which forced him to file an income tax return in 1970. It was the only time in his life that he reported income to the government.

Before skipping town, he encountered an attractive young student from nearby Kishwaukee College. By August, she was pregnant, his traditional views on his responsibilities in this situation leading to a New Age wedding "over a co-op grocery store by a gay guru named Nardi." For a honeymoon, the young couple hit the road. Erik, always prospecting for more opportunities, headed south this time.

* * *

Oklahoma to California to Indiana, 1970 – 1972

He turned up first in Stillwater, Oklahoma, where he raided the chemistry and chemical engineering laboratory at Oklahoma State University. A graduate student, William Metz, described his brief meeting with Erik. "I had a fellow come by who claimed to be in the biology or botany department or one of the life sciences departments, and he was looking to borrow some equipment for his research project, and seemed to be very knowledgeable about the kind of equipment we had, and also very knowledgeable about Oklahoma State. He seemed to be another assistant professor."

Metz helped find the equipment, and even carried some of it to Erik's pickup truck. "'I helped him load it up, and watched him leave. When my major professor got back, he'd never heard of this guy."

"That was the nuclear lab caper up at OSU where I relieved them of all the reactor control and counting equipment for a disused, shutdown reactor. They never intended to turn it on again, and didn't need it," Erik later explained with a shrug.

They reported the theft to the OSU campus police, but Erik was gone. He didn't travel back to DeKalb; that gig was over, and he wanted to avoid Illinois and any other state where the authorities might want to talk to him about missing items.

Indiana sounded promising, and he had never raided the University of Notre Dame. He headed for South Bend in January 1970. It didn't work out.

"Before I could even get a decent lab put together, I did some work for a fellow, installing some two-way radios. He didn't pay me, so I took his radios and his vehicle."

He headed out of town in the hot Ford Ranchero pickup, packed up his new bride and the equipment stolen from OSU, and then, leaving the Hoosier state behind, they headed for California.

They didn't get far. The victim reported his vehicle stolen, and when the Illinois police stopped the truck, they found OSU's pilfered electronic equipment in the back. That solved the mystery of the "assistant professor" who'd taken it.

Oklahoma issued a warrant for Erik's arrest, but Indiana wanted him first. They charged him with auto theft and returned him to the St. Joseph's County Jail. He had no money for bail, and his young bride wisely departed for home. On May 8, he pleaded guilty to the auto theft, and a South Bend judge sentenced him to serve one to ten years in the Indiana State Reformatory at Pendleton.

"Easy time," Erik says of his year in the reformatory. "I was fairly popular with the other inmates, and the staff let me do some electric work, repairing people's radios and televisions." Some of that work was off the prison grounds, where he established a working relationship with Anderson College and Indiana's Eli Lilly pharmaceutical company. Although he would later admit that he made "hallucinogens and methamphetamine" during his sentence, he denied doing any clandestine chemistry in the reformatory itself.

"I never made any such thing." He had a comfortable "electronics shop" in his cell in the prison, and wasn't "going to risk all that to make some dope for a bunch of losers on the penitentiary yard when I've got the director of research at Eli Lilly bringing in glassware."

He stayed out of trouble, and was out in just under a year. Oklahoma waited patiently for Indiana to be finished with their Pendleton inmate, then extradited him back to

Stillwater on May 19, 1971. He pleaded guilty to the OSU theft the next day.

His court appearance was an agreeable affair. "The judge gave me the minimum amount of time that he decently could. His son was my lawyer. It was funny, all of us trying to keep straight faces, and very nice. And the officer that did the extradition, he says, 'I know the DA. Are you happy with a couple of years on this thing?' And I said, 'Yeah, I think that'd be very reasonable, under the circumstances.' And he said, 'We can do that.' That's the way to go with these things, nobody getting mad or upset.

"They said, 'Where do you want to go?'" With recent and relatively fond memories of Pendleton, he said, "'A penitentiary.' So they sent me to McAlester."

The Oklahoma State Penitentiary, built in 1908 a year after Oklahoma became a state, and already more than sixty years old, had been constructed using the United States Penitentiary at Leavenworth, Kansas as a model. Informally known in Oklahoma as "Mac" or "Big Mac," by 1971, McAlester had a reputation for violence, overcrowding, and racial conflict. "It doesn't have a particularly nice reputation. It's an extremely dangerous place," Erik said.

He'd expected that time there would be harder, so he was pleasantly surprised when he arrived. "One had to tiptoe very carefully, and opportunities for mischief were fairly limited, but you mind your own business, and you sit in that cell, and you visit…they had a hot dog stand. They had a grocery store. You could get ice cream. You could get cigars and newspapers in there. I mean, it was just a wonderful place. A rather nice prison."

His wife sent some money, and he was able to acquire some items to make the time pass more easily. "I had a short-wave receiver that the lady sent in for me, a Magnavox stereo, and a big pile of classical records. There was a decent FM station in Tulsa at the time that played classical. There were rugs on the floors. Fix up your cell anyway you wanted. Never went anywhere near the prison chow hall. Guys had cells with knotty pine paneling on the walls. It's the kind of a prison you only hear about. Of course, that was before the riot."

The picture wasn't completely rosy. "I quickly found out the downside of it. The first cellmate I had, who was just temporary, he said, 'Don't borrow any money around here. You can get yourself killed real easy.' Every drawdown, somebody would get killed."

Violence was an almost everyday occurrence. "People fighting all the time, not enough staff. The inmates were really running the place."

Two hundred and eighty corrections officers were responsible for security at the prison, which housed more than 2,200 inmates inside the high, white walls, and another thousand in camps and a prison farm nearby.

The prison recorded "19 violent deaths, 40 stabbings, and 44 serious beatings" in the period between 1970 and July 27, 1973, when the pressures at Big Mac reached a boiling point. What followed was one of the worst prison riots in American history, resulting in the killing of three inmates, injuries to twenty-one inmates and guards, and $20 million in damages. A federal judge subsequently found the conditions at the prison to be unconstitutional and ordered changes. Those would take a decade or more to complete, all of which occurred after Erik's release.

Before leaving, he made note of a couple of potential opportunities. One stemmed from movie night. "I saw *Vanishing Point* in the chow hall/theater at McAlester in 1971. Remember one scene in particular, right before the end, where he stopped to score some 'road speed.' Was greatly impressed."

The scene had an impact because conversations with his fellow inmates produced the information that "road speed" and any other form of amphetamine was in great demand in Oklahoma, where the drug was cheaper than cocaine and more popular than heroin. Unlike the always marginal hippie LSD market, Erik thought, the meth trade might be quite profitable.

He filed the information away, and by the time he passed outside McAlester's walls in September 1972, he not only had plans to enter the meth business but had acquired several acquaintances able to assist with the distribution end in Oklahoma City and Tulsa.

Meth would eventually bring him back to the Sooner State…another stop on the long road that would, in time, lead to the lethal drug called fentanyl.

CHAPTER 14

Colorado, Kansas, Illinois, Michigan, 1973 – 1975

After Erik was freed from Oklahoma's prison in September 1972, he hit the road and perfected his new M.O. in fresh pastures. He found these in a cross-country swing that carried him out to the West Coast and back to the Midwest.

Although the divorce wouldn't be official until the following year, he'd split from his second wife. She'd given birth to a boy while Erik was locked up in South Bend. After the two prison terms in Indiana and Oklahoma ended, he took off without seeing his wife or his infant son.

"I don't think he ever saw or had contact with his son," his sister said.

Those travels carried him to the University of Denver and Kansas State University, where he lifted scientific equipment from both.

On June 6, 1973, police in Galena, Illinois arrested him for possession of stolen electronic equipment valued at $30,000 after tracing the items back to Denver and Kansas, as well as the University of Michigan. All three states issued arrest warrants, and he spent much of 1973 bouncing between jails in Denver (5-10 years, sentence suspended), Manhattan (case dismissed), and finally to Ann Arbor, where the court brought the hammer down.

He pleaded guilty in Michigan, accepting responsibility for a scam that had scored him a gas chromatograph, among other valuable scientific items.

At this hearing in Washtenaw County Court, the judge asked him about the particulars of the crime. Erik, as usual, was honest with the court.

JUDGE: It states here that you represented that you were employed at the department of radiology studying internal nuclear medicine.

MARQUARDT: That is correct, approximately correct.

JUDGE: What do you mean by that?

MARQUARDT: I don't believe that was the particular lie I used on that occasion.

After explaining the "particular lie" he had used, the judge accepted the guilty plea and set a sentencing date. That hearing, too, would be memorable.

JUDGE: Can you think of anything I should take into consideration, that you want to tell me before I sentence you?

MARQUARDT: Only one, and that is, after you folks get through with me, there are some other folks that are desirous of putting me in their penitentiaries, too.

JUDGE: Which do you think is better?

MARQUARDT: I don't know. I will have to try them out first. I couldn't tell you right now.

JUDGE: Well, how about two to ten?

MARQUARDT: That sounds reasonable.

JUDGE: Two to ten it is.

Happy enough with his "reasonable" sentence, he asked to be sent to the Marquette Branch Prison overlooking Lake Superior on Michigan's Upper Peninsula. "It sounded colorful," he said. "They immediately put me on an outside detail, put me to work."

Rather than toiling in farm fields or the prison's dairy ("Shoveling cow shit, where all the inmates start.") he was able to put his electronics knowledge to good use when the failure of a vital piece of equipment threatened the dairy operation. "The milking machine burned up, and I'm sitting in the office, and I said, 'Well, it's a 24-volt rectifier. What we need are two twelve-volt storage batteries from a couple of the tractors.' We hooked them up and they could milk the cows and didn't have to throw away the milk. That saved the prison some trouble, and got stories told about me over half of northern Michigan."

Now a trusted inmate with valuable skills, the prison staff rewarded him with additional freedom. "I lived at the barn effectively. On the grounds, but well away from the prison buildings."

He wouldn't have been Erik if he hadn't taken full advantage. "My girlfriend would come up to Marquette and come over and sneak up in the barn at night. This was really no bit at all."

Erik got out of Michigan's prison on March 12, 1975, but the system wasn't finished with him; he'd wrap up his sentence in a halfway house, making the transition back into the real world. It was a smooth passage, though probably not the one that the Michigan taxpayers had in mind. His designated home for the next six months would be a group residence in Battle Creek, a facility that housed about twenty inmates re-entering society.

Residents were supposed to spend their days at work or looking for work. Squeak saw this independence as an opportunity to make a little money, and he used the "looking for work" requirement as an opportunity for reconnaissance. "There was quite a lot of marijuana being smoked, and a lot of interest in drugs generally. And I had myself a comfortable little room and made friends, literally within hours, of the local dope-smoking crew. Their apparent interest lay along the lines of things like hash oil and speed. And well, I'm going to be stuck at this halfway house for a while, so I thought I might as well have myself a little fun, and wondered what I could turn up locally in the way of materials."

Something "turned up" on a bus ride to Kalamazoo College which had 1,400 students, laid-back attitudes, and a very trusting approach to its physical security. It provided a golden opportunity. In the chemistry department, deserted at lunch hour, he found "No one around, the stockroom wide open. I could not believe this. Well, it's time to get busy."

He eventually left with "quite a lot of stuff. Vacuum distillation equipment, fraction cutters, multi-neck flasks, a rotary evaporator, electric stirrers. Walking down the street, going in the back of the halfway house, with what was effectively most of a drug lab."

Within another day, he had the lab running. "A miniature one, and I got busy and extracted some hash oil, and then I made some amphetamine and dimethyltryptamine."

Things were going well, but his familiar problem had emerged. Like the hippies he detested, his new Battle Creek buddies showed little interest in actually paying for his product.

"For one reason or another, it became apparent to me that I wasn't going to develop a viable business. Everybody was fine with getting high, but they really didn't have a customer base. I decided the halfway house stuff had exhausted its usefulness and interest. So I packed up all my glassware and loaded my suitcase, and hopped the Greyhound bus for Oklahoma City."

This move marked his transition from a thief afflicting American universities to a full-time drug manufacturer plaguing everybody else.

CHAPTER 15

Oklahoma City, 1975

After a decade of wandering from coast to coast, periodically interrupted by stays in state custody, Erik had finally found a place where he wanted to settle down. Oklahoma, it seemed, had it all. It was centrally located, easy to get to, and seemed to have a voracious market for methamphetamine. He'd made some now-useful connections in the state when he'd been locked up in McAlester a few years before.

The state had one additional feature that appealed immensely to the boy who once dreamed of living out his life on a South Dakota farm: Oklahoma is, as its state song proclaims, 'where the wind comes sweepin' down the plains.' He felt right at home there on the Sooner State's wide-open prairie grasslands.

Best of all, from Erik's perspective, the state was home to a number of colleges and universities, with quite a few clustered in the Oklahoma City area. To get the materials he needed to start his latest lab, he visited most of these institutions, stealing equipment and supplies from all of them, including the most productive of all, the University of Oklahoma in Norman, where opportunity knocked.

Quite a bit of clandestine chemistry took place at OU's Chemistry Department at the time. "I believe that this was something of a rite of passage for young graduate students in this era," Erik said of drug manufacturing in college chemistry departments. "I seldom went into any chemistry department and failed to see someone's special project."

He suspected that most of these operations were non-commercial, intended to promote "knowledge for knowledge's sake," in the finest traditions of Bosch, Haber, Alles, and Niemann. "Although I'm certain that many of them felt the need to experiment with their products, and most wouldn't be above sharing."

Some of these labs had profit potential. "I saw a few that were exploring different syntheses for methamphetamine," he said.

A couple of chemistry education traditions bolstered this option. "These places had rules, unwritten perhaps, but very much honored by everyone in the department, students, and faculty. One of the most important was that one must never touch someone else's experiment." People might get curious about some of the reactions taking place on the new student's lab bench, but at OU and the other institutions he visited, they followed the unwritten rules and left it alone.

* * *

On January 15, 1975, Dr. Keith Hollenbeak, a professor in the University of Oklahoma's Chemistry Department, came across something unusual in room 407 of DeBarr Hall. The room had been allocated for storage, but when Hollenbeak opened the door, he saw a lab setup that included a heating element and liquid boiling in a flask. He immediately called the OU Police Department.

Investigator Mike Feuerborn responded to DeBarr Hall to find a gaggle of professors standing outside the storage room. They'd looked at the setup, the profs told Feuerborn, and concluded that somebody was operating an illegal drug manufacturing lab in their closet. Furthermore, they were pretty sure that all of the equipment in the room had been stolen from the chemistry department, and probably the chemicals, too.

Feuerborn settled down inside the room (without touching the experiment) to wait for someone to show themselves. Three hours later, someone did.

The man who entered turned out to be Jeffrey Scott Weimar, 23, and he claimed he'd just been looking for a quiet place for some peaceful meditation. He was carrying a couple of books as a student might. One of them was a chemistry textbook, and the other was an edition of the *Journal of Medicinal Chemistry.* Weimar said he didn't know anything about the lab equipment or the chemicals in the room, hadn't set any of it up. He denied making any drugs, or taking any of the chemistry department's chemicals or equipment. But Feuerborn wasn't buying it and arrested him on the spot.

The detective photographed all of the equipment, then seized it and the chemicals after giving a sample of the boiling liquid to Dr. Hollenbeak who'd first found it. The professor tested it, reporting that it consisted of 2,4,5-trimethoxy benzaldehyde and another chemical, nitroethane.

Dr. Hollenbeak also pointed out that Weimar's copy of the *Journal of Medicinal Chemistry* contained an article giving directions for the manufacture of 2,4,5-trimethoxy amphetamine, also called TMA. The article said that the first step in the process was combining 2,4,5-trimethoxy benzaldehyde and nitroethane. The next steps required several chemicals, including lithium aluminum hydride, all of which were also found in the room.

The OU police charged Weimar with attempted drug manufacturing, and he said later that he'd decided to try to make some TMA because he'd "gotten into a little trouble" and needed the money to pay for an attorney to represent him on a burglary charge. A jury convicted him, and he got two years on the drug case.

Later in 1975, Erik met Keith Hollenbeak, and the two became friends, finding they had a lot in common. The professor's description of TMA and Weimar's amateurish attempt to make it intrigued Erik, who decided this new substance might have commercial possibilities. "I knew immediately that TMA had potential," he says. "Manufacturing requires some relatively unusual chemicals, but only nitroethane was of any interest to the DEA, and I had sources for that, including Keith. It seemed to me to be a lucrative opportunity. Keith agreed."

The two chemists—a high school dropout and a PhD and OU chemistry professor—wouldn't forget the lucrative possibilities. They would stay in touch and eventually team up to produce a drug far more deadly than TMA.

That one was called fentanyl.

CHAPTER 16

Oklahoma City, 1975 – 1978

Still intent on breaking into Oklahoma's meth business, Erik found an opportunity in Oklahoma City. It started off well enough. A prison acquaintance introduced Erik to Robert Paul Harris, a World War II army vet and Oklahoma native who "wanted to talk about the possibility of making amphetamines." Since Harris, who ran a diagnostic lab in Oklahoma City, offered to finance the operation, Erik jumped on board. "We were fifty-fifty partners. I was supplying the technology, and he was supplying the money.

"Harris had a severe drug problem," Erik said. He'd been getting meth through a similar arrangement before his chemist "got a bad feeling off of Bob and bailed, leaving only his notes behind." These should have been flashing red lights for Erik, but need and greed took over, so he missed the warning.

He did shut down Harris' previous efforts at going it alone. "Bob was always buying chemicals, including phenylacetone from a chemical supply place down on the other side of the Santa Fe tracks and trying to make speed. It was beyond Harris' limited skills, and I said, 'Well, perhaps we can do this, but we're going to have to make all our own precursors,' because P2P[2] was not restricted at the time, but I knew the state was watching it. I managed to convince him that this would be a bad idea.

"We got a place over on Northwest 40th," and within a matter of days, Erik had filled the rented house with all of the equipment necessary to make methamphetamine in multi-pound quantities. "The whole operation was quite successful, and I thought that everything was running well, and we turned out a product and a rather good one. I guess the people he was selling to loved it."

But there were more warning signs. "I began to notice if I was asleep, for instance, Harris would creep in the house almost like a cartoon character and go to this drying oven where I stored the finished product and take some. I said, 'Bob, what the hell are you doing? You're a partner. You don't have to sneak off with the product.' Meth. You notice a lot of peculiar behavior around it."

And then it all fell apart.

"I took off with a lady for the weekend to have some fun, and when I returned, the laboratory had been cleaned out. All the equipment—which in fact belonged to me— the largest equipment, a 12-liter, plus some smaller stuff. Condensers, a vacuum pump, rotary evaporator, all the usual. I was mad about that rotary evaporator."

He'd stolen most of the stuff from Kalamazoo College, or later from institutions in Oklahoma, but all of it was gone, the chemicals, too. "Harris felt he had learned enough from me to run the operation by himself, and he ripped me off."

Standing in the empty house, the rage built.

Kimberly Dulany, the daughter of the woman he would marry a few years later, remembered her stepfather's temper.

---

2. Phenylacetone, also known as phenyl-2-propanone or P2P, is a direct meth precursor and key to one of the fastest and easiest routes to methamphetamine. It is closely watched by DEA and state agencies like OBN, and is currently a Schedule II controlled substance, as is meth itself.

"He was almost always very easygoing. It took a lot to set him off, but when it did, look out. Mostly he'd just ignore things that might be making him mad, and sometimes he'd seem like he was mad but just making a point. But folks who hurt dogs or little kids… Well, he always had a gun and I've seen him threaten people with it. They believed he'd use it, and so did I."

Erik might have scammed a few hundred people in his life up to that point, but he didn't like being on the receiving end, outwitted by someone far beneath him in terms of ability and intelligence. But standing in what had been their drug lab, although Erik might be plenty mad and sorely tempted to retrieve his faithful Colt .45, go find his one-time partner, and settle things the old-fashioned way, he was still smart and rational enough to know this wasn't a good plan.

"I had to get a lab up and running again. I had to get some equipment, and get it in a hurry. We didn't have a lot of cash available, and I needed that to live on. So, I did what I did."

Because he was rushed or just pushing too hard, things went catastrophically wrong. "I filched an oscilloscope from OSU and got caught trying to sell it."

Charged with grand larceny, a felony enhanced because of his criminal history, the arrest put him in a major bind. He already had seven felony convictions, including one in Oklahoma for exactly the same crime he was now being charged with. In fact, he was still on probation in Michigan, which had lost track of him when he'd ditched the Battle Creek halfway house; the authorities there issued a warrant for him at the end of April.

If nothing changed, he'd be returning to McAlester for stealing the OSU equipment, this time for at least ten years, and probably back to Michigan after that.

"This prospect did not appeal to me," Erik said. "I was thoroughly disgusted about the whole rip-off thing, and I ended up having a conversation with the captain in the jail who said, 'I'm going to have the OBN guys come around and talk to you,' and one day, who shows up but James Michael Birdsong."

Agent James "Jimmy" Birdsong of the brand-new Oklahoma Bureau of Narcotics and Dangerous Drugs Control went over to the jail to see what Erik had to say. The two men got along fine, and that first meeting was the beginning of a long, if unlikely, friendship between a career illegal drug manufacturer and one of Oklahoma's most notable narcs.

"I liked Jimmy right from the beginning. He never played the bullshit games other cops did. Always told you right where you stood with him. He made it perfectly clear that if he caught me in a lab, he'd be sending me back to McAlester, but he'd help me out if I helped him."

Erik needed all the help he could get. "We talked about this whole thing, and he found my tale sort of fascinating… or that part of it that I told him…and we hit it off."

Erik provided Birdsong with three key pieces of information. Although he disparaged Harris' talents and abilities, he detailed the exact method that Harris would be using to make meth, saying "It's the only one he knows." Second, he described the chemicals Harris would use, and which ones he'd be running low on and needed to replenish. Finally, he told Birdsong where Harris bought his materials, a chemical supply company in southwest Oklahoma City that called Birdsong when Harris showed up to buy some chemicals.

The OBN agents followed Harris to a home on Oklahoma City's northwest side where he lived with his wife and family. Birdsong quickly figured out that he'd hit the methamphetamine jackpot, following a distinctive vinegar-like smell to a small shack at the back of the property.

"Cooking dope in his own backyard," Erik laughed years later. "We'd been using acetic anhydride and phenylacetic acid, so there was a nice cloud of acetic anhydride vapor.

Jimmy got a snoot-full of that, so he knew they'd found the lab."

Harris had taken Erik's detailed notes on the process with him when he'd cleaned out the house. "You'd think the idiot would've put a condenser on it. I mean that was all in the notes, how to do that and how to set this thing up. But no, these amateur cookers like Bob, they tend to dispense with all this. 'Oh, I don't need this. I don't need that.' He can't follow simple instructions and look where it got him."

Birdsong got a search warrant, hit the shack, and found exactly what Erik had told them would be inside: equipment, chemicals, and forty ounces of finished methamphetamine.

OBN arrested Harris on a manufacturing charge, but he made bail and spent the next year getting ready for a trial that would commence in January 1977. His defense blamed a lab assistant who'd been making the drugs in the Harris backyard without his knowledge, pointing the finger back at Erik Marquardt. This was a further betrayal that Erik would repay in a memorable appearance on the witness stand at Harris' trial.

There, a captivated jury listened raptly as he told them that Harris had been a sloppy, barely competent chemist— but also one who had turned out the methamphetamine he was charged with making. Erik also provided the jury with some moral instruction, commenting on Harris' lack of talent and professionalism. "'One thinks that drug manufacturing…right or wrong, you know, I don't think that I am prepared to argue that question. But if it's carried out incorrectly, one can do a great deal of harm to a great many people very quickly," he said.

Harris was exactly such a danger to the Oklahoma community.

If Harris' attorney thought he could discredit Erik's testimony by challenging him on his own lengthy history of drug manufacturing and crime generally, he'd thought wrong. The state granted Erik immunity to testify in the trial, and he felt free to describe in great detail some of his previous adventures in fabricating pharmaceuticals.

Yes, he'd been doing exactly what Harris was charged with for more than a decade. He'd manufactured his first batches of mescaline and LSD only a couple of weeks after being kicked out of high school. He'd stolen equipment from schools and government labs across the country and made almost every controlled substance in the book—generally in university labs that he took over for that purpose, using chemicals and equipment he stole from the same institutions.

He freely—even proudly—told the jury that he'd even manufactured drugs while in Wisconsin and Michigan prisons, cheerfully admitting that he'd been a career criminal since he was a teenager. He was, he said with considerable pride, a professional criminal, and that's who Robert Paul Harris had chosen to go into business with.

The jury believed him, returning with a guilty verdict for Harris after only a brief deliberation. The judge sentenced the lab operator, then 48 years old, to five years in state prison, but Harris appealed the conviction and remained free on bail throughout 1977 and into 1978.

He didn't quit the drug business, however. Needing cash to pay his lawyer and meth to feed his habit, Harris got down to work in a new lab. He had to start from scratch; OBN had seized all of his equipment and supplies, especially the key precursors needed to make the methamphetamine he hoped to sell.

In May 1978, someone claiming to be a professor at Central State University in Edmond, Oklahoma telephoned a New Jersey chemical manufacturer and ordered a 100-kilogram barrel of phenylacetic acid, essential for making P2P. The laboratory supplier contacted CSU to verify the professor's bona fides. When CSU said they knew nothing of the order, the supplier called OBN.

"We didn't know this so-called professor," an OBN agent said. "But we told them to go ahead and ship the order, and we were waiting when it got here."

OBN attached a homing beacon to the barrel, had the freight company call the number on the order form, then sat back to await developments. The purchaser, an old acquaintance, showed up later that day. Bob Harris wrestled his beeping barrel into the back of a pickup truck and, surrounded by OBN cars and Jimmy Birdsong in an airplane above, drove to a storage facility on the northeast side of Oklahoma City.

"He'd learned a few things from hanging around with Erik," one of the OBN agents from the surveillance said. "He left that barrel in the storage unit for almost a month, letting it cool off, hoping if anybody was watching, they'd give up and go away."

But OBN knew they had a barrel of speed ingredients and a suspect who was already in that line of work, so the agents waited patiently for Harris to come back and move the barrel to the only thing they didn't know: the location of his new lab.

He finally returned in the middle of June, and drove the phenylacetic acid to a decrepit warehouse on Virginia Avenue, just west of downtown Oklahoma City.

"Right in the middle of town, but it was actually a pretty good location for a lab," an OBN agent said. "Only five or six miles from Harris' house, rough neighborhood right next to the railroad tracks in an industrial area. Any smells wouldn't be out of the ordinary down there."

Harris took the barrel out of the truck and muscled it into the warehouse. Convinced he'd discovered Harris's new lab site, Birdsong found a cooperative neighbor who allowed OBN to set up an observation post with a clear view of the warehouse.

Although the agents couldn't see what was inside the building, they saw Harris bringing in boxes of equipment and supplies to construct a lab. They didn't need to see inside because they had a key edge that Harris never saw coming:

Erik was about to nail his former partner for the second time.

As part of his cooperation with OBN, Agent Mel Sires asked him to outline on paper the exact process he, and presumably Harris, used to manufacture their methamphetamine. Erik gladly obliged, creating a six-page description, a virtual blueprint containing everything even an untested rookie like Harris would need to produce a batch of crystal meth.

Using Erik's formula, the OBN agents and a chemist from the Oklahoma State Bureau of Investigation monitored the electric meter on the outside of the building as Harris came and went. "He usually stayed inside for a couple of minutes, sometimes longer, adjusting his set-up or doing some chemistry," an agent who worked on the surveillance said. "Then he'd leave for long stretches. He had some of the equipment set up on timers so it would run without him being there."

By watching the ebb and flow of the power, and comparing that to the steps in Erik's blueprint, the OSBI chemist was able to point to the exact moment when finished methamphetamine was present at the lab. "Ideally what we wanted to do was get the lab when he was finished, to get the finished product, to get the best evidence possible," OBN Director Richard Hervey explained to the media.

That moment came just after seven o'clock p.m. on July 1, when Harris showed up to check on his progress. OBN arrested him without incident, and he clammed up and watched as the agents dismantled his second lab.

"It was a dump," a former OBN agent said. "Dirt floor. It looked like all the glassware and equipment was jury-rigged, hanging off the walls or on these plastic tables. Squeak would have looked down his nose at it, and of course, he hated Harris already. It didn't look like much, but he had finished meth and some more in progress, so it was definitely a working lab, and a pretty big one."

OBN charged Harris, who was still out of jail on an appeal bond from his 1975 lab case, with manufacturing a controlled substance, and this time they brought the charges to federal court. He didn't get bail, and the state revoked his appeal bond.

He pleaded guilty to the federal charges a month later and received an eight-year sentence. That ended the diagnostic lab owner's abbreviated career in drug-making, at least for a few years. Oklahoma would send him to serve his state sentence when the feds were done with him.

Harris never knew that he'd been undone in his second lab by the same person who did him the first time, or that Erik's detailed written recipe for methamphetamine had been the key to OBN's investigation.

OBN got a lot of mileage out of that blueprint that year, using it to nail another, much more dangerous clandestine chemist in a far more sophisticated meth lab.

That individual was named George Erik Marquardt.

CHAPTER 17

Washington, D.C., 1976 – 1977

Near the end of February 1976, the Washington Metropolitan Police Department and the FBI introduced the law enforcement world to a new undercover concept. Federal agents and undercover police officers began operating out of a rented warehouse on Washington, D.C.'s Northeast side, posing as mafia fences—buying stolen property, guns, and narcotics. Concealed microphones and cameras recorded every one of thousands of transactions with the undercover agents, who wrapped up their scheme by inviting their clientele to a party where they arrested everybody.

The media loved it, and so did the reading public, as Washington's *Operation: Sting* became the first of many similar programs conducted across the country in the months and years following.

In 1976, the Federal Law Enforcement Assistance Administration spent $2.2 million on sting operations in nine other cities. By the end of 1977, LEAA had funded operations in twenty-five cities. These "storefronts" are still commonly used in theft, drug, and money laundering investigations today.

In late 1976, the Oklahoma Bureau of Narcotics decided to set up a sting of its own, one with a reverse twist.

As Erik had discovered, Oklahoma had a problem with methamphetamine that year. "Speed," available in either powder form as "crank" or "crystal," and in tablet form as "white cross," or "meth tabs," was cheap, easily available, and ubiquitous across the state. Clandestine laboratories operated by outlaw biker gangs or their associates produced the vast majority of the methamphetamine on the streets, and OBN generally had one or two clandestine laboratory investigations, like that of Robert Harris, underway at any time.

Most of the lab operators, though often called "chemists," were relatively unskilled or unsophisticated. Methamphetamine isn't exceptionally difficult to produce, and most of the cooks were recipe-followers without a lot of chemistry background. But for all of these would-be manufacturers, actually making the meth wasn't the big issue they had to face.

The major problem for the underground chemists was the same one featured in *Breaking Bad*. They needed the precursor chemicals necessary to make methamphetamine, mainly methylamine and P2P.

The DEA and OBN closely monitored sales of both of these chemicals, and the two agencies had long-established relationships with all of the chemical suppliers in the state. These companies, both in Oklahoma and those outside the state, like the New Jersey supplier that had called OBN on Harris, who were shipping to questionable purchasers in Oklahoma, routinely reported suspicious transactions, usually before they even completed the sale.

Experienced meth makers knew this, and understood that getting a safe, reliable and, above all, discreet source for P2P or methylamine was a clandestine chemist's dream.

The brass at OBN wondered what would happen if the Bureau offered them one.

What if OBN set up a storefront selling chemicals, equipment, glassware, and anything else a clandestine lab would need? The undercover store proprietor could record the transactions, get the customer's ID or, at minimum, a license plate number, and provide them with the requested items. Agents could then follow the buyer to the lab site, and that could be raided later when the lab operator had a finished batch of meth ready for sale. It would even be possible to affix a transmitter to, for example, a barrel of P2P, and then track it directly back to the lab.

There were legal issues; defense attorneys in the Washington sting cases had raised entrapment as a defense for their clients, and those detectives had been doing what undercover agents always did: buying the drugs or stolen property. OBN was proposing to sell the precursors and equipment—things legal to possess—to people who would then, the Bureau hoped or at least expected, use them for some illegal purpose.

"Kind of like selling a legal gun to somebody you think is going to use it to shoot somebody," an agent said.

Ultimately, the attorneys decided entrapment could be avoided, and OBN went ahead with the plan, which involved setting up a storefront near the Max Westheimer airport in Norman. They needed an undercover agent, and picked one who hadn't had a lot of exposure in Cleveland County or with clandestine lab operators.

Their choice immediately raised some legitimate doubts.

"I had exactly one chemistry class in high school," the agent said. "I was a criminal justice major. Everything I knew about chemistry you could fit on one sheet of paper. And you could get everything I knew about manufacturing drugs on a three-by-five card."

"No problem," Jimmy Birdsong, the case agent for the investigation, said. OBN had an asset, an informant who knew all there was to know about clandestine labs and methamphetamine manufacturing.

"And that's how I met Erik Marquardt," the agent laughed.

Introduced to Erik as "Jay," the undercover agent settled in with a pad and pen, ready to learn at the master's feet. The initial session didn't go according to Birdsong's plan.

"Jimmy told me not to let on why we wanted all this information. 'Don't tell him about the store. He can't be trusted.' I was fine with that. You never completely trust an informant, never tell them any more than they need to know to do their job.

"But I found out pretty quick that that wasn't going to work with Erik. He was a very, very smart guy."

There were going to be problems.

"First of all, he figured out right away what the plan was," Jay said. "'You're setting up a trick store,' he told me. Took him about ten minutes."

Erik thought the undercover storefront was a terrific idea. "He jumped on it with both feet," Jay said. "He thought that anybody dumb enough to fall for our plan deserved what they got. He also really liked the idea that we'd be taking out his competition, clearing the field for him to do his thing. He never bought precursors; he told me that right away. He made his own, then used them to make meth or whatever else he thought he could sell."

Erik remembered the conversation. "I wouldn't buy anything on the DEA's watchlist, especially methylamine or P2P. Methylamine, for example, isn't that difficult to synthesize," he said. "I produced methylamine from ammonium chloride and formaldehyde—purified by distilling basified solution of HCl salt, removing the NH3 first, or I could make it from ammonium chloride and paraformaldehyde. That produces a higher yield, and the narcotics agents weren't monitoring any of those chemicals."

That last bit, the chemistry talk, raised another problem for Jay. "At our first meeting, I sat there and listened to him, trying to take notes. Finally asked for a break and went to find Jimmy. I told him, 'You're gonna need a new undercover for this thing.' He said 'Why? What's the problem?' I said, 'I just sat in there for three hours and I didn't understand a freakin' word that guy said.' I was in way, way over my head."

Birdsong had a chat with Erik, explaining that he didn't need to teach Jay how to be an organic chemist; OBN didn't have time for that. What Jay needed, he said, was to know his way around a clandestine laboratory, to know what lab operators would require—and how, as he'd just explained, a savvy chemist trying to avoid watchlisted chemicals might work around that.

"Like, if somebody came in and asked for ammonium chloride and paraformaldehyde, I was supposed to be able to figure out that the dude might be making methylamine," Jay says.

Erik, enthusiastically embracing his role as chemistry professor, never completely gave up on trying to teach his hopeless pupil advanced organic chemistry, but he did enjoy the challenge Birdsong had laid down. He also quickly knocked down Jay's fears that the store might fail to attract its targeted customer group.

"I shouldn't think that would be much of a concern," he told Jay. "If we set this up correctly, we'll have people coming from Alaska to buy our merchandise. They'll be knocking down our door," he said, taking some proprietary interest in "our" project.

OBN didn't need Alaskan customers, but it did want to identify those much closer to home and planned to use informants—Erik foremost among them—to bring the right people to the storefront's front door.

Erik threw himself into the project, making suggestions and offering advice, but most critically, outlining the ways that a real clandestine lab operator might stand out and how that person might try to circumvent the watch list.

"It had been my practice in previous years to synthesize all precursors from basic industrial stock," Erik told the agents. Getting all the way from these downstream chemicals to methamphetamine took longer and required skills—and a more sophisticated laboratory—that most bootleg chemists and meth cooks didn't possess.

"Those aren't the people we'll be seeing at the store. We'll get the clowns and the losers like Harris," he told Jay. "The smart ones will be doing it the way I do it."

Mel Sires, OBN's Agent in Charge in Tulsa, where Erik was living while he waited to testify against Harris, challenged him on that, saying in effect, "If you're so smart, how would you do it?"

That was when Erik produced his detailed description of his process: six handwritten pages of formulas that included the timing of each of several methods. It was an exact blueprint for making meth without ever buying a chemical on OBN's watch list.

Jay, who got a copy, said, "It read just like something you'd see in a scientific journal, with references to other articles, other chemists. Like he was writing for the *Journal of Forensic Sciences*, which he read religiously."

In his various meetings with Jay, Erik described alternate methods for manufacturing first methamphetamine, then a variety of other drugs. "Meth, acid, half a dozen others. Some really exotic ones. He was especially interested in one called TMA. He said these things were going to be the psychedelics of the future and anybody who mastered them—meaning him—was going to make a ton of money. Supposedly they had all the best features of meth and LSD or mescaline. He'd made it and tried it."

Jay tried to keep up. "I had a lab manual and later, DEA came out with a book, the *Clandestine Laboratory Guide for Agents and Investigators.* It lists six different methods for synthesizing methamphetamine. I sat in an interview room with Squeak and watched him come up with two more, just off the top of his head. No books, no papers, no math. Had it all in his head. One of them used Sudafed—pseudoephedrine—for the key precursor, which is all the rage now. In 1977, it wasn't even in DEA's book."

All this preparation, planning, and Jay's education came to nothing when, shortly after the conclusion of Harris' January 1977 trial, Erik stopped checking in and left Oklahoma, dropping off OBN's radar. Nobody at the Bureau had any illusions about what had happened or where he'd gone.

"Everybody figured he'd turn up in another lab sooner or later," Jay said. "Just a matter of time. But that was the end of our trick store."

The undercover operation might have been dead, but Erik had left some useful information behind when he vanished from Oklahoma. He'd given that detailed six-page description of his process for making meth and its main precursors, methylamine and P2P. "I went over that thing with him probably twenty times," Jay said. "I wasn't trying to learn how to do it, but by the time he up and vanished, I knew all the steps well enough to pull it off.

"I learned it the same way Jesse picked it up from Walter White in *Breaking Bad*. In fact, I had about as much background in chemistry as Jesse did. I can appreciate how frustrated Walt was. Squeak was the same way with me. But he gave me that process and a half dozen other complete formulas, like recipes, for acid, mescaline, meth. His favorites. All the chemicals, all the steps. Those things came in real handy when we wanted to bust Harris, because he was using the process he'd just learned from the same person who taught it to me."

Erik's blueprint would also come in handy if and when OBN found Erik in another lab.

"I don't think it ever crossed his mind that we might use it against him," Jay said. "He was arrogant about that. Ever since he was a little kid, he was the smartest person in the room and knew it. He always believed he was smarter than everybody else. He made that real clear."

"He's a brain when it comes to that chemistry stuff," Sires told a reporter later. "But he's dumb as a gourd otherwise."

Jay agreed. "He's brilliant on the chemistry, and he's been through the justice system so many times," he said. "He knows exactly how things work, how *we* work. That's an extremely very rare combination, a first-rate chemist and a professional criminal who's also worked with law enforcement. Someone like that is going to be very dangerous."

To catch him this time, OBN would need luck and patience…but when the agents caught up with him, they'd be using a tool Erik himself had given them to make their case. Until then, he was in the wind, and Jay went back to working undercover on other cases.

"Whatever happened to that trick store you and I were setting up back there in Oklahoma?" Erik asked much later.

"You did," Jay told him. "You and a meth lab in Beggs, Oklahoma happened."

CHAPTER 18

Seattle, Washington, 1976 – 1977

Erik wound up in the Pacific Northwest with the help of Jimmy Birdsong and OBN. "I told Jimmy that I wanted to move up to the West Coast," Erik said. "I was still on probation on the theft case, so Jimmy arranged it with the court. They had the Harris trial coming up, but I said I'd come back whenever they needed me."

Undercover agent Jay remembered, "Pretty much everybody at OBN felt like Squeak on the West Coast was a lot better than Squeak anywhere in Oklahoma, considering that wherever he was, he'd be in a lab making dope."

Jay's lessons in clandestine chemistry were suspended, resuming sporadically whenever Erik showed up in town. "He was playing us," Jay added. "Which is why you never trust an informant."

Erik thought Seattle seemed to be a good choice. "I looked around for laboratory space and found it at the King County Courthouse Annex, which was a former children's orthopedic hospital. They had the King County morgue there for a while, but then they moved it all over to Harborview and the building was put up for rent. This would've been right around Christmas of 1976. I leased the old pathology department laboratory and got busy."

The place, once a functioning laboratory, became one again as Erik, who'd made heroin before in another abandoned morgue, settled in. "I was still flying back and forth to Oklahoma City for the Harris case. Meeting with lawyers, talking to Jay and Mel and Jimmy. Helping with the trick store. When Jimmy told me I had to come down, I'd go out and hop on a plane and go. Jimmy thought they ought to cover my plane fare, but I wasn't interested in rocking that boat. I paid my own plane fare."

Paying his own way wasn't generosity toward the Oklahoma taxpayers; it meant the people at OBN, who didn't know exactly where Squeak was living, also didn't know exactly when he was coming or going. That was important because he was shipping meth back to the state where his market was, and where his customers lived.

* * *

OBN Agent Warren Henderson was a man on a mission. Before getting permission to move, Erik had been living in Tulsa throughout the wait for the Harris trial, and he was also hanging out with two men who were of interest to OBN and Henderson.

Bob Fearon, a long-time Tulsa resident, inventor, and quintessential American tinkerer, operated Electrochemical Laboratories, doing occasional work for Oklahoma's oil industry and providing a home for his experiments. He claimed to hold as many as ninety patents.

"He's got a rather distinguished record in the oilfield industries," Squeak said. "The inventor of neutron well logging. At one time a rather formidable actor in the oil field. Master's degree in physics from the University of Pittsburgh in the mid-'30s.

"Bob was an especially useful individual," Erik continued. "His business was very well established in Tulsa, and he had accounts at some of the major chemical suppliers that had existed for thirty years. Transactions, even for chemicals that the narcotic agents are watching, tend to not get as much scrutiny when a customer like Bob is well-known and reputable."

Fearon knew exactly what his new friend did, because Erik told him. "I worked for him in 1976, when I got out of jail in Oklahoma City. I'd moved to Tulsa, and I called him up on the phone and told him, I said, 'Well, I'm an out-of-work LSD manufacturer looking for something interesting to do.' And he says, 'Oh, did you make it from ergotamine?' I said, 'No, I made it from lysergic acid monohydrate. But I'm not interested in making any more LSD right now. What I'm interested in doing is getting a job.'"

Fearon obliged, asked him to build a magnetometer, and let Erik order chemicals and supplies on the company account.

His other cohort, Jerome "Jerry" McCoy, held a PhD in physics and taught that subject as a professor at the University of Tulsa. McCoy was equally useful with connections at the school, though not in the chemistry department.

"Jerry was a bit of a drinking buddy who became my co-conspirator. We had mutual interests, and one of them was money."

Henderson, a Tulsa resident assigned to OBN's two-man office in the city, thought both of Erik's new friends were dirty, at least accomplices if not full-fledged partners, so he kept track of the two men, expecting to see Erik sooner or later. In the meantime, he worked his sources, knowing that wherever he was, the chemist would be sending his finished product to his customers, and most of them were in Oklahoma.

Erik hadn't given up drug manufacturing just because he was working part-time for OBN, talking with Jimmy Birdsong about the Harris case, and giving Jay lessons in clandestine chemistry. "Summer of '77, and once they'd convicted Harris, I didn't have to go back down there anymore, so full tilt boogie. It was kind of nerve-racking. I was a prosecutor's witness on one end of the country and a drug manufacturer on the other, but that made the game a lot more interesting."

He was working with a twenty-five-year-old Tulsa resident who shared his interest in clandestine chemistry. Leroy Schumacher described their introduction: "My girlfriend was his next-door neighbor, and that's how I met him, from living with her. Oh, he took a liking to me. And I liked him, too, because he was kind of a strange character. He just kind of fascinated me, and it just took off from there."

Schumacher knew about the lab, and expressed his interest. "And then one day he asked me for my coffee, and he said 'I want you to try this,' and he put some stuff in there, just a little bit, and I drank it. And I went to the moon. And he said, 'You think you could sell this?' I said, 'Hey, you bet.'"

The two developed a bond close enough that Erik brought Schumacher into at least four of his labs in Oklahoma, and the one in the morgue in Seattle. Schumacher helped with the production as well as sales.

On one occasion, the two men set up a lab in Schumacher's parents' barn while they were away, then finished the batch in their kitchen. "My mom came home and asked me, 'What is that smell?' Cooking meth always has a hell of an odor. That batch came out looking like peanut butter. He couldn't clean it up. But it was some of the best-selling stuff we put out."

Erik's new distributor and part-time lab assistant was selling meth as fast as Erik could pump it out and the relationship, profitable for both of them, continued after Erik moved away from Oklahoma. Schumacher began flying up to Seattle to pick up each batch, and Erik flew back down to Oklahoma several times before Schumacher changed the plan.

"I was making beaucoup money. And I told him, I said, 'Well, I'll tell you what, I'm going to send my runner from now on.' I just didn't want the heat on me, right?"

In another effort to avoid heat and keep OBN at arm's length, the courier was flying into Wichita, about a two-and-a-half-hour drive from Tulsa. Previous trips had gone well, but this one in May 1977 would have a different ending.

Schumacher drove up to Wichita with two friends. They were expecting the runner—Lester Campbell—to arrive on a flight from Seattle with at least a pound of methamphetamine. Schumacher had prepped his customers in Tulsa, letting them know that a load was coming in.

Looking back, Schumacher thought this was a mistake. "My main partner who was working with me, I told him, and he told his brother who wasn't getting along with his wife, and she snitched us off."

OBN alerted the Wichita Police Department, which was waiting at the airport on May 20, and they arrested everyone when they collected Campbell's suitcase from the baggage carousel. The police found three jars containing 1.3 pounds of methamphetamine. "When they charged us, they said that it was the biggest methamphetamine bust in Kansas up to that time," Schumacher said.

"We figured Squeak was behind this. Who else do we know who's a meth chemist from Oklahoma, living in the Northwest and sending stuff to Tulsa people?" Henderson asked.

But although Henderson pressed Schumacher hard, he refused to give up his source. "I had the chance. They offered me full immunity to snitch, you know, to get after Squeak. I just told him no. I'd rather do my time in prison than snitch."

The uncooperative Mr. Schumacher would be sentenced to two to five years in the Kansas State Penitentiary at Lansing, but he would have been no help to OBN, because Erik knew about the bust.

"Leroy sent this guy up to pick up some dope, and we met him at the airport. This clown's got on this T-shirt with a badge, says 'Treasury Department, Narcotic Section.' To me, this is somebody that's trying to draw attention to themselves. He doesn't know what low profile is. It was all wrong. We didn't take him out to my house on Bainbridge Island or anything like that. Took him up to a local motel on Queen Anne Hill and got his suitcase packed with cosmetic bottles filled with amphetamine.

"So, take him back to the airport and dumped him off in the garage. I didn't want to go inside with this fool. Put him on the plane. Later in the day, I called up Leroy to ask him if he got in all right, if they picked the idiot up at the airport. I got Leroy's girlfriend, and she said, 'Oh, yeah. They picked it up all right, but they've decided to spend the night in Wichita.'

"'Oh. Well, okay.' Alarm's going off. I get off the phone and immediately dial up the Sedgwick County Jail. I said, 'I'm attorney so-and-so. I've been hired to represent…I'm trying to find out who these guys are.' They said, 'Oh, you mean that big drug bust out at the airport?'

"I said, 'Well, thank you very much.' The deputy actually said, 'I thought you said you were an attorney.' I said, 'Well, I'm really sorry about that.' Enough said. Time to go.

"I broke off all contact with those people. I didn't know it would be Mel and Warren, but I was fairly certain that somebody would be coming for me after the Wichita thing went bad. Even if none of those people they arrested gave me up, I was confident that Jimmy or someone else would be able to put two and two together and get Squeak," he said.

"We went off the top of Bainbridge Island over on the Kingston Ferry to the mainland, and we're sweating it all the way over. Got about fifty thousand bucks, left most of our stuff. We were towing a trailer behind the U-Haul that actually had the laboratory in it. Went over to Spokane, made a few loads of dope over there, one good load and half of another. And we were in and out of a motel one night, and somebody just picked up on us, and I felt it. 'Ah, well this is not good.'

"I was probably on top of my game as a hit-and-run drug manufacturer because I was very aware of police interest. I felt like I could sense the heat, and I found out later that those perceptions were accurate. OBN had tracked me over to Spokane some way or another, and had talked to local Vice over there, and put them on us. Time to move again, and next thing you know, we're rolling down the Columbia River."

Four decades before the fictional Walter White and Jesse Pinkman would hit the road in their mobile RV drug lab, Erik went there first, hitting campgrounds in state and national parks where he would stay for a few days or a week, then move on. "The conditions were fairly primitive, but that was a challenge I could overcome."

He produced batches every three or four days, distributed some of it in the area, stayed in contact with an Oklahoma connection, and shipped the meth out "after my representative told me payment had been received. Things all went very smoothly, finished a load of dope down in Cascade Locks, and then OBN knocked over Lasater."

In the Sedgewick County Jail in Wichita, Leroy Schumacher was trying to figure out what had happened. "I had been staying at Gary Lasater's, my number one customer, his apartment, and Squeak had the phone number there. That's where we was (sic) connecting with each other. Squeak called and Gary answered and told him we'd been busted. So him and Squeak hooked up. And I swear to this day, he's the one that got Squeak busted. I think he got caught and he decided, well, he's going to snitch and get a deal."

Gary Lasater had none of Schumacher's scruples about snitching. Henderson had already bought methamphetamine from Lasater, including some from the batch that looked like peanut butter, and described him as "kind of a zero" and at least two steps removed from Erik.

Convinced, however, that Lasater was somewhere on Erik's ladder, Henderson pressed hard, and Lasater said he'd been in contact with a chemist called Squeak who was currently somewhere in the Pacific Northwest.

"Just what we wanted to hear," Henderson said.

Lasater didn't know much more than Squeak's name and that he was a chemist and the source of Schumacher's meth, but that was enough for OBN, which wanted Squeak badly and was willing to send two agents to Seattle to try and get him.

Their quarry had warm memories of the episode, the pursuit he later described to a Tulsa reporter as "the last American folk adventure, the light of the moon, narcotics agents chasing you all over the land."

"I didn't know how close they were, but I had no problem keeping a step or two ahead. I led them a merry chase."

The agents didn't remember it as particularly merry as they drove from campground to campground asking about a big, unkempt-looking man in a pickup truck with Oklahoma license plates. Connecting with their counterparts in the Washington and Oregon State Police, they let them know how big a problem they had running loose in their states. One of the state police detectives, suitably impressed, said of Erik, "This guy could make dope from the dirt in your pockets," which wasn't far from the truth.

For a couple of weeks, they bounced from one park to another. "We had a picture of Squeak and a description of his truck, and we ran into people who remembered seeing him or the pickup, the Oklahoma tag. Some people remembered smelling chemicals on him and at his campsite, but we were always just a little short. The closest we got was a state park where the people said, 'You just missed him.' He'd pulled out just minutes before. Maybe going out one entrance when we were going in another one," Henderson said.

Because they didn't know where Erik was headed next, the agents stayed one jump behind, and after "a bunch of near misses," they were out of money and out of time. OBN told them to come home.

CHAPTER 19

Faribault, Minnesota, October 25, 1977

At about the time his pursuers gave up and headed out on the long drive back to Tulsa, Erik figured he'd worked this road scam to its useful end; it was time to go home. He disposed of all his chemical waste, packed up everything he could still use, and set out on I-90, heading east across the Rocky Mountains and his beloved plains with Carla, a "Road Suzie" from Oklahoma and her brother Rex, his "semi-partner." It was a "fine drive" through western Washington, the Idaho Panhandle, and Montana, a "very enjoyable trip" that he still remembered fondly forty years later.

But the cross-country trek ended outside Faribault, Minnesota, a farming community on I-35 south of Minneapolis, when Erik wrecked the pickup on October 25, 1977.

"Rolled it end over end. It was a mess. Me, too."

The Rice County sheriff's deputies who responded to the accident scene became suspicious when the only party in the crash—an injured man who reeked of a toxic chemical spill—could not produce a driver's license or any other ID. While an ambulance took Erik to the hospital in Faribault, deputies went to his room at the Lyndale Motel. There they found Carla and Rex who "demanded a warrant, but the cops tried to force or talk their way into the motel room. And this guy got belligerent with Rex when Rex wouldn't let him in. And so they just essentially pushed over the top of him, and went in there and started searching."

The searchers had the right place: they found plenty of evidence, but none of the methamphetamine they'd been hoping for. "All they got was the glassware and lab equipment, and there was a bunch of that. But it was all fruit of the poisonous tree. No warrant," Erik said.

By the time a sheriff's sergeant reached the scene, the damage had been done. "The guy that was running the arrest felt terrible about it," the sergeant told Erik later, but it was too late. The cops scored in the motel room, so they hit a second place at a lakeside resort nearby and got more glassware and chemicals. Then they sent everything up to the Minnesota Bureau of Criminal Apprehension in Saint Paul, which reported that it was exactly what the BCA would expect to find in a methamphetamine laboratory and about what they'd see in a year's worth of seizures.

Everybody was convinced that they had a major drug manufacturer—and the biggest criminal to hit little Faribault in years—in their hospital bed.

There were just those two small problems.

"I had the dope mostly finished and was going to bring it out of solution that morning, but it wasn't in the room," Erik said, explaining the absence of methamphetamine. "Luck, mostly. And those ducks."

So the police had no crime but plenty of evidence, all of which had been obtained by violating their only suspect's Constitutional rights.

"I was following this investigation from my bed while I was all busted up from this accident. I had called over to my motel room, and some guy answered. I said, 'Where's my girlfriend?' and he said she wasn't there. He said he was a police officer and I said, 'What are you doing in my motel room?' And he says, 'Oh, we think you were making amphetamines.' Okay, 'Well thank you for telling me that. Why don't you come over here and read me my rights? I'm all busted up. Obviously, I'm not going anyplace.' He says, 'Yeah, we'll probably get around to that.'"

There was no meth at either crime scene because Erik had just relocated from a third location, and hauled the idle equipment and chemicals to the motel rooms in Faribault. "I had just come out of shutting down another lab, a very nice setup in the basement of a feed mill in Albert Lea. I had tumbled to the fact that somebody had made a surreptitious entry into the lab, and there was an argument over the rights to some space."

The dispute was with a local resident who was storing wooden duck decoys in the building. "His ducks shouldn't have been there. He was told to take them out."

Convinced that the duck man was snooping and "heating us up with the Albert Lea police," he packed up his lab and headed up to Faribault, about forty-five miles north.

Before going, though, he left some surprises for the owner of the decoy ducks. "Went in there and took a couple of ducks, and cut their heads off and put them on backwards and glued them on there. Made the rest of them smell real bad."

This fairly juvenile response turned more serious when they left the duck man a bigger surprise. "Probably not a real good thing to do in retrospect, but we drilled out one of the ducks and put about two ounces of metallic sodium in the bottom of it."

Metallic sodium is another of those substances that "reacts violently" with water, a duck decoy's natural habitat. Two ounces would have created an impressive and unforgettable start to that year's duck season.

"I don't mind law enforcement guys, no problem with that, but citizens don't belong in a game between serious players. I won't shoot a policeman. Citizen sticks his nose into my business? He could get shot."

Feeling pretty good about his situation despite the injuries and the loss of his labs in an illegal search, Erik did something out of character: he dialed a local attorney. He'd always displayed an almost pathological aversion to lawyers, but this time he thought some legal representation might be useful.

"I got the nurse to prop me up, and got on the phone. The first attorney that I get, he stopped me and said, 'Look, I'd like to take your case, but in a sense, I've already got it. I'm the acting district attorney down here this year.' And I said, 'Well, I guess I came to the wrong shop.' He laughed and said, 'Between you and me and the gate post, there's not much of a case, but why don't you call up Mike Gillen.'

"And so I call up Mike, and he came right over. I told him what the deal was, and he says, 'Okay, on my way.' He found out they had my girlfriend and her brother over at the local police station. They weren't doing any good with Rex at all. He went hard. And they got on Carla so bad, they just scared her. If they would've been half nice to her, she probably would've told them everything. But they didn't, they overdid it. About that time, Mike shows up and springs them both. And here they come, waltzing into my room with big smiles on their faces, and Mike behind them. And I took a line from the old Hays movie code and said, 'The law, defeated.'"

The law may have been defeated, but Rice County law enforcement had had enough of Erik and his two friends. Three days after the crash, police escorted Carla and Rex to the Iowa state line and watched them disappear down I-35 toward Oklahoma. Erik, still in the hospital, had money left after paying Gillen and his hospital bill, so he found a used truck, this one a bit shabbier but sound enough to make it to Tulsa. Then he resumed the journey down I-35. "Got back in November, glad to be out of Minnesota."

* * *

Warren Henderson was back in Tulsa, too, still waiting, and a month later, his patience paid off. While working another drug case on Tulsa's south side, Henderson had parked in a strip mall across the street from the meet at the Camelot Hotel. The surveillance was dragging. "Nothing was happening, and everybody was bored…and then he shows up."

Nobody paid much attention to the battered pickup when it pulled up and stopped next to a payphone almost directly in front of Henderson's car. But the agent perked right up when a familiar figure climbed out of the truck and walked to the phone. "I'd rather be lucky than good," Henderson laughed. "There's Squeak, bigger than life."

Henderson abandoned the other investigation, and carefully followed the pickup out of town down US Route 75 into the Oklahoma countryside. The trek that had taken him on a 2,000-mile quest across half of the United States ended at a small blue farmhouse about 25 miles south of Tulsa, just outside the little town of Beggs.

Henderson, both lucky and good, thought he'd found Erik's new lab.

CHAPTER 20

Beggs, Oklahoma, 1977 – 1978

"OBN rented us a trailer on a property a couple of hundred yards away, and we set up where we could monitor comings and goings," Henderson said. There were quite a few of those: Erik leaving to go up to Tulsa and Fearon's business, to chemical supply companies, and "a hippie chick who said she was an artist and sculptor, but she worked with glass."

Jerry McCoy came into the picture, too. "Squeak was getting his glassware from McCoy, who was getting it from the university where he worked," Erik's distributor, Leroy Schumacher remembered.

By early January, Henderson and Sires had almost everything they needed, and made the final preparations to raid the lab as Erik put the final touches on his latest creation. Sires had Erik's blueprint for methamphetamine, and OBN put another meter on the electric line leading to the farmhouse so they could track the power consumption inside as they drew up the search warrant that would get them through the front door.

Hoping for final confirmation of the blue house's secret purpose, Henderson sent two agents in for a closer look. On the evening of January 16, Elaine Dodd and Lonnie Wright drove into the farmyard and went to Erik's front door. Both agents were relatively new at the time, which was important because in his earlier work as an informant, Erik had met or at least seen most of OBN's workforce and, being Erik, he had carefully filed the names and faces away for future reference.

The agents said they were on their way to the Tulsa airport when they had car trouble, and asked to use Erik's phone. He said he was sorry, but he couldn't let them in the house because of the strong chemical odor coming from inside the residence. They asked what was making the smell.

"I wish I could tell you," Erik said.

That was all the confirmation Henderson needed. He took his affidavit to a judge.

* * *

Early on the morning of January 17, 1978, OBN Agents Warren Henderson and Mel Sires, carrying a search warrant, approached the front door of a small blue farmhouse that lay five miles northwest of tiny Beggs, Oklahoma.

Sires knocked on the door and waited for Erik to answer it. As the first two who would be entering the lab and shutting it down, he and Henderson were wearing respirators. Their glass faceplates fogged in the frigid early morning air.

When Erik opened the door, he peered at both of them through his own clouded faceplate. "Is that you, Mel?" he asked.

"Yeah, Squeak. Got a warrant."

Shrugging, Erik passed the flask he was holding to Henderson, turned around, and put his hands behind his back. "Well, you got me fair and square," he said, conceding defeat.

"I was glad to see them, strange as it may seem to say so. I knew I'd been busted the night before when the young couple on their way to the airport stopped by. I was glad it was OBN and not people I didn't know."

He showed his appreciation by stepping back into the doorway and blocking Sires from entering the house. But this wasn't resistance to the search warrant or his arrest.

"I saw right away that the cartridges on their masks were not appropriate for the chemicals in the house. There was cyanide gas present, and any number of other things that wouldn't have been good."

"He didn't want any of us to get hurt," Henderson said. "I busted plenty of people who would have said 'go right ahead, officer,' and laughed while we choked out. But that's not Squeak."

He told them where in the house they could find his .45 Colt and the correct cartridges for their masks. After exchanging masks with Henderson, who went in to collect the cartridges and the gun, Erik stayed on the front lawn and chatted with Sires, telling him where he was in the process and how to shut down the lab safely.

"Mel read him his rights, but there's no shutting Squeak up when he's on a roll," Henderson said. "And his attitude was that we'd caught him: the game was over—for now— and he was ready to move on."

The agents and OSBI chemists who entered the house found a far more sophisticated setup than the Robert Harris lab. And although they'd caught him with finished methamphetamine on hand, he was quick to tell them that meth was only a stepping-stone on his way to a much more ambitious project.

"I was going to create the recreational drug of the future. Speed and a hallucinogen in one package." TMA, he thought, would attract both the many customers who sought meth—and were willing to actually pay for it—as well as the less lucrative "hippie market."

"Hollenbeak was very excited about it, and I reviewed the literature and found it had tremendous potential," Erik said. He had some personal experience to offer after taking a small sample of his first batch. "I knew it was going to be good when I watched the car's windows melting."

OBN photographs of the lab show chemical equipment, scales, electronic gear, and racks of glassware on almost every wall of the house. He had re-routed electric and water lines to service pieces of equipment, and built storage for bottles and boxes of chemicals.

Erik walked through the place in handcuffs, identifying the contents of the various containers for OSBI chemist Don Flynt.

"This wasn't some fly-by-night operation," Henderson said. "He was planning on being there for a while."

Elaine Dodd described the scene inside and Erik's response. "He was very nice to everyone. He took us through the house, and like a proud papa, told us about each room. Each room had its own particular drug that he was making. There was a room for the methamphetamine and a room that was 2,4,5-trimethoxyamphetamine. There wasn't much space that was not used for drugs in that home."

Dodd said Erik had a surprise in his TMA space. "When he showed us the room where he was making the 2,4,5-trimethoxyamphetamine, he had [a printout from] a mass spectrometer. That was a paper with charts to show the composition of the TMA. He had run his own tests or had a buddy do it. He was proud to have this proof of what the drug was, because he told us that even the DEA would not be familiar with this particular drug."

"I had a finished batch of methamphetamine, and a separate area set aside for the TMA I was in the process of developing. I explained all this to Mel and Warren and Don. They found the spectrograph we'd run on the TMA. Warren was sure that McCoy had run the mass spec, or had it done on equipment at the University of Tulsa. I wouldn't confirm that. It was actually run by my friend Keith. He ran samples I gave him through the mass spec at his work. I kept his name out of it, so Warren and Mel were chasing the wrong rabbit. They were focused exclusively on Jerry McCoy."

Erik fell easily back into his role as an OBN cooperator, waived his Miranda rights to silence and an attorney, and told the agents anything they wanted to know. Almost.

He never mentioned Keith Hollenbeak at all, and claimed Bob Fearon and Jerry McCoy had no knowledge about the goings-on in Beggs.

"He wasn't being honest with us about his partners in the lab. We asked him about Fearon and McCoy, and he admitted he knew them but said they weren't involved," Henderson said. "We knew that was bullshit, but he wasn't budging."

"Warren, I think, had some special grievance because of Jerry's position at the University of Tulsa," Squeak said. Henderson, who had been a football standout at that same university, admitted he would have liked to have added McCoy as a co-conspirator since he correctly believed the Tulsa PhD was "in it up to his eyeballs," but Erik was no help at the time.

"Jerry lost his job over this incident, but I let him peddle the story that I had fooled him and deluded him and used him completely, and I wouldn't testify against him. Warren offered me the sun and the moon for that, and I was not going to do it. Told Mel and Warren both, I just can't do this. Because the guy was sort of a friend of mine.

"I protected him from going to the penitentiary. He was my co-conspirator on the Beggs case, but I stood up and took the rap," Erik said years later, admitting that he and McCoy had been 50/50 partners and intended to split any profits from the lab equally.

It had been McCoy's daughter who was bringing breakfast to Beggs that morning, and OBN had stopped her on her way to the house. But that was as close as the agents would get to the physicist.

Although they knew of Fearon's role, that Erik was ordering chemicals through Electrochemical Laboratories, Erik loyally maintained that Fearon himself hadn't known anything of the Beggs lab. "I knew right away that I'd be going to prison on these charges, but I also knew that I'd be getting out again. And when I did, I'd need the same sort of services that Bob had provided in this case, so it did not benefit me to burn that particular bridge."

Remaining faithfully silent about his two partners, Erik stood alone in the indictment handed down later that month and again on February 2, when he pleaded guilty in United States District Court in Oklahoma's Eastern Judicial District.

He didn't stay completely quiet, though. The next day, he gave an interview to reporter Doug Hicks from the *Tulsa World*. In the most memorable quote from the piece, Erik said that he viewed "drug manufacturing as 'the last American folk adventure…the light in the moon…narcotics agents chasing you all over the land. It's a fantasy made real.'"

"That's exactly how he viewed it," OBN's undercover agent Jay said. "It was all a great game, an adventure: him doing what he loved while we tried to catch him. The moral question? He didn't see one.

"I saw him after he was sentenced and before he left for prison. We talked about what he'd said before, that people in the drug business—the users and the people like him who made drugs or sold them—were all taking the same risks. 'You pay your nickel, and you take your chances,' he told me. People who take drugs know they could be harmed or killed, and prison's a possibility. But it's their choice. And he knows he could be poisoned or get cancer or blown up; making drugs could kill him, too, or send him to prison. But nobody forced him; he made a free choice. He said he paid his nickel, too, and if he loses it, he can't complain.

"He lost this time, and went to prison, but he never complained," Jay said. "That's Squeak."

CHAPTER 21

Muskogee, Oklahoma to Leavenworth Penitentiary, Kansas, 1978 – 1979

On March 16, 1978, Erik came to court for yet another sentencing—his eighth.

His appearance before United States District Judge Joseph Morris would be his second in federal court. At age thirty-two, he had reached the Big Leagues.

John Osgood, a young assistant United States attorney, was trying his first clandestine lab case. Erik made an impression. "The first time I saw him, he came into the courtroom for the bond hearing. He was wearing an old Army GI coat, and he stunk beyond belief, it was terrible. And, of course, he was held without bond."

When he pled guilty on February 2, Erik was still wearing the clothes from the morning of his arrest and, as Osgood remembers, "still smelled badly because of the chemicals that were just so fully in his clothing. And we had a real issue with that in the courtroom there."

The hearing went quickly. "He agreed to waive counsel, and to plead guilty," Osgood said. "When you plead guilty, there is no trial, so we didn't have to put on any evidence. You have to give a factual basis for the crime, and that's pretty straightforward. You just tell the judge, 'Do you admit that you were attempting to manufacture amphetamine?' 'Yes.' 'Were you doing it in a laboratory in Beggs, Oklahoma?' 'Yes.' 'Tell me why you were doing this.' 'Well, I'm a chemist, and I like to make drugs.' That's pretty much it. The judge says, 'Okay, I find you guilty.'"

The guilty plea didn't surprise the OBN agents who had made the case and knew him personally. Osgood remembered, "He was bragging about what he was doing at the time of his arrest, and how he was making fancy designer drugs that were a little bit different than amphetamine, even though it was an amphetamine lab. He was very proud that he was capable of doing that kind of work. He didn't feel he had any defense."

Like a kid who'd been tagged on the playground, he told Henderson and Sires on the day of his arrest, "You caught me fair and square."

Now it was time to play the next phase of the game. Elaine Dodd recalled. "He called it 'cops and robbers,' and he waxed poetic when he was talking about it. So I think he saw it just a game. He failed to see the people that were impacted and hurt by his actions."

Judge Morris, who did see the people who were harmed by his defendant's actions, accepted the guilty plea and set sentencing for March 16.

With no plea bargain, Erik had pled "straight up" to the most serious offenses charged and the ones carrying the stiffest potential penalties. In this case, these were manufacturing methamphetamine, and possession of TMA with intent to distribute. Both carried five-year maximum terms.

Osgood remembered talking with Erik before the hearing and offering some advice. "At the time of sentencing, I talked to Mr. Marquardt, and I said, 'You need to show a little contrition here. Judge Morris is a tough judge. If you can come in and kind of *mea culpa* a little bit, and say you're sorry, and that kind of thing, you might do a little better on the sentencing.'"

Erik wasn't having any of that. "He wasn't offensive in his answer, but he said, 'No, I'm not going to do that. I make drugs. I'm a chemist. I'm good at what I do, and I'm going to do it again when I get out,' or words to that effect. And that's actually what he told the judge."

Most of the hearing went by the routine, but it got interesting for everyone when the judge asked Erik the standard question.

THE COURT: Before I pass sentence do you have any statement that you wish to make, or any information which you wish to give me in mitigation of punishment?

DEFENDANT MARQUARDT: A very brief one.

THE COURT: I want to hear you.

DEFENDANT MARQUARDT: I have been a drug manufacturer for a number of years. If I did not believe in manufacturing drugs, I would not have manufactured them. I assume responsibility for my act, and I ask for no consideration from this Court in sentencing. If the circumstances were the same as they had been before, I would do the same thing over again.

Warren Henderson laughed about this later. "Everybody there was just stunned. Especially the judge. That's not what he was used to hearing. You know, most people are asking for leniency, saying how sorry they are, how they've changed, how they'll never do it again. But Erik isn't like everybody else, and he wanted them to know it. Mel and I were the only ones who weren't even a little surprised. Because we knew Squeak."

When Judge Morris got over the initial shock, he gave Erik exactly what he'd asked for, "no consideration from the court."

"I think the judge made some comment about, 'Well, it's going to be quite a while before you do it again.' He gave him what he thought, at the time, was a fairly substantial sentence: ten years. Again, by today's standards, you could expect twice that," Osgood said.

Judge Morris handed down the maximum five-year term for each count, then ordered that they be served consecutively, one following the other. Erik would be going inside for the full ride.

"Sires felt bad about me getting ten years rather than five. Of course, ten years turned out to be just about six because I don't get into any trouble in prison. I got all the good-time credit they could give me at the time."

Osgood spoke with Erik before he was led out of the courtroom. "I think after the sentencing was over, I told him, 'Maybe you ought to try to get into a new line of work after you get out of prison.' But he was bound and determined."

"I said, 'Oh, I don't know. I figure I'll be bringing out my next batch in about seven years,'" Erik said. Then he turned to Henderson. "You chased me all over the West Coast this last time. How about a change of scenery? How about if I go along the Gulf Coast next time?"

"If I'm still here, I'll be waiting for you," Henderson told him.

Osgood remembered mixed feelings. "My recollection of Marquardt as a person was an intelligent individual, a likable individual. I hate to say that, as the federal prosecutor's not supposed to like the people he's prosecuting. And I think he was honest. Anybody that tells a judge 'I'm going to do it again' and then does it again obviously has a certain degree of honesty about him.

"I might say also some stupidity, but that was him. He was the most unusual person being prosecuted that I have ever met as a prosecutor, or even as a defense attorney now. I've been doing both now for decades, and I've never seen anybody before or since like him."

* * *

It took about a month for the Bureau of Prisons to get Erik to his new home. This would be his first extended stay in federal custody, and he'd be spending it in a legend, the United States Penitentiary at Leavenworth, Kansas. Already over a hundred years old in 1978, the penitentiary was the largest maximum-security institution in the federal system and had housed some of the worst—and most infamous—of American criminals.

Erik began serving his sentence, as was common practice at the time, in solitary confinement. His cell, the staff helpfully informed him, had previously been occupied by Robert Stroud, known to America as "the Birdman of Alcatraz." He considered his stay in the Birdman's cell as "hard time," and when he compared his miseries in his early school days to his time in custody, solitary at Leavenworth was his benchmark.

In solitary, the prison staff assessed him, deciding where to put him for the long haul. He didn't make this easy for them.

As part of the evaluation, his counselor learned that not only did Erik not have a college degree, he had never graduated high school. That was a problem, the counselor told Erik, because Leavenworth based job decisions at least partially on their educational attainments. The prison routinely received prisoners like Erik who hadn't finished high school, and offered classes for these people to obtain their General Educational Development certificate. With Erik's background and obvious intelligence, the counselor said, passing the GED test should be a snap.

To the counselor's surprise, Erik turned the offer down flat, refusing to say why, but of course we know.

It might not be a PhD or even a driver's license, but the GED was a credential, a certificate from the Kansas Department of Education, and Erik did not do credentials.

He was going to do it this time, the counselor told him, because to get out of solitary and earn some privileges, you have to work…and in order to work, you have to at least be studying for the GED exam. There wasn't any flexibility; those were the rules.

"It was blackmail, essentially," Erik said. "I fought it through their system, but the answer was always the same, so I eventually told them I would take their test under protest."

He claims he finished the examination in fifteen minutes and "received the highest score ever recorded by the Bureau of Prisons." Now holding the only official certificate he would ever possess, Erik moved into Leavenworth's general population.

Soon afterward, he ran into Bob Harris, and couldn't resist confronting him and gloating a bit. "I found out he was in Receiving, and I went down there, and pulled right up on him and I said, 'What'd you rip me off for?'

"He was scared to death. Leavenworth scared the shit out of him. I think he believed that he might cause problems for me with the other residents. I thought that anyone hearing our stories would be more inclined to take my side, if it came to that.

"Finally, this came to the attention of the administration. They called me up to the lieutenant's office and they said, 'Are you all right on our yard?' Went, 'Yeah, I like the place. I get along good at Leavenworth and get along with the people that run it. I like my job.' He said, 'Well, we'll put him outside. Keep you inside.'"

Moving Harris to the adjacent camp "suited me fine," Erik said.

At his new job in the electrical shop, he met Laurence Alden Blakeslee, a Californian and fellow chemist. Erik didn't think much of his abilities as a drug manufacturer, but Blakeslee did have excellent references from the distribution end of an operation. "Larry was making meth for the Hell's Angels," and Erik filed Blakeslee and his contacts with the outlaw motorcycle gang for future use.

Another Californian had references of a different sort. His new cellmate was Thomas Silverstein, someone who had already acquired a reputation at the prison, and not a good one.

"I was advised by other inmates who knew him that I should use extreme caution around Mr. Silverstein. They told me I should remove myself from that situation as quickly as possible, and I did so."

Tom Silverstein had arrived at Leavenworth the year before to do fifteen years for armed bank robbery. Although he'd been in and out of custody for much of his twenty-six years, he hadn't yet earned the reputation for extreme violence and murder he would carry for the rest of his life. Erik's fellow inmates assured him that celling with "Terrible Tom," who would be called "the most dangerous inmate in the country," was a terrible idea.

"We weren't together long. I moved down the run, and I stayed out of his way until the murder, and then he went back to solitary."

Erik got advance warning of that murder, a heads-up that might have saved him but not Silverstein's victim. "I was in a cell with Danny Atwell, who was the first guy that Tommy Silverstein killed at Leavenworth when he went on his rampage. George Perkins, who was a friend of mine and an old Aryan Brotherhood guy, he sent a message down the run. He said, 'Whatever you have to do, get that fuck out of your cell. Either you go or he goes. You don't want to be living with him.' Apparently, he knew something was going to go down. So I told Atwell he had to go, which he did."

That something did "go down" on February 17, 1979, when the prison said Silverstein and two other AB members stabbed Atwell multiple times. Erik said, "Everything I had heard was that Tom didn't do it himself. He organized it, though, because Atwell stopped smuggling heroin for them, which was definitely something for which one could be stabbed to death in Leavenworth."[3]

Like many of the inmates Erik encountered in prison, Silverstein took an interest in his cellmate's chemistry skills. He didn't want to make alcohol or drugs, however. Some of his associates were interested, instead, in lead acid storage batteries kept in the electrical shop.

"There were pallets of batteries there. They were sealed, but you could drill them out and steal the sulfuric acid and try to cook it down to do some silly ass prison shit. Either as part of some half-baked escape attempt or just because they just wanted somebody dead, I don't know which. But I obviously had no interest whatsoever in doing anything like that."

Silverstein continued to ask about chemistry when he'd see Erik after the move. Still, (as Danny Atwell found out) "one has to be extremely careful about saying 'no' to a person like Tom. But I knew if I gave him anything at all that he subsequently used to kill guards or other inmates, the investigation would lead back to me. People were smart enough to know that he didn't have the capacity to do the chemistry, and they would look closely at his associates. As his former cellmate, and with my background, I'd be immediately suspect."

Although he had no problem associating with people like Mel Sires, Jay, and Jimmy Birdsong, and even liked and respected them on the outside, he avoided any hint that he might be willing to give information to the "cops" within the walls. "These people don't like informers." Snitching against someone as dangerous as Tom Silverstein only reinforced his resolve to keep his mouth firmly shut.

But the pressure was building, and Atwell's murder ratcheted it up even further.

---

3. Silverstein was ultimately acquitted of the murder.

"I went to the boss, and I told him, get rid of that sulfuric acid and those batteries. Put them someplace and lock them up. He immediately understood right away."

But Erik had violated the code, "so they locked me up for my own protection, because there were some rumors going around that these folks were going to do something bad to me. The administration wrote it up as a conflict between inmates and resolved it by transferring me, and that's how I ended up getting shipped to Lewisburg."

It's also how America took a big step closer to its fentanyl epidemic.

CHAPTER 22

Lewisburg Penitentiary, Pennsylvania, 1979

"Is this real, or just more cop bullshit?"

Erik considered the question and the man posing it very carefully. He'd been warned about this person by an authority no less than the Godfather of New York's Bonanno crime family. "Be careful with that guy," Philip 'Rusty' Rastelli had cautioned. "Better you don't do anything with him, especially alone."

Stories about Louis Cirillo circulated in the underworld, inside Lewisburg and out. One possibly apocryphal—but definitely thought-provoking—tale described how he'd bitten out the Adam's apple of another hood in a fight.

Alone now in a Lewisburg prison cell with that very man, Erik weighed his answer.

* * *

Within the federal prison system, the United States Penitentiary at Lewisburg—known as "The Big House"—had a fearsome reputation that equaled or even surpassed that of Leavenworth, the institution Erik had just left. For the vast majority of the 1,200 inmates at the Big House, Lewisburg meant doing hard time in austere and difficult conditions, with dangerous men serving long sentences for violent crimes.

That's what Erik expected in April of 1979 when he left the hell of Leavenworth and its solitary for the rolling hills, green farm fields, and high brick walls of central Pennsylvania.

The penitentiary, built in 1932 to accommodate the growing number of prisoners in the federal system, became known as the East Coast Cosa Nostra's "home prison," housing mafiosi and other mobsters for decades. Within the prison, most of these men were confined together on "Mafia Row" in J Block, described by *Goodfellas* hood Henry Hill as the "Honor Dorm," a "three-story building... more like a Holiday Inn than a prison." This was Erik's new home.

"Mafia? Oh yeah. I lived on J-2 initially, and then I moved down to J-1. This was the center for the Italian community at the prison. Bunch of very nice people, actually, and fun to do time around...always eating something or playing some amusing stunt. Took the thing in stride, didn't cry or complain about the fact that they were in prison."

When Erik arrived, most of the East Coast mobsters were on the first floor, J-1. He fit in quickly, moving downstairs after catching the eye of the ranking Mafiosi in the joint, Philip "Rusty" Rastelli, then the boss of New York's Bonanno family.

"I knew Phil Rastelli quite well—or as well as you could know him under the circumstances. Absolutely wonderful. Nothing but good things to say about Phil. Still miss him. He was an extremely intelligent guy with a dry sense of humor, able to deal with the slings and arrows of outrageous fortune with a great deal of patience and deliberation. Nothing to not respect about him. I think Phil was a great man."

Rastelli outlined J Block's rules and customs, and he made it clear to the new arrival that fitting in meant not rocking the very agreeable "Honor Dorm" boat, not talking out of turn to the cops, and paying the proper amount of respect to those fellow residents who were also following these rules.

No one on J Block wanted to mess up a good thing.

"J Block was the most pleasant of places. You had a wooden door on your room; in theory, they had the capacity to lock them, but the locks were seldom used. On a few occasions when parties took place down there, they would just shut the door at the end of the unit, wait 'til everybody cooled off, and come in and sort things out in the morning. The people who lived there were assumed to be reasonable and sensible and didn't do things that were inappropriate in a prison environment. Nice place to live."

His fellow J Block residents included mobsters from all of the five New York families: a couple from New Jersey, and two major players from the Philadelphia family.

The block wasn't exclusively Italian; besides Erik, there were criminals from as far away as Kansas City, but all of them "connected" in some way.

"I've been to a couple of prisons that I considered very civilized, and Lewisburg was that way in spite of the fact that you had some very dangerous people there. But they all declared a truce on each other. If they had issues on the outside, those stayed on the outside, and it was understood that they would take them up elsewhere."

As was the case in other institutions, word circulated quickly about the new resident to all the other inmates on the block. "There's a substantial rumor mill in a prison, and you find out what people are there for. Or in the case of a place like J-1, they will find out what you are there for because they're always concerned that someone could show up there who might be interested in their affairs and taking tales to some investigative agency or another."

Erik's close relationship with Rusty Rastelli cushioned any potential conflicts with others in J Block. "I did a couple of major favors for Rusty early on. I was happy to help, and he was very appreciative." One of these favors was simple: Rastelli's television wasn't working. "It was a simple fix, and it led to similar work on electronics for both the inmates and later, for the prison."

That had been easy as well as cheap. Rastelli's next request was more complex. "He said his people had a shipment of cocaine, quite a lot of it, two or three hundred pounds, two million dollars' worth, that had somehow been contaminated with diesel fuel. As things stood, it was useless. Rusty wanted to know if it was possible to clean the coke."

Erik assured him it was and explained the method, but also stressed the risk. "The process required ethyl ether, among other things, and I emphasized how dangerous this was, especially since these wouldn't be trained chemists performing the work. I recommended they do the reactions in small quantities. A pound or two at a time with a reasonable amount of ether. I understood later that they thought that might take too long—these people had very little patience—so they obtained a barrel by some means, fifty gallons. I'm still surprised they didn't blow up half of Little Italy."

But luck was with the mobsters, and Rastelli was most pleased about his clean cocaine. He spread the word around J Block and greater Lewisburg that Erik was "with Rusty," a status guaranteed to make the time go even easier. It did, and Erik hung out in Rusty's cell and with the other mob guys. Both men thought quite highly of each other.

Erik held no illusions about his new friend; Rastelli was a hardcore gangster with dead bodies behind him. Only three months after Erik arrived at Lewisburg, Rastelli had ordered the murder of Bonanno underboss and Rusty's rival Carmine Galante, who was gunned down in a Brooklyn restaurant, famously pictured very dead and bloody with a cigar still clenched in his teeth.

A key figure in the American heroin business and a Lewisburg alumnus himself, Galante had been trying to take control of the New York narcotics market, annoying the other families while attempting to usurp Rastelli's position as Bonanno family boss. Rusty took care of both of those issues with one murder ordered from J Block.

In one of the more whimsical moments of his Lewisburg life, prison pals Erik and Rusty went to the movies. The prison showed films in the massive dining hall, and the movie that night was the original *The Godfather.* Surrounded by a thousand of the hardest criminals in America and a sizable chunk of the East Coast Cosa Nostra, Erik took in the epic mob film with the real-life godfather of the most powerful Mafia family in the country.

What did New York's Godfather think about the film? "He was amused, maybe a little contemptuous. He'd really been there and really done that. He said that before the movie, nobody called people like him 'Godfather.' Before, it was always 'Boss.' And that kissing-the-ring thing? That didn't happen until after the movie came out. Then it was a thing. That goes back to art imitates life imitates art. He liked the movie, but he knew what was real and what wasn't."

As at Leavenworth, inmates at Lewisburg were supposed to work, and thanks partly to Rastelli's influence (and his GED credential from Leavenworth), Erik got a very good job early on.

"Phil put out the word that I could fix things, and I had people from all over the prison bringing me items that needed repair. I wouldn't say I knew everybody who was there, but I was well-known in the prison population."

Erik did most of this work for free, and soon caught the eye of the prison staff. "This was an old prison at the time, built before World War II, and all of the systems were from the same era, and so obsolete that no one on the staff or even outside knew how to fix things when they went wrong. But I'd been working on equipment from that generation since I was a kid. I could fix everything."

He needed a few things, he told the staff: tools and diagnostic equipment, including oscilloscopes. He eventually got so much of it, and had so many pending jobs, that the prison gave him a second cell to house the accumulating clutter. He paid them back by keeping the prison's alarm, security, and communications systems functioning.

"Sometimes I'd be alone in a control room and had the ability to open every secure area in the prison."

This trust and access led to another privilege as the staff allowed Erik to work unsupervised outside the prison walls. "They used me for everything. Electrical maintenance of all kinds. In fact, my boss used to get mad. 'Look, he's our electronic serviceman. We don't want him fixing electric welders and bakery ovens. And you got him doing everything in the world because he does good work.' Those years weren't really like being in prison. Good times."

Asked whether he ever thought of exploiting this quasi-freedom to escape or bring in contraband, he had a ready answer. "Never crossed my mind. I was certainly aware that the Bureau of Prisons had places far worse than Lewisburg where they could send me. I liked it, and a number of the other people that went to prison there, they were having such a good time, like the Philly crew, their wives were mad at them because they were struggling to deal with daily issues on the outside and not having so much fun. Why would I ever do something to jeopardize that?"

An incident with a passing acquaintance illustrated his attitude toward parole and probation. "I was casually familiar with one of the ladies on the parole board. She used to stop down through the mechanical services and looked in at the shop I had, and said, 'What in God's name is this? A research laboratory?' I said, 'Actually it's a communication shop.'

"She was always very friendly, and she asked me, 'Are we to see you in front of the board?' I said, 'No, I refuse to see the parole board. Nothing personal or anything like that. But when I go out, I'm going to return to a life of manufacturing drugs.' And she was just absolutely fascinated by that statement. She probably didn't hear that much."

But behind all of the electronics work and the story swapping with the elite of the East Coast Mafia, drug manufacturing was still the key to Erik's appeal with his curious fellow inmates. "I was a representative of a relatively new and novel type of criminal activity, and this was becoming of considerable interest to the people in Philadelphia. And New York people had their own variant of interest in it, and the people up in Boston. Lots of consulting got done mostly on an informal basis. Occasionally funds were made available for these, presents were purchased, and it was just a nice place to do business."

And business was exactly what the man who lived down the hall wanted to talk about.

CHAPTER 23

Lewisburg Penitentiary, Pennsylvania, January 8, 1981

Louis Cirillo thrust the *Newsweek* magazine at Erik, pointing at an article titled, "A Deadly New Drug Passing as Heroin."

"So is this real, or is it just more cop bullshit?" Cirillo asked.

That was the question, and Erik took a few moments to read the article and form a response that might be acceptable to the man now waiting impatiently for an answer.

That individual was an intense beetle-browed, short-fused thug called Louie who claimed to be a bagel baker from the Bronx. He peered expectantly at Erik through a pair of thick glasses. Above all, Erik had to understand who was asking and why, because this man was perhaps the most dangerous in Lewisburg on two levels: his question was at the heart of the danger.

Louie looked impatient as he waited for an answer.

"The guy that first brought it to my attention was a local low-grade loser named Gaetano Licata, and he had been asked to approach me by Louis Cirillo. He said Louie wanted to see me in his room. It was just down the hallway, but I'd never been in it before. Never had anything to do with Louie.

"I got there, and he had a *Newsweek* magazine, with an article about China White, the alpha methylfentanyl that had been killing people in California. There was something in the article to the effect that it was 80 or 100 times more powerful than heroin, and was totally legal. This was obviously before the government passed the Analogue Act."

Erik read the story that appeared in the January 5, 1981 issue of *Newsweek*, focusing on its close. "Police and DEA officials suspect a single source, probably in the San Diego area – a renegade chemist skilled enough to synthesize the Fentanyl derivative and greedy enough to ignore the consequences. 'It's not an easy compound to make,' says Darrell Clardy, a drug official in California. 'It takes somebody who knows a lot about chemistry.' Finding him, authorities say, will not be easy."

He waffled a little, hedging. "There wasn't enough information in the article. I'd never looked into fentanyl and didn't know what the process for making these substances would be. I said I'd look into it, but as to whether I thought I could make it or not, I told him I thought perhaps I could. He told me to find out.

"As I expected, the prison library wasn't especially helpful, but I was able to determine through some discreet correspondence with my friend in Oklahoma, that fentanyl was a piperidine derivative. Piperidine is at the root of any number of useful pharmaceuticals, pethidine and loperamide, for example. I had never worked with these substances, but morphine has a piperidine ring as part of its structure, as does PCP, so I was able to form a rough idea about the structure of fentanyl and the analogue discussed in the *Newsweek* article as 'China White.'"

He shared this information with Cirillo, "who didn't understand it, of course."

But he was able to answer the original question; yes, "China White" was real, and no, the rest of the article was not "more cop bullshit."

Not long after, he got a visit from his mentor. "Rusty came and asked me what I was doing with Louie. I said he'd called me down to his house and asked me about this new drug. Phil advised me that Louie was exceedingly dangerous to do business with, warning me that, 'You need to be careful with that guy.'"

Louis Cirillo had been born in the Bronx in 1923, and although he had ties to Florida and Canada, had been a lifelong resident of New York, not counting several long stretches—including the current one—in various prisons. First arrested for larceny in 1942, his first drug arrest, for selling heroin, came in 1945. Although he'd served time afterward for armed robbery and assaulting a union organizer with a hammer, Cirillo's primary focus in the 1950s and 1960s had been heroin trafficking.

Though closely linked with mafia types from at least two of the New York families, as well as Santo Trafficante in Tampa, Florida, Cirillo himself wasn't a "made guy." He'd forfeited that option in the early 1940s when he'd pulled an armed robbery on someone he knew *was* a made guy. This might ordinarily have been a capital offense, but Cirillo already had a reputation as a "good earner," someone with very, very good connections in the drug business, and worth more alive and making money than dead and making a point. Not being a member meant he could cultivate ties to more than one family, which Cirillo did.

Louie was at Lewisburg serving a 25-year sentence for his role in a 1972 case in which prosecutors charged him with smuggling 1,500 pounds of pure heroin in cars shipped directly to New York or via Montreal, Canada. Agents of the Bureau of Narcotics and Dangerous Drugs who searched his family home in the Bronx found over a million dollars in cash in the walls of the house and buried in the yard. BNDD regional director Frank Monastero said after the seizure that Cirillo was the "most substantial narcotics trafficker the Bureau has ever found."

The U.S. Attorney alleged that Louie alone had been responsible for supplying one-sixth of the entire American heroin market with narcotics valued at $293 million on the street. He was, U.S. Attorney Whitney North Seymour said, "the most important heroin distributor ever tried and convicted in New York."

Aside from his first venture into drug manufacturing in Waukesha and hawking Robe with Frank in Milwaukee, Erik had avoided the heroin business. "Obviously there was a lot of money in it, but the people who ran it wouldn't have appreciated any competition from me."

That definitely included people like Louis Cirillo, who had lived in that world as far back as the 1940s. "He was a bitter individual, but civil, polite, never saw him discourteous to anyone or anything like that. Kept to himself pretty much. I had several discussions with him, and became aware of the fact that he was involved in this French Connection thing in some way or another. I really didn't know all the details about it, but I was told by other people that he had been bringing heroin in from Europe. I knew that's what he was at Lewisburg for."

In fact, Cirillo was much more than just "involved" in the French Connection. He was one of the central figures on the American end who had put the whole thing together in the 1950s, and maybe, with the late Carmine Galante, *the* key player. Cirillo organized the direct importation of heroin from Europe and connected the New York crime families with their Corsican and Italian counterparts to move opium from Turkey to France and then the United States.

In the late 1960s, Cirillo restructured the business again, cementing connections between the New York Italian Mafia families and black traffickers, particularly Frank Matthews and Leroy "Nicky" Barnes, who would control packaging and distribution of heroin on the streets, not just in New York but other American cities.

Others on J-Block, notably Martin Angelina of the Philadelphia family, were also interested in the *Newsweek* article. Erik remembered. "Marty was just absolutely fascinated by this whole fentanyl thing. It's probably a good thing that Marty and I never got together after I got out, because Marty's not a bullshitter, and he's a person who could have gotten the deal done."

Angelina's heroin links may have been solid, but they were nothing like Louis Cirillo's. If there was any one person in the entire world who had the resources and connections to completely restructure the American narcotics business from a model based on opium poppies, morphine, and heroin to one centered on fentanyl, that man was sitting in a cell in Lewisburg Penitentiary, waiting expectantly for the answer to his second question.

"Can you make it?" Louie Cirillo wanted to know.

Wary and guarded, Erik said he believed he could, saying he'd try to find out more.

What he learned has changed the world.

PART II

Squeak—By the Light of the Moon

CHAPTER 24

Squeak and Dr. Paul Janssen, though drastically different in both personality and their life stories, had a couple of things in common. Deeply involved in medicinal chemistry, they each spent a lifetime in the laboratory. Both did their chemistry using that "intuitive approach to complex scientific problems" described years earlier by Erik's court-ordered psychiatrist. And both synthesized a drug called fentanyl.

The late Sir James Black, M.D.—physician, pharmacologist, researcher, and winner of the Nobel Prize for Medicine—described his friend and colleague, Paul Janssen, and that intuitive approach to chemistry and pharmacology he shared with a self-taught American underground drug manufacturer:

"As Dr. Paul grew in experience, he, too, filled his head with chemically reactive groups that he called 'pharmacophores.' I often watched him at meetings, when bored with the proceedings, finding solace inside his head as he doodled new chemical compounds."

Janssen, a Belgian medical doctor and pharmacologist, has been described as "the most prolific drug inventor of all time." Over forty-eight years, he and the company he founded synthesized an astonishing 147,000 new chemical compounds. Eighty would be determined to have significant value as new drugs. Eight of these, including fentanyl, are on the World Health Organization's List of Essential

Medicines. One of them, loperamide (Lomotil), an anti-diarrheal, accompanied America's Apollo astronauts to the moon.

Janssen's company, Janssen Pharmaceutica, a subsidiary of Johnson & Johnson since 1961, is now a multi-billion-dollar organization with tens of thousands of employees and operations across the globe...but it all began in the head of its founder.

Janssen was born in Turnhout, Belgium in 1926, received his medical degree from the University of Ghent in 1951, and followed that with a PhD in pharmacology in 1956.

After founding his own independent research laboratory with a modest loan from his physician father in 1953, he produced his first new drug, ambucetamide, useful in the treatment of menstrual pain, the same year. By the late 1950s, he was focused on an opioid called pethidine, and sold in the United States as Demerol.

First synthesized in 1939, pethidine had narcotic properties like morphine. The drugs had a similar chemical structure, and both contained a structural element, piperidine, a common organic compound that occurs in many alkaloids.

Janssen believed that piperidine was the key to the narcotic effect in both drugs and thought pethidine's simpler structure might make it easier to manipulate. He started creating piperidine-based compounds that were chemically similar, but which he hoped would be more powerful and have fewer of the negative side effects well-known in both drugs.

One result, phenoperidine, produced in 1957, proved to be twenty-five times more potent than morphine, and was at the time the most powerful opioid in the world. Fast-acting and short-lasting, phenoperidine was an effective anesthetic, and it's still in wide use, though not in the United States.

Janssen didn't quit there. In 1959, he produced another piperidine-based substance, 1-phenethyl-4-N-propionylanilinopiperidine. He called this one fentanyl.

From a medical standpoint, it proved to be almost exactly what the doctor ordered. Substantially more potent as a pain reliever than morphine or even his own phenoperidine, fentanyl also acted more quickly, and its effects wore off faster than morphine. Injected intravenously, fentanyl's analgesic or painkilling effects occur within one or two minutes and last two to four hours.

Surgeons found that fentanyl used as an anesthetic had fewer side effects than morphine. Unlike morphine, fentanyl had minimal effects on blood pressure, which morphine depressed—something that could cause problems in surgeries. Patients anesthetized with fentanyl awakened more quickly after surgery and were generally breathing on their own, requiring less time in recovery and in the hospital. Fentanyl revolutionized cardiac surgery, with cardiologists saying that modern heart procedures like bypass surgery or valve replacement would not be possible without it.

Janssen put the new drug, fentanyl citrate, on the market in Europe under the trade name Sublimaze, and it was an immediate hit with surgeons and anesthesiologists. Although it received the American Food and Drug Administration's approval in 1964, it was not widely used until 1968, partly because of fears that the drug would be abused. Because of these concerns, the FDA approved fentanyl in combination with droperidol, a drug used in surgery to prevent nausea and vomiting which had a reputation among abusers for being a "bad high." The combination, first trademarked by Johnson & Johnson as Innovar in 1964, quickly took off and by the early 1970s, American surgeons were using fentanyl in 80 percent of operations requiring general anesthesia.

Those initial concerns about potential fentanyl abuse were not without some foundation. The World Health Organization identified fentanyl "as being capable of producing addiction or of conversion into a drug or other substance capable of producing addiction," and the Treasury Department regulated it as a narcotic in April 1964. This regulation required manufacturers importing, exporting, or producing fentanyl to register with the Bureau of Narcotics as they would for other narcotics, and sale and possession of the drug outside a hospital or medical setting became a criminal offense.

Abuse didn't seem to be a problem at first, although warning signs were there. Because it was approved solely for use in surgery, the only people who had regular access were generally anesthesiologists or anesthetists and hospital pharmacists.

These people sometimes abused it. Dr. G. Douglas Talbott, an addiction specialist who treated physicians "suffering from the disease of addiction," reported in 1986 that "nearly 90 percent of the 125 anesthesiologists he has treated in the past three years were addicted to fentanyl."

Outside medical practices and the hospital setting, the only real abuse of fentanyl was taking place at the track, where trainers of thoroughbreds used fentanyl and its analogues to dope racehorses. Difficult to detect in blood tests, fentanyl use spread and by 1978, a number of trainers had been suspended for doping horses with the substance.

Janssen continued to work with his new drug, developing other compounds from the piperidine structural element, and discovered that the possibilities for new forms of fentanyl were almost endless. In 1974, he synthesized sufentanil and carfenatnil, followed by alfentanil in 1976. All three of these substances, substantially more powerful than fentanyl, had some use in human or veterinary medicine.

As this is written, over 1,400 fentanyl analogues have been discovered, each with different properties, dosage, and effects. Some have uses in medicine, but most do not.

Other chemists also explored the piperidine ring and its fentanyl offspring. At the University of Mississippi, Dr.

Thomas Riley, a professor of medicinal chemistry, developed 3-methylfentanyl, a stunningly powerful analogue with thousands of times morphine's potency.

Although Riley patented his new compound in 1974, no one could find a medical use for his drug, but as with Albert Niemann's sulfur mustard, someone else looked at Dr. Riley's compound, saw an opportunity, and put the substance to a bad use. And like mustard gas, 3-methylfentanyl was very effective at killing people.

* * *

Orange County, California, 1979

In January 1978 when DEA Agent John Maher warned his class of the risks of super-narcotic drugs like Etorphine and fentanyl, he made two predictions. First: someday, someone would lift the lid off Pandora's Box and release these substances onto American streets. Second: the result would be "a lot of dead junkies. Hundreds of them, maybe thousands."

Just under two years later, someone lifted the lid.

On December 28, 1979, ambulances in Orange County, California responded to two calls to assist men, both in their thirties and suspected of having overdosed on narcotics. One, found unconscious in a motel room, was transported to Anaheim Memorial Hospital but pronounced dead on arrival. The second got home from work, fired up a spoonful of white powder, and died on the spot.

Police and EMTs found signs of previous intravenous drug use, as well as drug paraphernalia and packets of white powder. Surprisingly, the forensic chemists in Orange County, expecting heroin, couldn't identify any narcotic drug at all in the packet. Nor could the pathologists find any substance present in any amount sufficient to kill in the men's blood. It was a mystery, one that would not be solved for almost a year.

Samples were sent to DEA's Special Testing and Research Lab in Virginia, where the best forensic drug chemists in the world worked to solve the puzzle, even as more people died: thirteen in southern California and others as far away as Phoenix, Arizona. All were victims of something users called "China White," the street name for the highly prized, almost mythical pure white heroin from Southeast Asia.

Chemists analyzing seized China White did discover heroin in some of the samples, but in others they found no narcotic at all…only the materials like lactose that dealers used to dilute heroin for sale on the street.

Nobody doubted the lethality of this unidentified substance because as 1980 passed, this baffling new drug racked up a body count and as the death toll mounted, everybody finally got an answer from DEA's STR lab. China White was a new drug making its first appearance on America's illicit drug scene.

It was called fentanyl.

CHAPTER 25

California, 1980

The China White discovery, though obviously welcome, immediately raised another issue. That was because the new drug wasn't *exactly* fentanyl, a substance that had been regulated since 1964. It was a fentanyl analogue, chemically similar and with, as researchers would soon learn, comparable effects and potency. And although the STR chemists had finally identified the key ingredient of the "China White" on California's streets, police weren't having much luck in finding the source for the lethal substance.

Paul Janssen discovered alpha-methylfentanyl in the early 1960s, and the process for manufacturing the drug had been published in patent and scientific literature by both Janssen and Thomas Riley. But, like most other fentanyl analogues, it had not been adopted for use in medicine.

This raised the other serious issue with the "China White" killing addicts on the West Coast; alpha-methylfentanyl was totally legal.

"You could walk around with a shopping bag full of this stuff," one agent commented, and there wasn't anything the DEA or any other law enforcement agency could do about it.

Since a little alpha-methylfentanyl went a very long way, it didn't take a shopping bag full to cause major problems. Some experts believed that the unknown chemist who'd manufactured the drug might have produced as little as a few grams or a couple of ounces, then closed up shop and moved on, possibly shutting down before the first overdoses hit the morgues. Finding the responsible party in that scenario would be virtually impossible—and even if they found him, the law didn't allow a prosecution.

Under American law, both federal and in all of the states that adopted the Uniform Controlled Substance Act in the early 1970s, a new drug could be placed under legal control only by Congress or a state's legislature. Legislators routinely added drugs, usually following a move by Congress that was based on a recommendation by the DEA.

Once DEA had identified alpha-methylfentanyl as a problem, it made the recommendation and Congress added the drug to Schedule I, the section reserved for substances like heroin and LSD that had a high potential for abuse and addiction, and no accepted use in medical practice. But by September 1981 when the scheduling went into effect, it was already many months too late.

California cops still saw China White on the streets, but alpha-methylfentanyl had been replaced by other fentanyl cousins similar in structure and effects. These drugs were just as legal as alpha-methylfentanyl had been when it first appeared in 1979. This totally new phenomenon quickly got the public's attention.

* * *

The well-publicized China White deaths did not deter those like Louis Cirillo who wanted to duplicate the China White success. Several researchers in California studied the phenomenon, and foremost among these was pharmacologist and associate professor Gary L. Henderson. He became an early authority on fentanyl and his lab at the University of California-Davis was the only one in California capable of detecting the fentanyl analogues and he performed over three hundred tests to identify specific analogues responsible for overdose deaths.

"What some very clever people have done is take fentanyl, patented as Sublimaze—a drug much used by anesthesiologists—and with very simple and inexpensive modifications, created derivatives, new chemicals which are not illegal: the China White series," Henderson told a reporter in 1983.

In news stories, reporters called these "designer drugs," a term credited to Henderson. It was one of these articles that caught the attention of Louis Cirillo in far-off Lewisburg, but he wouldn't be the only one who read about these new drugs with interest.

The *Chemical & Engineering News* is an official publication of the American Chemical Society, offered weekly to the Society's 155,000 members worldwide. Squeak, never much of a joiner, wasn't an ACS member, but he was a faithful reader of *C&EN*. The prison library at Lewisburg was not a subscriber, however, so he missed the January 19, 1981, issue which announced the DEA's solution of the year-long China White mystery.

In an article titled "Structure of bogus 'China White' solved," *C&EN* writer Steve Stinson reported: "The hitherto puzzling structure of a potent but deadly new drug of abuse, called erroneously 'China White,' has been solved by forensic chemists at the U.S. Drug Enforcement Administration's special testing and research laboratory at McLean, Virginia.

"Chemically, the drug is N-phenyl- N-(1-phenylethyl-3-methyl-4-piperidinyl) propenamide... DEA officials call the new drug "3-methylfentanyl."

Much of the article was technical, describing the process DEA chemists used to identify 3-methylfentanyl, helpfully pointing readers to the literature where 3-methylfentanyl synthesizer Thomas Riley had published his formula, and noting that "methods of production have also been published by Janssen Pharmaceutica."

The secret of this compound, which *C&EN* reported could be "about 6,700 times more potent than morphine," was now out. Although he hadn't seen Stinson's *C&EN* article, which appeared two weeks after the *Newsweek* story that prompted Louis Cirillo's question, Squeak heard about it when he reached out to his chemist friend in Oklahoma. The response, watered down to pass the prison censors, was still detailed enough to identify the drug – 3-methylfentanyl – and give some idea about the process for making it.

With this information, Squeak returned to Cirillo with an answer. The drug was everything the *Newsweek* article said it was—a heroin substitute, very powerful, and totally legal to make, sell, or possess. Critically, although *Newsweek* didn't mention it, the *C&EN* article clearly said that the processes for manufacturing the drug had been described in the chemistry literature.

"If it's in the literature, I can do it," Squeak said, although he suspected that Cirillo wouldn't understand the significance. He told Cirillo he thought he was capable of making fentanyl or its cousin.

He said the same thing to Martin Angelina, a Kansas City hood named James Harvey "Junior" Bradley, and to his friend Rusty, who told him not to give Cirillo any more information, saying, "I'll take care of this."

Knowing that Squeak and Rastelli were close, Cirillo went to the Bonanno boss, asking what Rusty thought. "He'd asked whether I could do such a thing. And [Rastelli] says, 'Ah, I don't know.' He said, 'He makes drugs for those hippies.'"

Rastelli, knowing that Squeak really didn't want to partner with anybody like Louis Cirillo, or the much less menacing Angelina, either, covered for his friend, and much to Squeak's relief, "The word I got back was that Louie thought I probably couldn't do it. I'm really glad that Louis

Cirillo thinks I couldn't do it because Louis Cirillo's killed more people accidentally than most people in here have on purpose."

* * *

While the Stinson article provided enough information to give a would-be chemist a solid start on synthesizing 3-methylfentanyl, it would take a second, much more detailed exposé to really launch the new drug. That one came in *C&EN*'s September 9, 1985, issue in an article titled, "New Variety of Street Drugs Poses Growing Problem."

The article's author, Rudy Baum, provided a detailed history of fentanyl and its analogues, and described how these fit into the market for narcotics. One quote would catch the eye of several chemists: "According to Frank Sapienza, a chemist at DEA headquarters in Washington, D.C., in rough numbers a $2000 investment will yield about a kilogram of heroin worth about $1 million on the street. A similar $2000 investment in glassware and chemicals can be turned into a kilogram of 3-methylfentanyl, currently the most common fentanyl analogue being sold, worth about $1 billion (yes, billion!) on the street."

One doesn't ordinarily see a lot of exclamation marks in *Chemical & Engineering News*; it's about as far a cry from publications like the *Weekly World News* or the *National Enquirer* as you can get. But this statement and its excited "about $1 billion (yes, billion!)" got every bit of the attention its author hoped for.

* * *

Wilmington, Delaware, 1985 – 1989

Michael C. Hovey, a 33-year-old chemist employed by the DuPont Company at its Experimental Station outside Wilmington, Delaware, was a regular *C&EN* reader, and he caught the September 9 issue that suggested that one could, "tinker with a side chain here, add a halogen there, and the result is still probably a chemical that packs a powerful wallop, a chemical that can be sold on the street as heroin, and a chemical that might very well be as legal as sugar."

Hovey had a solid background in his field, with an undergraduate degree from the University of Illinois and a PhD in chemistry from the University of Wisconsin-Madison. He'd been employed by DuPont for over five years, working on agricultural products, and had full access to DuPont's extensive library and laboratory facilities—together with the education and training to appreciate the possibilities in this new substance.

When asked later why he had gone from researching insecticides to producing one of the deadliest drugs ever put on American streets, Hovey said it was all about the money, and he'd gotten the original idea from a piece in a magazine.

"An article appeared in *Chemical & Engineering News* roughly two months ago," he told a DEA interviewer.

"What struck you about the article?"

"What struck me was that it was easy to make. It seemed to be very potent, and it would be worth a lot of money."

Hovey needed a lot of money because he thought civilization was destroying itself, and the collapsing society would descend into chaos. A doomsday prepper long before that activity became popular, Hovey's plan for coping with The End of the World as We Know It was to: 1) make a batch of 3-methylfentanyl, 2) trade it for a million dollars in gold, and 3) obtain property in some remote part of the United States, possibly in the Rocky Mountains, where he and his family could survive the coming apocalypse. It was an ambitious plan and Hovey, with his PhD in organic chemistry and access to a world-class laboratory, had the first base well covered.

Getting to second, however, would prove more difficult, and ultimately fatal.

Once he'd decided on 3-methylfentanyl, he researched the literature thoroughly, then ordered the chemicals he would need through DuPont's system and set up some lab space in his work area to do the synthesis. Then, two months of work produced about a quarter pound of high-quality 3-methylfentanyl.

He also made a small amount of methamphetamine and was finally ready for phase two of his plan: the sale of his creation. For that, Hovey needed a buyer, someone with two essential attributes. This person needed to be well-connected in the heroin business, and have a million dollars to spend. In short, he needed Louis Cirillo.

But Hovey, a married square with a three-year-old daughter and a house in a quiet Wilmington suburb, didn't know Louie or anybody like him. He also had negligible actual experience in the drug trade—most of which, judging by his actions, he obtained from watching 1970s television programs like *Starsky & Hutch* or *Mission: Impossible*.

Hovey kicked off his million-dollar-quest by writing an anonymous letter to a fellow DuPont employee. The letter began, "Would you like to earn $10,000 or more? If so, I have a business proposition for you. This is no joke."

To demonstrate his seriousness, he included a small sample of 3-methylfentanyl, and instructions on how to establish contact.

His co-worker, who didn't know who had written him or why he'd been chosen for this special opportunity, notified DuPont's security department, which in turn called someone well-connected to the narcotics business and with money to spend on "synthetic heroin."

Squeak had confronted the same issue. "Yeah, that was my problem too. How do you find a gangster? Do you advertise for one in the newspaper? No, I don't think so. I had to go to prison to meet a gangster."

In Delaware, DEA undercover agents followed the letter's instructions and placed an ad in the *Wilmington*

News-Journal classified pages. The "Happy 31st Birthday Vermillion, Love, Joy, Kisses," ad ran on October 31. A help-wanted ad two weeks later contained an address and telephone number where the undercover agents could be reached. Hovey called the number the following day, and arranged to drop an ounce of 3-methylfentanyl in a buried ammunition can behind a hotel off I-95. The agents, in turn, left $40,000 in cash.

Hovey expected to pick up another $960,000 before delivering the remaining three ounces of 3-methylfentanyl and six ounces of methamphetamine, but DEA agents watching the drop arrested him when he attempted to collect the money. The DEA seized all four ounces of 3-methylfentanyl, so none of it—the equivalent of 240 pounds of pure heroin—made it to consumers.

On February 5, 1986, Hovey entered a guilty plea to two counts of manufacturing 3-methylfentanyl. The court sentenced him to two consecutive nine-year terms, but Hovey, who had been in jail since the day he was arrested, hadn't given up. He filed an appeal of his conviction, claiming that the DEA "lacked the authority to temporarily schedule drugs."

The court agreed, ruling that at the time he committed the offenses, Hovey fit into a narrow window when 3-methylfentanyl wasn't legally controlled. Released from the custody after serving twenty months, Hovey returned to Delaware. His ordeal wasn't over, however, as the state of Delaware indicted him for identical charges in January 1988.

Citing double jeopardy issues, Hovey's attorneys argued that he should not be tried again, but appeals courts denied these claims, and on September 1, 1989, Delaware police found the now-divorced Hovey at his girlfriend's apartment. He had no intention of going back into custody, however, and armed himself with a paring knife that he used to slash his own wrists and throat before confronting four state troopers in the building's hallway. "You'll have to kill me!" he shouted, and advanced on the troopers with the knife until one of them with a twelve-gauge shotgun did just that.

The episode illustrated how a qualified chemist with access to a first-rate laboratory and the ability to obtain the necessary precursor chemicals could manufacture this extremely powerful new substance. Hovey also demonstrated why such a chemist needed connections to the drug trade to successfully market the drug.

* * *

Suitland, Maryland, 1986

Daniel Hodes had quite a bit in common with Michael Hovey. They both had advanced degrees; Hodes obtained his PhD in organo-metallic chemistry from Boston University. Both worked in world-class research laboratories; Hodes was employed at the United States Naval Research Laboratory in Suitland, Maryland. Both used their training and lab access to pursue 3-methylfentanyl…and like Hovey, Hodes was arrested before any of his fentanyl analogue could hit the street.

Unlike Hovey, this wasn't Hodes' first time in a clandestine drug lab. He'd been busted before in a Tufts University fraternity house in 1970 where he was finishing a batch of LSD. Hodes said he expected to get $50,000 for the acid before the cops interrupted him. He pleaded guilty and received a two-and-a-half-year sentence, which the judge suspended because Hodes "provided police valuable information and cooperation."

Also unlike Hovey, when Hodes went into the 3-methylfentanyl business, he already had connections to "professional narcotics distributors with possible ties to organized crime." Hodes didn't entirely trust these people, however, saying he "believed he would be killed after he delivered the 200 – 300 grams of 3-methylfentanyl "to ensure that no others would be entering the market."

Like Hovey, Hodes had used his employer's laboratory facilities, chemicals, and equipment to produce both the methamphetamine and 3-methylfentanyl—and as had been the case with Hovey, none of Hodes' fentanyl analogue made it onto the street. Thanks to the DEA and the Naval Criminal Investigative Service, the American public had dodged the fentanyl bullet for a second time.

We wouldn't always be so lucky.

The two cases seemed to show a trend, and DEA developed a "profile" of the chemist who might go into 3-methylfentanyl production.

Gary Henderson, by then a DEA advisor, described a "typical" 3-methylfentanyl producer. "They've got to be talented chemists. Three-methyl is a different and much more difficult creation than most designer drugs. I'd look for a good pharmaceutical chemist. But you need a talented chemist who has a link to a drug distribution network. I can make the stuff, but if I tried to sell on the streets of San Francisco, it would be a race to see whether I got killed or arrested first."

* * *

California, 1985 – 1986

Two chemists arrested in 1986 in California seemed to fit the profile perfectly, and agents in Los Angeles strongly suspected that one or both of these two were behind the original China White outbreak five years earlier.

Luther Dickson, with a PhD from the University of the Pacific, was a former assistant professor of chemistry at California State University, Bakersfield. Dickson had done underground chemistry before; he'd been arrested in March 1977 for manufacturing phencyclidine (PCP) in his lab space on the Cal State campus. He eventually pleaded guilty in 1983 to manufacturing PHP, a phencyclidine analogue and received a five-year sentence—but he didn't leave the drug manufacturing business.

He got arrested again in Los Angeles in 1980 for operating a clandestine lab making methaqualone, the key ingredient of the then-popular sedative Quaalude. Dickson won that case when some of the evidence was suppressed, and he turned to 3-methylfentanyl, a drug that was still legal at the time. State and federal law enforcement agencies caught up with him in June 1985.

Like Dickson, Kenneth Marvin Baker, 43, had been down this road before. Baker, a "chemistry whiz" who dropped out of UCLA after two years, had been arrested in a drug manufacturing case in 1972 after a house explosion in the San Fernando Valley north of Los Angeles.

Three years later, state and federal narcotics agents arrested Baker again in connection with the seizure of a half-ton of phencyclidine (PCP), the "largest angel dust haul in West Coast history." Agents also seized over a thousand pounds of piperidine, a key PCP precursor. Baker pled guilty to conspiracy and possession of PCP with intent to distribute in March 1976, and received a four-year and eleven-month sentence.

Also like Dickson, Baker went back to manufacturing drugs when he got out. The DEA arrested him again on June 7, 1985, at his North Hollywood apartment after neighbors reported a "horrible odor." They found ten pounds of what was first suspected to be 3-methylfentanyl, linking Baker to the earlier China White cases and over ninety overdose deaths.

Analysis of the seizure, however, found eight different fentanyl analogues, none of which were then listed in state or federal statutes as controlled substances.

Originally charged with manufacturing a controlled substance, those charges were dropped because the fentanyl variants weren't scheduled at the time, but federal prosecutors indicted Baker in February 1986 for manufacturing sixty pounds of "synthetic heroin." The actual charges, however, were Food and Drug Act violations, like "mislabeling drugs with the intent to defraud," that carried much weaker penalties.

Both Baker and Dickson were caught after ordering essential fentanyl precursors from a southern California chemical supply company, one that was already the subject of a two-year investigation by state and federal agents.

Chemical Shed, Inc., operated by Burton W. Farrell, was an established business that came to the attention of law enforcement after police encountered containers bearing the company's label at clandestine labs and sites where waste from drug manufacturing operations was dumped.

"Forty-one of the 84 times Los Angeles police were called to investigate illegal drug labs or dump sites from 1983 to July 1985, they discovered Chemical Shed labels on the containers."

A year-long investigation of Chemical Shed that included wiretaps on the business' phones and video surveillance outside the stores uncovered several lab operators making phencyclidine (PCP), amphetamines, and methaqualone. Of Chemical Shed's $1.5 million in 1985 sales, "Seventy-five to eighty percent was illegal business." People from as far away as Minnesota came to southern California to take advantage of Farrell's "no questions asked" policy for cash customers.

In July 1985, investigators seized Farrell's home, other assets, and all three stores, putting Chemical Shed out of business. Before that, however, the investigation had uncovered both Dickson and Baker who, unlike the other customers, were buying chemicals that investigators knew could be used for the production of fentanyl and its analogues.

"We heard someone order some chemicals that we'd never heard of before—stuff like methyl acrylate and aniline. We did some research, and came up with a formula for methylfentanyl," LAPD Detective Roy Wunderlich told a reporter. "We went back to the Chemical Shed and had a long, heart-to-heart talk with (Farrell), and convinced him that he could be involved with a lot of deaths from China White, so he had better tell us who was buying those particular chemicals. He said Luther Dickson had bought six pounds of methyl acrylate and gave us an address."

Police obtained a warrant for Dickson's North Hollywood house, served it a few days later, and found a lab setup and enough chemicals to produce "more than 100 million units of the fentanyl analog (sic)."

There was a problem, though. At the time of the seizure, 3-methylfentanyl hadn't been listed as a controlled substance, so Dickson was charged with those Food and Drug Act offenses that carried much lower penalties. Even those lesser crimes had a major impact on the traffic, removing Baker and Dickson from the business for several years.

Taking out Chemical Shed may have also contributed. Its owner, Burton Ferrell, was charged with conspiring to aid and abet the manufacture of illegal drugs, income tax evasion, and running a business through a pattern of racketeering (RICO). Farrell pleaded guilty on April 15, 1986, and admitted that he knew he was selling to clandestine lab operators. He was sentenced to six years in federal prison.

Los Angeles narcotics investigators noted that after the closing of Chemical Shed's operations in 1985, the price of PCP doubled in the area, and it became very hard to find on the streets. Deaths attributed to China White also fell sharply following Baker and Dickson's arrests.

DEA Chemist Frank Sapienza credited the cases against the two chemists with ending the China White episode. "We think they were the ones primarily responsible for it.

It seems rather coincidental that we took down the labs in L.A., and analogues dried up on the street."

* * *

Rochester, Michigan, 1986

A year after Chemical Shed's closing and Baker and Dickson's arrests, David Demeglio, a Michigan dentist, reached for the 3-methylfentanyl ring. Demeglio maintained an office in the Detroit suburb of Rochester, and on November 3, 1986, another dentist in the building called the fire department to report noxious fumes coming from Demeglio's suite. When the Rochester fire chief ordered the rooms opened and entered, he found a working laboratory with "chemicals hissing and bubbling through a labyrinth of tubing." The police called the DEA and forensic chemists determined that the lab contained "enough equipment and chemicals to produce up to 25 million dose units of 3-methylfentanyl."

Larry Bunting, the assistant U.S. attorney who handled the case, said, "Demeglio apparently found the formula in the library, and bought the chemicals a little here and a little there, and went into the business." Subsequently convicted of attempting to manufacture controlled substances, Demeglio received a five-year sentence.

None of his product reached the streets or killed any customers. So American addicts and consumers had dodged the fentanyl bullet once again.

They wouldn't be so lucky the next time a chemist opened the lid on this Pandora's Box.

* * *

Pennsylvania, 1978 – 1988

On June 2, 1988, Jay Duschl, 38, died of a suspected drug overdose in Pittsburgh, Pennsylvania. A month later, another overdose claimed Daniel Kostopodis, 41, of Bellevue. Police and coroners suspected heroin, but chemists analyzing the drugs recovered at the scene were shocked to find 3-methylfentanyl, almost undetectable in either the samples found or in the blood of the deceased.

Law enforcement in Pittsburgh went looking for the source of the drugs. That investigation ended in the arrest of Thomas Schaefers and several others in November and December 1988.

Although the DEA's investigation would show that Schaefers, a 48-year-old research chemist at the Calgon Corporation, had manufactured the drug at his workplace and in the basement of his parents' home, the arrest came too late for the eighteen people killed by 3-methyfentanyl, and as many as sixty others who overdosed but survived the experience.

Schaefers did not have a PhD but did possess extensive experience in research chemistry and had access to Calgon's facilities, so he was an almost perfect fit for the profile of a fentanyl manufacturer. Convicted, he received a 40-year sentence for his part in the operation—and with his arrest and conviction, 3-methylfentanyl disappeared from Pittsburgh streets.

* * *

With one key difference, Joseph Martier was a much better fit for the profile. Martier was born in April 1950 in Harrison Township, a Pittsburgh suburb, and attended Kiski High School in Vandergrift, another Pittsburgh bedroom community, before attending the University of Pennsylvania. He wasn't a chemist; he had started law school at the University of Pittsburgh, dropping out before graduation.

In 1977, Martier created a solar heating business, and persuaded a "long-time friend" and college classmate,

Christopher Jastrzebski, to join him. The business, Solar Instruments, encountered financial problems and by 1978, with the business failing, the two men were looking for another source of income. They turned to drug manufacturing to get it.

Unlike Martier, Jastrzebski had some background in science, including a master's degree in chemical engineering from Lehigh University and employment as a chemical engineer for the Exxon Corp. before leaving to join Martier in the solar heating venture.

They focused on PCP and MDA, another hallucinogen, researching the subject at the Carnegie Library and eventually creating a process that produced "the most profitable PCP possible." It would only be profitable if they could actually sell it, and this was a problem until Martier contacted another acquaintance, James Boyd, who had the necessary connections to market the drugs.

Operating a laboratory set up by two associates in a remote rented cottage in the nearby Laurel Mountains, they ordered chemicals through Solar Instruments and two dummy companies they had created in Ohio and New Jersey. When all the pieces were in place, the group cranked out significant quantities of PCP and MDA. The operation was a success until May 1979, when the DEA pulled the plug.

During a four-month investigation, undercover agents and informants purchased PCP from members of the group. One informant bought twenty-four pounds of the drug from Martier and Jastrzebski just a few days before the agents rounded up the group. Arresting officers seized another twenty-two pounds of a PCP precursor and five pounds of MDA.

In a post-arrest confession to drug agents, Martier described the agreement between the four principal conspirators in which he and Jastrzebski were responsible for manufacturing the drugs while Boyd and another man "supplied the necessary chemicals, the laboratory site, and lab apparatus." The four had agreed to split the profits four ways in what the DEA called a "multi-million-dollar operation."

Martier and Jastrzebski fought the case in a three-week trial that began in late September, and the jury deliberated for two days before finding both men and their partner Boyd guilty on most of the charges. At sentencing in November, both men were given fifteen-year prison terms. Their appeals were denied, and Martier and Jastrzebski were ordered to prison in November 1981.

Initially assigned to the Federal Correctional Institution at Ray Brook, in upstate New York, after ten months both were transferred closer to home. They were bound for the United States Penitentiary at Lewisburg.

In what would be bad news for drug addicts across America, the two Pennsylvanians would discover that they had plenty in common with another inmate doing time in the Big House.

CHAPTER 26

Lewisburg Penitentiary to Danbury, Connecticut, 1982 – 1986

The word "conspiracy" comes from the Latin *conspirare*, which means to "breathe together," and a conspiracy is just that: people breathing together in the pursuit of a common (and usually illegal) goal.

In order to be legally complete, a conspiracy requires two or more people, an agreement to commit a crime, and some overt act to further or advance the agreement. Some conspiracies conclude quickly, some go on for years, and others may take weeks or months to move past casual talk to something more sinister.

The one hatched at Lewisburg in early 1983 was only an idea, percolating idly for more than five years before its schemers ultimately breathed together. When they finally did, a lot of Americans would stop breathing altogether.

Late in 1982, Lewisburg moved Squeak from his comfortable situation in J Block to the even more congenial setting of the adjacent minimum-security camp. He had no problems fitting in, and soon after he made the move, he met Joseph Martier, also incarcerated for making drugs. Martier had arrived at the prison two weeks earlier, a first-time offender feeling his way through his first prison sentence.

"My relationship in prison with Martier? Friendly, but obviously motivated by mutual interest," Squeak said. "Several days after we met, it became known to Joe and his partner that I was incarcerated for a similar type of offense. They became curious, and conversation was struck up at some point about the technical details relating to their offenses."

Squeak was not impressed. "Joe was an intelligent enough individual, but he had minimal laboratory skills. You get that when some people think themselves very bright. Joe had a reasonably high IQ score and he thought, 'I'm quite a bright person, I can do anything.' This perception collided with reality in the case of organic chemistry. Everything he tried, basically, he would muck up or fail except these PCP operations that they were carrying on in garbage cans. It didn't require any high level of chemical talent to do this."

Despite Squeak's contempt for his new friend's chemistry skills, the two were pushed closer when the institution assigned Martier to drive Squeak around for his maintenance job. "I may have been at camp perhaps eighteen months, and we talked constantly," Squeak said. "He lived right next door to me, and we went practically every place together around there, and we were constantly in each other's company during that period of time.

"We talked about manufacturing drugs, MDA and synthetic cocaine, amphetamine precursors and amphetamine. Just everything you can imagine, but drug manufacturing was certainly a large portion of the conversation."

He also met Martier's crime partner, Chris Jastrzebski. "Chris had quite a bit of training as a chemical engineer. Very bright. No decent lab skills, but he had some experience. They were making PCP and got arrested for that. I'm quite certain that Jastrzebski must have carried Joe through that, or one of their other accomplices. I doubt Joe could have managed it on his own."

The three would be together for the next year, but Squeak tried to maintain some distance from his new buddies, both of whom were novices at the prison game that Squeak had been playing since he was nineteen.

"Martier and Jastrzebski were hated and distrusted by the prison staff. They were viewed as privileged members of the upper middle class, Ivy Leaguers who had fucked up. Joe and Chris had an aloof attitude towards the people who worked there. Constantly smuggling hooch, which amused the admin, and from time to time, drugs, which did not."

Squeak, zealously guarding his access to his precious instruments, refused to permit either man to compromise his own comfortable relationship with the prison staff. "I would not allow them to store their contraband articles in my shop or any spaces to which I had access. Lose my oscilloscopes over that? I don't think so!"

Martier remembered their relationship similarly, saying later that he and Erik became friends and "continuously talked about chemistry and electronics. We talked probably ten hours a day."

Erik remembered the moment when fentanyl first came up. "Sometime in the first year, Martier made mention of 'China White,' fentanyl, etc., and that it might be an interesting possibility to explore. I said, 'You guys get me a structure, and I'll look at it to see if we can make it.' And nobody came up with a structure at that time. They said it was fentanyl and alpha methylfentanyl and 3-methylfentanyl, and there were lots of discussions about them."

The subject came up because Martier read a magazine article about the drug and showed the article to Squeak who, thanks to Louis Cirillo, Martin Angelina, and the other interested parties on J Block, was already thoroughly familiar with the subject.

These discussions, brief and mostly in passing, did not advance past idle prison talk. The seed had been planted, however, and though it was still dormant when Squeak left Lewisburg in December 1983, neither man forgot the subject or each other when they were separated. No one was yet breathing together in conspiracy, but they were getting closer.

That would have to wait for Martier's release from prison. When he was transferred from Lewisburg to the Federal Correctional Institution at Danbury, Connecticut in September 1984, Martier found another opportunity to meet new people, and he promptly encountered two who would be helpful in his future efforts. Initially assigned within Danbury's medium security "walls" section, he became "good friends" with another inmate, Benito "Benny" Febre.

Febre, who was also known as "Brooklyn Bob," was at Danbury serving a seven-year sentence for conspiracy in a marijuana smuggling case, and he talked up his connections which he claimed included Italian organized crime and Latin American traffickers in New York and Los Angeles. Febre gave his new friend phone numbers where he could be reached after both men got out of prison in case future opportunities knocked.

Martier met his second useful contact after his move in the spring of 1985 to the adjacent Danbury camp. Barry Wilson was a bearded, balding Boston criminal defense attorney that local newspapers called, "flamboyant" and "volcanic." Wilson was at Danbury doing four-and-a half months for refusing to testify before a Federal grand jury.

He and Martier hit it off, becoming "good friends"… the former law student and a prominent criminal defense lawyer living "back in the same corner of the dorm," and sharing some common interests. Martier said they never discussed criminal activity, but as with Febre, he kept Wilson's number for possible future use.

Wilson did his time and returned to his practice in October 1985, leaving Danbury before Martier, who was discharged to a halfway house in Pittsburgh in early 1986.

* * *

Norman, Oklahoma, 1983 – 1984

Lewisburg released Squeak on December 9, 1983, almost six years after OBN grabbed him off his porch in Beggs.

"After I was released from Lewisburg, I went back to Oklahoma and leased myself a house, then set up a laboratory in back of it, making amphetamine precursors. Joe and I stayed in contact. He phoned me from the prison. In fact, many times I was running reactions when I got his phone call, and I would sit there and converse with him with my feet on the table, watching the pots boil."

Despite his promise to Judge Morris and John Osgood at his Muskogee sentencing, he didn't turn straight back to manufacturing TMA or even methamphetamine. Instead, he set his sights on an idea he got from the Oklahoma Bureau of Narcotics.

Before doing that, maybe hoping the third time would be the charm, he tried marriage again.

Squeak already knew free-spirited Peggy Dulany, a lively and attractive divorcee with wavy brown hair and brown eyes and a love of animals and flowers…a literal flower child who sold them on the street in Oklahoma City. They exchanged letters throughout his prison term and talked about marriage, and in January 1984, they tied the knot.

Squeak got along well with Peggy's daughter Kimberly, who remembered her stepfather fondly. "I was fifteen when he married my mom. We knew what he did, knew he was making drugs. He'd been in prison for doing the same thing. But he warned me about using drugs and tried to keep us away from that kind of thing. He never gave any drugs to me or my friends, and I had some who'd have been happy to get them.

"He was always very laid back. Reading books, doing quiet things, listening to classical music, but he could get mad. He loved animals, especially dogs. At one point we had I think twenty dogs and cats. Mostly dogs. My mom found them and brought them home, and he did, too. It took a lot to get him upset or angry, but somebody hurting a dog or a little kid, that could set him off. He didn't have much patience for that.

"Somebody shot one of the dogs once, and I'll bet he spent a couple thousand dollars at the vet. It was a dog that had been a stray, but it was his dog and somebody hurt it, so he wanted to take care of it. I'd hate to have been the person who did it if he found out. He always had a gun, and he'd probably have shot him."

It didn't take long before he had his lab up and running again. He kept some of his equipment and supplies in the house he now shared with his new bride and her two children but ran his reactions from a rented house nearby.

He wasn't exactly hiding out from old friends who'd been helpful in the past. He immediately reconnected with Bob Fearon in Tulsa and Keith Hollenbeak at the Halliburton Company's laboratory in Duncan, Oklahoma. He also didn't neglect his acquaintances from the other team, and talked occasionally with Jimmy Birdsong and Lonnie Wright from OBN.

Wright, who had been on the Beggs raid and was working his way up through the ranks at OBN, introduced a younger agent, John Duncan, to Squeak.

"John was from Norman," Squeak said. "I think Lonnie introduced me because he knew I was living in Norman and thought John could keep an eye on me. We ended up keeping an eye on each other.

"I caught them watching the house, and we were about ready to move on anyway, so I packed my things and we moved out toward Tulsa. Put a little distance between myself and my pursuers."

OBN agent Duncan remembered his conversation with Squeak. "I said, 'I was watching you when you were in Norman.' He says, 'Yeah, I saw you guys out there sitting around with your binoculars.' And I said, 'Well, what were you doing over there? I thought you were running a lab.' He says, 'I was.'"

Squeak had a surprise, though. "It wasn't a meth lab or amphetamines," Duncan said. "He told me, 'I'd gotten out of jail, and I was watching television, and one of the first stories on the news I saw was that people who had AIDS and HIV were not able to get this new experimental drug, AZT, and they were protesting. I thought if I can get my hands on some of that, I'll just make some and sell it to them. And so that's what I was doing over there.'"

Squeak managed to scrounge a small amount of AZT. "I got a sample of it, and then had Keith run it through a mass spectrometer at Halliburton and give me the results. And then I figured out how to make it, and set up a lab at the house, and was making bootleg AZT and selling it to people that needed it."

When asked later about this apparently altruistic flip from making dangerous, even deadly drugs of abuse to a life-saving medication for desperate people with a fatal disease, Squeak scoffed and said it was all about the money. "I was not in it for fun or trying to win some humanitarian of the year award. And I certainly enjoyed undercutting the Burroughs people. I thought the amount they were charging was much too high, especially since the original patent had expired and anyone could make it. They should have been giving it away, but if they weren't, I wasn't going to, either."

Five years before AIDS activist Ron Woodroof created his Dallas Buyer's Club to provide unapproved medications to patients with HIV, Squeak went there first.

AZT, or azidothymidine had been synthesized in 1974 as a cancer treatment, but Burroughs Wellcome, one of the oldest and largest drug manufacturers in the world, tried the drug for HIV/AIDS, found some success, and put the drug on the market in 1987. The cost was $10,000 per year. That might not sound like a lot in 2024, but at the time, AZT was the most expensive pharmaceutical in history.

"I was charging a fraction of what Burroughs was asking, and still making money. As you can imagine, people were glad to get it. My motives were, on a vastly smaller scale, exactly the same as the legitimate manufacturer. Make a pile of geet. And I love the adventure."

Duncan thought the AZT episode cemented Squeak's reputation as a dangerous—and different—underground chemist. "He did not just understand meth and amphetamine chemistry, LSD-type chemistry. He understood chemistry on a larger scale. He could make bootleg AZT because he just got a mass spectrometry of it, and figured it out on his own. No telling what else he could make you if you wanted it—and were willing to pay for it."

Duncan remembered one of Squeak's more sinister projects. "He told me, 'If you're up in the northwest part of the country, there's a lot of survivalists up there. And a long, long time ago, I made a precursor for sarin nerve gas and sold it widely up there. A lot of them have it.'

"He said, 'If you ever go on a raid and you're in that part of the world, and they have a sprinkler system, and it really doesn't look like it ought to be there…they'll run into a hide. They'll put their gas mask on. They'll flip a switch, it'll break two vials, bring the chemicals together, and then they'll use a pressuring device to spray nerve gas out. Just be real careful.' And I'm thinking, *Wow*."

Another OBN agent remembered the same thing from his experience with Squeak. "The clandestine chemists we saw were all strictly one-trick ponies. Not Squeak. He'd make whatever he thought he could sell or, more often, whatever interested him. AZT wouldn't surprise me. Or nerve gas for Idaho Nazis."

Another OBN agent remembered the same thing from his experience with Squeak. "The clandestine chemists we saw were all strictly one-trick ponies. Not Squeak. He'd make whatever he thought he could sell or, more often, whatever interested him. AZT wouldn't surprise me. But that's what made him different. That's what made him unique."

Although Duncan enjoyed his memorable conversation with the man he called a "great genius," but one who "got caught up in the mad scientist model," he and the other OBN agents who met him were aware of how dangerous he and his chemistry skills were.

The subject of fentanyl came up, Duncan recalled. "Marquardt was particularly interested in something that I mentioned called 3-methylfentanyl. And I said, 'Do you make that kind of stuff in labs? Have you ever made fentanyl?' And he says, 'Well, I don't know. I might have. I'm not sure. Not something I'd talk about.' And so, we didn't talk about it much more, but sadly, I think maybe I put the idea in his head to make fentanyl."

Duncan needn't have worried. When asked about the conversation, Squeak remembered, "Duncan raised the fentanyl flag, which did not catch me by surprise. I obviously didn't tell him about my conversations with Louie Cirillo or Martin Angelina, or Joe Martier, for that matter. Some things are better left unsaid."

And even though the subject kept popping up, Squeak didn't need fentanyl. "I dragged my feet on it for years. I wouldn't do it. I had local customers for nickel-dime speed deals that provided me with enough rent money. I'd make a couple of ounces of speed here, a couple of ounces of speed there…just avoided the whole question. It wasn't necessary."

* * *

In 1980, while Squeak was safely locked away at Lewisburg, Congress placed phenylacetone or P2P into Schedule II of the Controlled Substances Act. Oklahoma followed suit, making the chemical a Schedule III controlled dangerous substance.

Sale and even possession of P2P by clandestine lab operators became a felony carrying penalties identical to those for methamphetamine, cocaine, morphine, and fentanyl. Finding a supplier willing to violate these laws became much more difficult, and underground cooks sought out alternatives.

Squeak saw an opportunity, and he got the idea—not from John Duncan, who worried that he might have planted the fentanyl bug during their chats—but from Jay and OBN's proposed "trick store" of six years earlier that would have supplied things like precursors and other lab supplies, "no questions asked."

Squeak had no problem making P2P, methylamine, or other precursors; he'd been doing it for years. The new rules meant lab operators would, he thought, have an even more difficult time than before acquiring key precursors. They would be looking for a safe source, one that would not take their cash and call OBN or the DEA.

He could supply this need: could safely acquire phenylacetic acid, the chemical needed to make P2P, convert it in a fifteen-hour process, and sell the key meth precursor to lab operators for almost as much as he could get from producing the methamphetamine itself.

His customers, including the Pagan outlaw motorcycle club and other Oklahoma bikers were quite happy with their new source for P2P.

No questions asked.

CHAPTER 27

Oklahoma, 1984 – 1986

Squeak hadn't forgotten his discussions in Lewisburg about fentanyl—and neither had Martier, who reached out by mail in cloak-and-dagger fashion.

"They sent me this letter and told me to heat it up with a candle or some such thing, and somebody had written a secret message on the back, and there was the name of the stuff, fentanyl citrate, and showing the structure."

Martier wanted to know if Squeak thought he and Jastrzebski were capable of making the drug and in a later, carefully worded phone conversation from the prison where the staff monitored both phone calls and mail, asked the question more directly.

Joe asked me. "'Do you think I can make it?' I opined that I thought he could. He was an intelligent person, and I had no idea what kind of laboratory competence he and Chris had, but I assumed from discussion with the two that it was greater than it turned out to be."

Squeak told Martier in a phone call that he would do a literature search to get more information. He found some good news, but enough bad news to cause him to express some doubts. "The first paper I unearthed was a general reference in the *British Journal of Anesthesia*. It gave a description of the effects and talked about the overdose potential. I did not like what I saw, and reported this to

Martier in a later phone conversation. We had no further discussion about fentanyl for some time after that."

All that changed in the fall of 1985 when Keith Hollenbeak called his attention to a piece in the *Chemical & Engineering News*. It was the same September 9 article that had seduced Michael Hovey and Daniel Hodes. Hollenbeak thought they could manage the manufacturing process for the lethal 3-methylfentanyl, and based on his previous reading of the literature, Squeak agreed…though not without some serious reservations.

"Overdose seemed to be a problem. Hollenbeak believed it could be solved, but I remained unconvinced.

"I don't think that these extremely potent opiate replacements are suitable targets for a street drug. They're too difficult for the dealers to handle, the chances of overdoses are too high, and this makes for bad market."

In saying so, Squeak wasn't arguing that they shouldn't make fentanyl or 3-methylfentanyl because it would kill its consumers; in his view, those people knew the danger and accepted the risks of being drug users. Instead, he was recalling the warning given him by his first drug partner, Frank in Milwaukee, that dead junkies bring heat, which was something he didn't need or want.

He would repeat these misgivings—especially the ones about the lethality of 3-methylfentanyl, numerous times over the next several years. His warning seems especially prescient as we view the current fentanyl problem—a crisis he predicted in 1985—that is now killing two hundred Americans every day.

After his first dive into the fentanyl literature, he warned Martier that, "I think we've got something here that's going to make PCP look nice. And I think if we make this stuff, we're going to kill a bunch of people."

Despite his reservations, Squeak continued his research, leaving the question of right or wrong aside, concentrating on the chemistry as the German chemists of the nineteenth and early twentieth centuries he idolized had done. There was no idle musing about the moral ramifications of their project, no soul there…only chemistry. And he found enough of that to resolve some key questions that did matter.

"I did a further search of the literature, and unearthed a good preparative method by Janssen and other authors in the *Journal of Medicinal Chemistry*. The most interesting paper, from my standpoint, was a journal article which described in some detail a workable method for production of fentanyl precursors."

He concluded that the process described in the journals—the so-called "Janssen Method"—was fairly difficult, required a well-equipped laboratory, and was, in his words, "beyond the abilities of the average clandestine chemist, especially Joe Martier." He did think, though, that he himself could perform it if he had enough money.

Baum's article reinforced this view. In it, DEA Chemist Sapienza said, "Making these fentanyl compounds is not the same as making PCP or methamphetamine. I don't think that the average bucket chemist would be able to follow a set of instructions to make 3-methylfentanyl."

In another 1985 article, designer drug expert Gary Henderson said of a hypothetical fentanyl manufacturer, "He's clearly a state-of-the-art chemist. He'd have to be, or he'd kill himself making the stuff. It's that potent."

Several of the articles stated that the process required at least a master's degree in chemistry, which cheered Squeak up considerably when he read them. "I was not considered a candidate for being the person who is manufacturing this because of my lack of academic credentials. I thought, *that's just absolutely wonderful, and I hope that's the official mantra because that absolves me*. I'm just a tinkerer on the backside of nowhere and, consequently, won't be looked at with any particular amount of attention."

But with Martier still incarcerated, the fentanyl project remained on a back burner as Squeak concentrated on making AZT, P2P, and methylamine.

In January 1986, Martier was released to a halfway house in Pittsburgh. He and Squeak stayed in touch when Martier's time in the halfway house ended in April. They weren't exactly breathing together yet.

But they were getting close.

George Erik Marquardt, c. 1958, in the basement laboratory, 500 Grand Avenue, Waukesha, Wisconsin. *Courtesy, Marquardt family*

Erik, c. 1951, on the Olson family farm, outside Sisseton, South Dakota. *Courtesy, Marquardt family*

Erik, c. 1955, with chemistry set Christmas present. *Courtesy, Marquardt family*

Resthaven, Waukesha, c. 1910-1919. The morgue and laboratory where Marquardt produced heroin were on the ground floor at the right side of the image. *University of Wisconsin, Madison*

Erik, with his sisters, Mary and Gini, c. 1961. *Courtesy, Marquardt family*

OBN Agents Jimmy Birdsong (l) and Lonnie Wright (r), c. 1979. *Oklahoma Bureau of Narcotics*

OBN Agent Elaine Dodd, in Marquardt's Beggs laboratory, January 17, 1978. Note the lack of personal protective equipment. *Oklahoma Bureau of Narcotics*

Squeak, transported to Muskogee County Jail following his arrest at the Beggs laboratory, January 17, 1978.

Philip "Rusty" Rastelli, Bonanno Family
boss and Lewisburg inmate. *NYPD*

Louis Cirillo, Lucchese Family associate and Lewisburg
inmate. Federal narcotic agents called Cirillo "the most
substantial narcotics trafficker the Bureau has ever
found." *Bureau of Narcotics and Dangerous Drugs*

Squeak, with wife Peggy Dulaney (l) and step-daughter, Kimberly Dulaney, c. 1986. *Courtesy of Marquardt family*

Squeak in his April 1988, mugshot, at Norman, Oklahoma, *author's collection.*

DEA surveillance photograph showing
Marquardt approaching PrairieLab. Chemical
containers observed by DEA outside PrairieLab,
c. January 1992. *Courtesy of Troy Derby*

Tango & Cash fentanyl packet, seized in New York
City, February 2, 1991. *Author's Collection*

Laboratory equipment and glassware, seized at
PrairieLab, February 3, 1993. *Courtesy of Troy Derby*

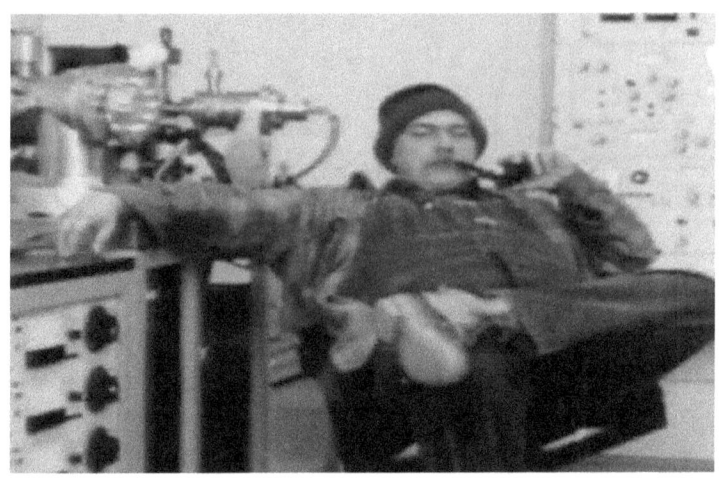

Squeak, at PrairieLab, with the Micromass VG-70-70 mass spectrometer that he purchased from Wichita State University and restored to working condition. c. 1992.

PrairieLab building, Goddard, Kansas. *Author's collection*

Christopher Moscatiello and sister Cynthia,
Courtesy Moscatiello family

Joseph V. Martier, high school yearbook photo

CHAPTER 28

Davenport, Oklahoma to Norman, Oklahoma to Seagoville, Texas, 1987 – 1989

The fentanyl project bubbled along in desultory fashion through 1987 and 1988, going nowhere as Squeak talked with Martier periodically by phone, neither taking any positive steps toward making the plan a reality.

In Oklahoma, the marriage to Peggy Dulany was in trouble. They were living in Davenport, a town on the famous Route 66, about halfway between Tulsa and Oklahoma City. He was careful to never bring any precursor chemicals or finished product home. But he still had a lab setup in the house, and ran "some preliminary, but non-criminal reactions" there and this might have contributed to some of the marital tensions.

"One time my buddy Keith turned up with some cyanide, and I got it set up and make some initial preparations. I turned my back for a second, then turned around and there was hydrogen cyanide pouring out the top of the flask. And I grabbed that thing in my hand, froze my breathing full stop. Went out the back door into the solarium we had, and Peggy was coming up the stairs. And I made it clear she should get out. No argument. She turned around and like a cartoon character, legs moving in the air, shot down. Just vanished.

"I just set it down outside and let it boil itself off. And left the house and ventilated the place. Cyanide disperses rapidly. It's lethal as hell, but you can get rid of it."

Peggy apparently didn't regard a houseful of cyanide gas with the same nonchalance, and the stresses of living with Squeak—combined with the ever-present risk that she might be gassed, blown up, burned up, or busted along with her two children—eventually persuaded her that the marriage wasn't working out. Especially since Squeak was moving away from meth precursors to something much more deadly.

"My ex-wife heard a lot of the discussions. I suspect she remembers very well that I did the literature search, because it was when I broke up with her that I had first started to acquire precursors for fentanyl. And then I was headed down a long dark tunnel when I just acted in a fashion that was guaranteed to run her off," he said.

The separation went quickly and amicably. Squeak stayed in touch with stepdaughter Kimberly, but cleared out all of his stuff and left what would be his last marriage behind. "I was kind of at loose ends about this time, and I moved back to Norman, to a little apartment there."

He hadn't stopped any of the chemistry, although he recognized the need to be more discreet. "I knew Jimmy and the OBN people would be all over me if they got even a hint of where I was operating or what I was making."

He'd always been a fast learner, and he'd picked up quite a bit from his 1978 bust in Beggs. He had a very good idea about how OBN, in particular, operated. That didn't deter him, just made him more cautious. "At one point they were trying all the old electric company stuff on me in that place. But I had storage batteries and auxiliary power supplies. A real quiet generator, and then I had a hookup with the house next door. So, anyone watching my meter, as I assumed the OBN people would be doing, wouldn't see anything out of the ordinary. I was doing all kinds of insidious shit like that. I love the game."

He knew the electrical issue wasn't the biggest of his problems, and went to even greater lengths to avoid the one that was. John Duncan, hot on Squeak's trail, said a clandestine lab "is one of the worst-smelling things you'll ever encounter. We could always catch people by the smell."

Squeak knew all about that risk. "By this time, I'd spent so much time running reactions, more than twenty thousand at that point, I'd completely lost my sense of smell. But I knew Jimmy and Lonnie hadn't lost theirs."

He took steps to deal with that issue. "Ran the reactions under negative pressure, took some other steps I'm not going to describe. My objective was that somebody could stand in the next room or at the front door, and not smell anything except the pipe and the dog."

That pipe, ever-present, became something of a trademark. He would keep it lit, and his technique refined, in the future fentanyl operation he and Martier had discussed.

And suddenly even those occasional conversations stopped altogether.

"We always talked," Martier recalled, "once we were both out of jail, probably once every month or two on the telephone. Sometime in the late eighties he disappeared. As it turns out, he was arrested for a firearms violation."

Squeak was back in prison.

This incident occurred on April 12, 1988, and in Squeak's words, "That was just one of those stupid things people do. I lost my temper, pulled my pistol, and chased the fellow down the street in front of about two hundred Chinese students. Just a generally foolish thing."

The Norman Police Department, called to the scene by a shocked onlooker, arrested him without incident. Squeak gave up as soon as he was confronted by the law, and called Jimmy Birdsong at OBN to let him know what happened.

"Jimmy and Lonnie took care of it with the Norman police, but I knew I was going to have to do some time over it. The OBN agents all got a big laugh out of it. They'd been used to playing their game as best they could, chasing me, and I hadn't been famous for doing a lot of stupid things—but when I picked something to do, I really picked a good one."

The arrest put Squeak in a tough legal bind. Convicted felons aren't supposed to have guns at all, and facing state firearms and assault charges, and a federal charge for being a prohibited person in possession of a firearm—he cashed in a favor.

"I was, at the time, acting as a technical consultant, unofficial or semi-official for OBN. I'd been giving them information about people making suspicious purchases at the places where I did my shopping. I also told Jimmy about some people who were planning to make some heroin out of codeine, something I knew a little about."

Recalling his long-ago adventures in Waukesha, Robitussin, and codeine tablets, Squeak described the process for converting codeine to heroin for the OBN agents and advised them on what to look for and where.

The OBN agents went to bat for their informant. "Jimmy and Lonnie went down to the prosecutor's office in Norman and told them they wanted me in federal custody, and I'd be doing time even if the state dropped its case, which it did."

At federal court in Oklahoma City, Squeak's special parole term from 1978 was revoked on August 15, and Cleveland County's charges were dismissed a week later. By that time, Squeak was at the Federal Correctional Institution in nearby El Reno, on his way to FCI Seagoville, twenty miles southeast of Dallas.

"Seagoville, uneventful trip. It's kind of pleasant. Met some interesting people. Throughout my confinement there, Martier and I talked over the phone intermittently. One must be somewhat circumspect in these conversations. The staff is always listening. But I made it clear I was going to be ready to go to work when I got out, and he led me to believe that the fentanyl project would be funded upon my release."

In mid-February 1989, Joe Martier's phone rang. "He called me very shortly after he got out," Martier said. "He said that while he was in prison, he got divorced, he lost his car, and his house. He said he was broke, and that he wanted to get something going. He needed some cash. And he asked me if I could lend him some money to help him get on his feet."

Martier knew exactly what they were talking about.

"It wasn't like he was going to spend this money on rent. He wanted some money to buy some chemicals."

The fentanyl project was about to shift from idle chat into something else, and there's a name for that.

The law calls it a "criminal conspiracy."

CHAPTER 29

Oklahoma to Milwaukee, 1989

Squeak returned to Oklahoma facing a discouraging picture. He was flat broke with no equipment or supplies, and his acquaintances at the Oklahoma Bureau of Narcotics had made it crystal clear that they were going to be watching his next moves—and the ones after that—very closely. This was now critically important because over the four years following Squeak's release from Lewisburg, Congress had been busy amending the country's drug laws. In doing so, it had substantially raised the stakes in the game Squeak loved so much.

Squeak was aware of these legal changes. "I paid close attention to the Analogue Act, of course, but it just made things more interesting," he said much later. "I did recognize that my potential legal exposure was greater."

Other statutory changes pushed that exposure even higher. A 1984 law abolished parole for federal crimes and drastically reduced the "good time" credit inmates received for behaving themselves in prison. A ten-year sentence like that he'd received in 1978 now meant almost nine years in prison rather than the six he'd actually served.

Penalties for drug crimes were doubled or more, and many offenses now had mandatory minimum sentences. Someone making or selling a mixture or substance containing *a detectable amount* of 400 grams or more of fentanyl or

100 grams of a fentanyl analogue faced a sentence of ten years to life.

There was a *minimum* term of 20 years up to life if "death or serious bodily injury results from the use of such substance," and all of these penalties doubled for repeat offenders.

Squeak's prior conviction for a drug felony in Oklahoma's 1978 case now meant a mandatory life sentence if the fentanyl he planned on creating killed anyone. For someone who had warned his putative partner that, "If we make this stuff, we're going to kill a bunch of people," this was sobering indeed.

None of it, however, convinced him that he should, as John Osgood suggested in 1978, "get into a different line of work." In a perverse twist that Congress didn't anticipate, the legal changes pushed him *toward* the much deadlier fentanyl.

"When I got out, it was pretty apparent that I had a lack of opportunities. OBN had been quite successful in infiltrating the speed market in the state, so I thought the manufacturing of amphetamine in Oklahoma was tantamount to a long stay in the penitentiary. Why did I decide to manufacture fentanyl? Because the penalties on the lighter weight stuff became so enormous that it made very little difference whether I made fentanyl or made amphetamine. I was taking the same risk because I was going to get an enormous amount of time, probably a life sentence, no matter what I made."

With eyes wide open, he started from scratch, heading up to Tulsa to reconnect with an old friend. Although Bob Fearon never became directly involved in Squeak's drug manufacturing, his business would play a major part in the unfolding scheme since Squeak used Fearon's accounts to order chemicals and supplies. He also counted on Fearon to notify him of any law enforcement interest, the eccentric inventor serving as a trip wire and alarm.

Now that he was fully focused on fentanyl, Squeak thought he knew what would be required to make the drug. He needed money to investigate the manufacturing process further, and to obtain the equipment he'd need to set up an experimental lab. He turned back to Joe Martier.

Martier moved in 1987 to Boston, where both he and his girlfriend had jobs. In early 1989, he received his general contractor's license, and started a construction business. In a reprise of the solar enterprise in Pittsburgh, this one promptly failed, too.

And then Martier's phone rang in Boston.

Squeak said the fentanyl project they'd been discussing aimlessly for five years was on. He asked for a loan or investment to cover startup costs, saying he needed $15,000. Martier said he could only afford to invest $5,000. Squeak said that wasn't going to be enough, and suggested that Martier seek out some other source of funding.

Martier, recalling the conversation later, said, "What he asked me to do, and what I agreed to do was, to try to find an investor who was willing to invest that amount of money in him. To prime the pump to get him going. And he told me to negotiate any deal that I thought was appropriate."

To firm things up, Martier wired Squeak $500, and arranged for Chris Jastrzebski to wire an additional $500. Martier also sent a plane ticket, and Squeak flew to Boston.

"I was picked up at the airport by Martier and his girlfriend, Erin. I hung around for a number of days in which nothing seemed to get done, loitering about his apartment on the North End of Boston waiting for a construction deal to materialize, and finally we grew somewhat testy and unpleasant with each other."

Frustrated at the slow pace, and skeptical that Martier could put the deal together, Squeak got tired of waiting, and flew back to Milwaukee. "A day or so later, I received a phone call from Martier who told me that we were 'funded.' The project was a go."

Martier had reached out to fellow former Danbury inmate, lawyer Barry Wilson. They had stayed close after Martier moved to Boston. "Practically daily, we would go out and have a drink after work," Martier said.

When he met Wilson at the lawyer's Boston law office, Martier didn't tell him what he needed the money for or his "specific intentions," but he said enough that he believed Wilson, who knew all about Martier's previous conviction for manufacturing PCP, understood Martier needed the money to finance a drug deal. "I mean, he's a damn lawyer. I can infer that he had some idea that what I was doing wasn't remodeling buildings," Martier said.

When he returned to Wilson's office two days later, Wilson arranged a meeting between Martier and someone he and Marquardt hoped would be the solution to their money problem: Charlestown marijuana smuggler Christopher Moscatiello.

The two met on the Boston Common, where Martier outlined the plan for fentanyl. "I told him that I was in contact with an expert drug manufacturer. I told him he needed $18,000 seed money to get started up, and I told him he (Marquardt) could manufacture anything he might want.

"He was interested. During that conversation, we went through the whole gamut of everything that Marquardt could do, and we eliminated everything except fentanyl. He said it was the only thing he was interested in.

"I didn't really know it at the time, but as I got to know him, I learned that he was a large marijuana and cocaine dealer. And I guess the nature of his connections was such that he wasn't interested in pills. He thought he could move the heroin. And then he told me that he believed that heroin was like the market for the nineties. It was going to be a mover."

With three people on board and in agreement on fentanyl as the drug of the future, the conspiracy had finally come together.

CHAPTER 30

Charlestown, Massachusetts, 1989

Christopher Moscatiello was a "townie," the name given to people from Charlestown, the Boston neighborhood north of the Charles River that is home to Bunker Hill. Mostly residential in 1989, Charlestown had a large population of working-class Irish Americans, as well as many of Italian ancestry like Moscatiello, who was thirty-six that year.

"He wasn't brought up in the city. He grew up in a middle-class family in a North Shore suburb," his girlfriend later recalled, playing hockey and football as a kid and then attending high school in Wenham, about thirty miles north of Boston.

After graduation, Moscatiello headed back to Boston, enrolled as a philosophy major at Boston University, driving a cab in the city to help cover expenses. He was described as "bright," and "very smart," and he was on B.U.'s debate team. He seemed to be doing well until he suddenly dropped out in his final semester at the school.

His girlfriend, later his wife, Maryann, remembered Moscatiello's description of his early family life and a possible motivation for his turning away from school to something darker. "He had it pretty hard. A mom that was very abusive. I remember him telling me that she told him, 'You're a bum. You're never going to be anything but a bum.' I think he believed her. And so I think that's one of the reasons he dropped out of college. I mean, who drops out of college right before your last semester? I think he was stunted by his mom."

Moscatiello didn't have a college degree. But he had something that worked better in working-class Charlestown. Like many townies, he had connections, and those would be very useful when he went into the drug business.

* * *

Wichita, Kansas, 1989

Back in Oklahoma, Squeak waited to see whether Martier and his new friend could actually produce the money they'd promised. While he waited, he made some important preparations. "Remaining in Oklahoma was clearly no longer a viable option. OBN was monitoring me closely. I needed some distance," Squeak said. "Every narcotics agent in the state of Oklahoma knew me by sight."

He quickly settled on Wichita, Kansas. It was the closest big city not in Oklahoma, and "it was still in the Southwest," Squeak said. He wouldn't need to leave his beloved prairie.

"I returned to Tulsa and waited around the office of Electrochemical Discoveries until a U.P.S. package arrived containing $5,000. I thought that was reasonable enough and would suffice to make some samples, and set about removing myself from the state of Oklahoma. I drove down to Norman, picked up my son-in-law, Kevin Donovan, and we left for Wichita to find a house. Kevin had vague knowledge that I was 'up to no good,' but knew better than to ask inappropriate questions."

He found a suitable place—a small frame house at the end of South St. Clair Avenue, a cul-de-sac ending at an open field and a major highway. After renting the house, which he put in Kimberly's name, he had Donovan rent two storage units nearby.

Since he was still on supervised release for his firearms conviction, Squeak rented a small apartment in Norman to report to his probation officer. Then he headed back up I-35 to Wichita with a load of laboratory equipment and furniture. "Reduced pressure distillation equipment was set up, and the synthesis of 3-methylfentanyl began."

Squeak was in his element. With Wagner playing in the background, he worked alone amidst his hand-blown glassware, humming vacuum pumps, electric stirrers, and a clutter of mostly non-functioning electronic devices he planned to restore to working condition.

He didn't view fentanyl or even its far more lethal cousin, 3-methylfentanyl, as any great challenge but his efforts in the early months of 1989 were not directed at producing fentanyl or 3-methylfentanyl—the work of a chemist—but at the creation of a lab where he could perform the necessary processes to make the drugs.

This is normally the job of a chemical engineer, and the American Chemical Society describes the chemical engineer's job: "The main role of chemical engineers is to design and troubleshoot processes for the production of chemicals, fuels, foods, pharmaceuticals, and biologicals, to name just a few."

Unlike most chemists, Squeak had the ability to perform the functions of a chemical engineer, especially designing and planning equipment layout and getting the most out of the production process.

He needed these skills in the spring of 1989 when he created the country's only underground fentanyl laboratory.

* * *

Most schemes of this sort, even those much less grand in scope, take time and effort to pull off. They usually require a lot of money, too, and Squeak ran out of that essential element barely two months into the operation.

"Towards the end of May, it was apparent that I was going to run out of funds before I had a product. Martier and

I discussed this, and he advised me he would re-negotiate the deal."

Martier recalled that putting this arrangement together "actually took a while because what Marquardt had in mind was a one-shot deal. I told him that Moscatiello was interested, but only in fentanyl. Marquardt said, 'Fine. Whatever he wants. Just get the cash.' I said, 'What do you want me to offer him?' And he said, 'A one-shot deal, ten keys for a half million, and that's it.'"

"So I took that offer back to Moscatiello, and he said that it sounded like a good price, but ten wasn't sufficient. It was too much trouble to make all the contacts necessary to sell the stuff if he was going to quit after ten. He wanted to have an ongoing business: ten a month, or twenty a month, or something like that.

"So I went back to Marquardt and told him that, and he said, 'Fine. Whatever he wants. Just tell him to send me the money.'"

More meetings followed. "Very typical in the drug business," a retired DEA agent said. "And the bigger the deal and the more money involved, the more roadblocks and hiccups you'll see. It can take a while before everybody's on the same page."

Martier, trying to build trust with someone he'd only just met, assured Moscatiello that if he produced the $18,000 in "up-front money," his chemist would produce the initial ten kilograms of fentanyl, roughly the equivalent of ten kilos of pure heroin, within ninety days. Martier never identified Marquardt in these conversations, but only said (at Squeak's insistence) that the chemist and lab were located "somewhere in the Midwest."

Whatever he said must have been persuasive, because Martier recalled that at a meet in the food court at Lafayette Place in Boston, Moscatiello gave him "$18,000 in cash in an envelope, a down payment on the agreed-upon $500,000."

Martier express-mailed $16,000 to Squeak in Tulsa, and kept $2,000 for himself.

Now that he had some cash in hand, Squeak began experimenting with fentanyl precursors in the Wichita lab. After five years of talk, the fentanyl project was finally underway.

Martier and Moscatiello both expected results, and Squeak promised they would get some.

"He said that in ninety days, he would have the first ten kilograms," Martier said.

* * *

Squeak's biggest secret wasn't keeping his name and location hidden from his own investors, and his production of the drug was only part of a much bigger and more ambitious scheme. He wasn't shy about his ambition. He aimed to engineer the most sophisticated clandestine drug lab ever built.

To get there, he needed more cash. "I didn't have enough to finance a proper laboratory."

He'd spent some of Martier and Moscatiello's money on his rented house and enough chemicals to do some preliminary workups. To get to the next step, he needed premises. "I've never had a proper physical plant… I've been manufacturing in bedrooms for years."

While this had been good enough for methamphetamine and other less hazardous substances, fentanyl and 3-methylfentanyl were much more dangerous.

As he'd never worked with the two new drugs, he was wary. "I've been conducting these manufacturing operations under conditions that were considered probably more hazardous to me than they were to the consumers." Not this time. Now, he wanted to create a lab that would, he believed, be like nothing the opposition—the narcotic agents at OBN and the DEA—had ever seen before. And he intended to use it to play a high-stakes game against the people he saw as his true peers and most dangerous adversaries: the DEA's forensic chemists.

So, in the spring of 1989, the idea of Prairie Lab was born.

CHAPTER 31

Kansas City, Missouri to Wichita, Kansas, 1989

"Moscatiello was patient for the first ninety days, probably for another thirty days thereafter," Martier recalled later. "It was probably late spring, early summer, he and I met in a restaurant in Quincy Market, and he told me he couldn't wait anymore. He was tired of dealing through a middleman. He wanted to talk to the chemist." He also said that if he didn't see some fentanyl soon, he wanted his $18,000 back.

Martier had stayed in contact with Squeak, and although Squeak had sent him "some papers and articles relating to the manufacture of fentanyl," Martier had the uneasy suspicion that Squeak hadn't done any actual manufacturing. Moscatiello's patience had worn thin. If he wanted to talk to the chemist, Martier would set it up.

He reached Squeak through Bob Fearon and explained the issue. Then he put Moscatiello on the phone. It was the first time he and Squeak had any direct contact.

They agreed to meet the following day at the airport in Kansas City, Missouri.

Squeak said, "I flew to Kansas City to meet with Joe Martier and Chris M. (I did not, as yet, know his last name.). We met outside the airport security gates and then took a cab to the Westin Crown Center Hotel where we discussed the project at length. While on the way to the hotel, Martier passed me a package of money which I later discovered contained fifteen thousand dollars."

Martier recalled that it was around the beginning of May when "we made the arrangements on a Saturday, and then—it was a Sunday when we flew to Kansas City. Moscatiello was picking up the expenses for flying from Boston. And we rode into Crown Center and we went into a bar-restaurant there. While we were in there, I definitely wanted them to settle this thing themselves. I was tired of being in the middle. So I let them talk at a table while I sat at the bar. When they were through talking, I sat down with them again to see what they resolved."

They had a deal, and everyone understood their roles and goals. Squeak would produce fentanyl samples and, ultimately, enough of a fentanyl analogue to produce the equivalent of 10 kg of pure heroin to start with. Squeak said he believed at the time that it would require on the order of fifty grams of fentanyl and 950 grams of cut to make the equivalent of one kilogram of pure heroin, and only five grams of the much more powerful 3-methylfentanyl and 995 grams of cut to produce the same heroin equivalent. Squeak said he could do that.

Recalling the meeting later, Martier told a jury that, "Marquardt convinced Moscatiello that he could produce this stuff, you know, literally without end. So, Moscatiello elicited from him a promise to make a thousand kilograms of this stuff to be distributed over a two-year period."

All three men were seeing dollar signs. Moscatiello and Martier estimated the wholesale/distributor-level sales price of a kilogram of heroin at about $125,000, making the proposed package worth $125,000,000. They agreed that the profits from sales would be divided up four ways: 25 percent for each of the three, and the final 25 percent reserved for Barry Wilson. Although both Martier and Moscatiello later offered Wilson some of the proceeds from the scheme, the lawyer declined the money and disclaimed any interest in their activities.

A satisfied Squeak returned to Wichita via Tulsa, and set to work on producing the promised sample in the bedroom of his rented house. He quickly got evidence that this operation wouldn't be safe, easy, or much like anything he'd ever done before.

"First batch I made, I was poisoned by 3-methylfentanyl. I crystallized the product and put it on the evaporator to see if I could pull it off without it oiling out. And apparently I got some contact with it on the glassware. First, I got the sick feeling in the pit of my stomach. Then I went in and sat down in my swivel chair, and I hit the floor. I woke up in that condition I don't know how long later. And well, gee, look at this, one damn fool is still alive."

More convinced than ever of a need to have a proper laboratory, he came to some other conclusions about the deadly substances he was creating, warning Martier about the potency and emphasizing that overdoses were likely, if not inevitable.

When they evaluate a new drug, pharmacologists want to answer two key questions about dosage. First, how much of it does it take to get the desired effect? For a drug like fentanyl, a pain killer, how much will take to relieve the pain? This is called the "effective dose."

Pharmacologists also want to know about the drug's lethality. How much does it take to kill someone? For fentanyl, a 2mg dose—about the equivalent of 30 grains of salt—is generally regarded as lethal for most people.

As for 3-methylfentanyl, the analogue that almost killed Squeak, pharmacologists believe 50 micrograms— an amount smaller than a single grain of salt—would be a lethal dose for most humans.

The road to mass production of any of these compounds did not run straight or true. Throughout the summer of 1989, Squeak said he produced "numerous samples of both 3-methylfentanyl and fentanyl" and shipped these to Martier and Moscatiello. He said, "the product report was highly favorable," but Moscatiello "was reluctant to advance the cash for the product, insisting on a total front." Squeak responded by "dragging my feet on any deliveries." And once again, he was running out of funds.

Moscatiello added to Squeak's expenses in late summer when he said he wanted the fentanyl pressed into the form of a block or brick. Squeak, who thought this was unnecessary and "stupid," told him he lacked the skills, and would have to farm the job out. When Moscatiello insisted, Squeak asked eccentric inventor Bob Fearon to help.

Fearon had a friend do the work for $1,300, but the man asked the kind of questions that led Squeak to believe he "suspected we were smugglers," and had reported the job to the DEA or OBN in Tulsa. He told Moscatiello, who "indicated that he wanted to have the man whacked."

"I thought it was just 'gangster talk,' but I began to wonder about the good sense of Mr. Moscatiello," Squeak said. "I reminded him that I hadn't wanted to do it at all, and that it would arouse suspicion."

Moscatiello dropped the matter, but the remark set off alarm bells for Squeak. Was that how these Boston mobsters conducted business, by hiring someone for a job and then killing them when it was finished? How would that scenario play out for the chemist they'd hired for a much bigger deal?

"I was very doubtful that I was going to be paid after the fact," Squeak said. "Which is why I was so insistent about being paid up front."

While he mulled over these doubts, Moscatiello sidetracked the project even further.

"Late in the summer (or early fall), Moscatiello became temporarily disinterested in fentanyl and obsessed with something called 'ice.' I knew little about it, but surmised that it was 'free base' methamphetamine, and probably the d isomer prepared from ephedrine. I advised them that 1) ephedrine was unavailable and 2) resolution of the isomer was impractical and cumbersome."

Moscatiello, annoyed at the delay in producing fentanyl in quantity, and already with more than $32,000 invested in the project, asked if Squeak could make something that "looked like ice." He grudgingly agreed and produced a pound of "amphetamine HCl & isopropyl alcohol that had a slushy appearance."

Squeak took it up to Kansas City in a liquor bottle, and met his two partners at the Westin Crown Center hotel. Moscatiello paid $3,000 for the "ice," and Squeak gave him another fentanyl sample, then said he needed $10,000 more to ramp the fentanyl production up. Moscatiello gave Squeak the cash and he and Martier returned to Boston, but the tensions that had developed over the past few months were about to boil over.

A few days later in Boston, a "very angry" Moscatiello, now at least $35,000 in the hole, reported that the "ice" was worthless; he couldn't sell it, and he was turning back to fentanyl. Martier called Squeak to pass along the complaint, saying Moscatiello "wanted two kilos of product (200 grams of fentanyl), and would pay us 'in several months.'"

Squeak said he blew up, and severed communication with Martier.

Martier remembered Moscatiello's frustration. "I mean, at that point, he had probably, if you count all the flying around, the money he sent to Marquardt, and some other expenses, he probably had close to $35,000 invested in the thing, and all he had to show for it was a five-gram sample; so he was angry, yes."

That lasted for a few weeks until Martier reached out to Squeak. He had a proposition and a new customer. Could Squeak make the equivalent of a single kilogram of heroin consisting of either fentanyl or 3-methylfentanyl? Martier said he also had another distributor, "some fellow named Benny in Los Angeles."

Squeak agreed, producing forty grams of 3-methylfentanyl cut with 960 grams of sorbitol, and Martier flew to Kansas City to pick up the finished kilo. That fell apart when Bob Fearon, Squeak's tripwire in Tulsa, hinted in a telephone conversation that the DEA or OBN might be onto them. Thinking that "something was amiss, and not overfond of Martier flying out of Wichita airport with a kilo of cut product to L.A., I advised Martier to go home. A screaming match ensued, and he was left with no choices. I dumped the product down the sewer, cleaned up my pots, and vowed to stick with amphetamine precursors."

With each of the three partners angry with at least one of the others, the fentanyl conspiracy appeared to be dying before it had even been born.

CHAPTER 32

Boston, Massachusetts, 1989 to 1990

By the middle of September 1989, the three principals in the fentanyl conspiracy were no longer breathing together. Or even talking to each other. None of them, however, were quite ready to give up the dream. It was Moscatiello who brought it back to life.

Squeak, who was fed up and disgusted with both of his partners, re-configured the lab on St. Clair Avenue to crank out P2P and methylamine—solid, reliable sellers that he could move down to Oklahoma.

He'd barely finished when he got a troubling call from back East. "A week or so later, Martier and I have a phone conversation in which he advises me he is in 'deep shit' with Moscatiello and his backers, and he must produce something to get Moscatiello off his back."

This was the first time that Squeak heard there might be other players in the game. "Chris always tried to leave the impression that he was the big money man. The cars, the clothes. Came to find out that wasn't so."

More disturbing was the implication that these people might be far more dangerous—and have less patience—than Moscatiello.

"Joe left me with the impression that [his wife] Erin might get hurt, too. Wonderful position to put your family in, eh?"

Martier wasn't saying who these dangerous mystery backers were, but he knew. "Chris went to one of his partners in his reefer and coke business who I think knew about this thing from the get-go. Mike Murray."

Michael F. Murray and Chris Moscatiello went way back. Like Moscatiello, Murray was a townie, a Charlestown boy, and they had both been involved in criminal activity together for years. When asked if Murray was "involved generally" in business with Moscatiello, Martier said, "Generally in business with everyone. He is, I guess, what you would call a big guy in the rackets in Charlestown."

Mike Murray was indeed big in local organized crime. In Mike's case, this was mostly the marijuana business he operated with his brothers Joe and James. Joseph Paul Murray was widely believed by Massachusetts law enforcement to be the biggest marijuana smuggler in the state, and possibly in the entire Northeast. By 1989, both Mike and Joe had been busted in previous marijuana cases, and the amounts involved—sixteen and thirty-three tons— were eye-opening. If either man was backing Moscatiello's play with cash or other support, their involvement raised the stakes considerably.

Squeak knew nothing of this, but he was prepared to listen to Mocscatiello's proposal. It actually sounded pretty good. Moscatiello wanted to move the entire operation to Massachusetts, where Martier would perform the chemistry under Squeak's remote supervision from Kansas.

Martier recalled that, "In that whole timeframe Moscatiello and Marquardt were in communication with each other, and Marquardt convinced Moscatiello that it wasn't really necessary for him to spend all his time in Massachusetts. He felt that by sitting in Kansas, that he could coach me, via phone calls, notes, letters, and whatnot, to actually do the work."

Squeak would provide a detailed description of the synthesis and a list of all the equipment and chemicals required, but Martier, Moscatiello, or someone else in Boston would purchase everything a thousand miles from Wichita. Squeak wouldn't have to leave his beloved prairie for unfamiliar New England, and Moscatiello would have much tighter control over how his—and the Murrays'— money was being spent.

As 1990 loomed, they put the plan in motion. Martier started on his end, while Moscatiello went looking for a place to put everything.

Squeak liked this idea quite a lot. He would be getting paid the same, but wouldn't have to do any of the riskiest work operating or even setting up the lab. Martier and Moscatiello would be buying the chemicals and equipment where there was always a chance that the DEA or state agents would be watching. And someone else would be doing the actual chemistry, working in the lab that Squeak had agreed to come east and help set up. After that, he could return to Kansas and turn back to his own projects.

There were just a couple of issues. The biggest was that Joe Martier, the designated chemist, wasn't confident that he could actually do the work.

"I wasn't convinced that I could do it; in fact, I knew I couldn't do it. I mean, he's a chemist; I am not. I know the buzz words (sic). I understand what's going on, but I am still not a chemist," Martier said. Fentanyl was hard, more difficult than anything Martier had tried before.

Martier said Moscatiello "made several demands at that time. One was, he wanted a copy of the synthesis. He wanted a printed copy of exactly what he [Squeak] was doing. He felt that was some sort of security. Another thing he wanted was a copy of the synthesis for amphetamine, seeing that amphetamine, as opposed to fentanyl, was—is—relatively easy to manufacture."

The responsibility for equipping the lab fell to Martier, who needed "equipment and chemicals, glass reaction vessels, flash reactivators, vacuum pumps, glass condensers, and whatnot." Squeak provided a comprehensive list of everything needed, and Moscatiello paid for a plane ticket to fly Squeak up to Boston in November to help look for a suitable lab site. He wanted something out in the country but close to a major university, and didn't like anything he saw in Boston.

Martier drove him down to Providence, Rhode Island, a slightly more rural setting close to Brown University, but that didn't satisfy either. So while Moscatiello started a search of his own, Squeak headed back to Kansas and kept in touch by phone after helping his partners with a few chemical purchases.

Martier got down to work on his end. He knew that some items—like fentanyl precursor chemicals—were going to be more difficult to acquire. "It's not really simply a matter of walking out and buying equipment. They [suppliers] are used to selling it to businesses. It's possible as an individual to go out and buy those things to a certain degree, but basically, they like to sell to businesses," he said later. "The other problem with it is that some of those chemicals are on a watchlist."

This would especially include three key precursors. Danger lurked. The chemicals at the top of Squeak's list, methyl acrylate, methyl methacrylate, and aniline, were also at the top of the DEA's.

He could get all three through Bob Fearon, or just make some himself. He didn't offer to share these sources with his Boston partners. If they wanted to do their chemistry in Massachusetts, they could do it—all of it—their way. If anything went wrong, he planned to be 1,600 miles away on the prairie.

Up to this point, he had both of his partners believing he lived in Oklahoma. It was a deception he intended to keep going as long as possible. If things went bad in Massachusetts, "as I expected they would, given the personalities involved," he hoped his partners would steer the cops to the wrong state.

Martier and Moscatiello had none of Squeak's sources, but Martier had a plan. "What I did was set up a shell company in Cambridge, which was nothing really more than a mailing address, a telephone answering service." He called the company TX Green, printed out some stationery, and got down to business.

"We never had to order anything. We would call chemical companies, ask for things in stock, try to sound like purchasing agents, argue about price, quantities, and breaks, but only buy what was available in stock," Martier said. "Some of the things we ordered were on the watchlist. So if we would call, and an hour later come and pick up something, the chances of there being a surveillance were minimized. Stuff like glassware and equipment, most of what we did was drive to New Jersey and pick it up. All the manufacturers are down there."

They ordered glassware, too, picking some custom items…again, larger capacity than the stuff used in most legitimate labs, and most significant, TX Green began making purchases of precursors: methyl acrylate, methyl methacrylate, and aniline.

In most cases they followed Martier's script, not ordering anything directly but walking in and purchasing the items after a preliminary phone call. Although this did protect them to some extent from the DEA surveillance, it did not prevent their suppliers from reporting suspicious transactions after their customers walked out the door.

The DEA received several reports of purchases made by well-dressed "preppy-type" young men representing an unknown and brand-new company. These buyers, the callers said, did not appear to know how their purchases were going to be used, or in fact, know much about chemistry themselves. But they were buying equipment and chemicals that would work perfectly in a clandestine laboratory manufacturing fentanyl or its analogues.

"Those are exactly the kind of people we were hoping we'd get in our undercover operation...the Oklahoma trick store," OBN agent Jay remembered. "They're obviously up to no good, and only buying the items you'd need to run a clandestine lab and nothing else."

Red flags went up in Boston.

Jack Fasanello, a chemist in the DEA's Northeast Regional Laboratory in New York, spotted one of these red flags early on. "I was fishing on a boat in Cape Cod with a friend, and my pager went off and they asked me to call the Boston office. So we went to shore and I called and they said they have a list of chemicals they'd like me to look at. They were going to fax it to the Barnstable Sheriff's Department. I received this fax and I looked at the list, and I immediately called them and said, 'This is a big fentanyl laboratory,' and it was going to a company called TX Green."

By January 1990, only a few months after Squeak agreed to mentor the project from long distance, and mere days after Joe Martier rented a P.O. Box for the company in Harvard Square, the DEA was already onto TX Green.

The DEA's Boston Field Office, believing there was a "big fentanyl laboratory" somewhere out there in their area, opened an investigation into the unknown persons behind TX Green and began looking for the lab site.

The DEA would still be looking three years later.

CHAPTER 33

Boston, Massachusetts, Early 1990

Early in 1990, the search for a suitable lab site ended at a beach house on Indian Ridge Road in Falmouth, Massachusetts. Located seventy-five miles south of Boston, Falmouth sits at the west end of Cape Cod, with the Indian Ridge house set just back from the beach and overlooking Buzzards Bay. The house was quiet and secluded at the end of a cul-de-sac, some distance from neighboring homes, an essential feature according to Squeak, and it had a full basement, also useful.

The property had been owned by Ric Ocasek, singer, songwriter, and front man for his Boston-based new wave band, The Cars, and his wife, Suzanne. But the band broke up in 1988 and Ocasek left Suzanne to marry Czech supermodel Paulina Porizkova, with Suzanne getting the Falmouth beach house in the divorce. She leased the property out and Moscatiello arranged to rent the house, which wouldn't be available until March 1.

In the meantime, they needed a better place to store the equipment and supplies piling up rapidly in Moscatiello's apartment in Boston. And with Martier doubting his own abilities, they also wanted a more qualified chemist to work with Squeak long-distance.

Moscatiello though Michael Murray was the answer. He and Murray had smuggled marijuana together and

Moscatiello considered Murray his best friend. Murray, "a big guy in the rackets," could help with both problems.

"What Murray did, he found another guy who had a chemistry degree, and that changed the plan to where he would be the chemist. I would be sort of a liaison translating Marquardt's instructions," Martier said.

Martier got a cloak and dagger introduction to Murray's man, Moscatiello arranging a meet at a Boston restaurant. As Martier waited outside, a black Cadillac with heavily tinted windows pulled up with Moscatiello and another individual in the back seat. Martier could not see the driver, a tiny detail that would have life-altering significance farther down the road.

The passenger, Robert Paul Rubino, climbed out of the car, introduced himself as "Bobby" and the two of them walked toward Martier's apartment. Rubino said he had a Bachelor's degree in chemistry, and he reviewed the nine pages of instructions Squeak had provided, then said he "couldn't understand the theory of fentanyl" but he understood the reactions, and thought he could manage the process. They talked for a few minutes, then Rubino climbed back into the black Cadillac, which had been "circling the area," and drove off.

"I assume that was Michael Murray driving the car," Squeak said, after hearing about the meeting from the participants later. "But he was keeping Moscatiello in the middle, between everybody else and him. I was doing the same thing with Martier down in Wichita."

The fentanyl project wasn't Murray's only iron in the fire at the beginning of 1990; he was also deep into a separate conspiracy to import marijuana in multi-ton quantities by truck across the Texas-Mexico border. One of his partners in this scheme, Richard Baker, operated Baker's Boat Services in Pembroke, about halfway between Falmouth and Boston. During the winter of 1989-1990, Murray stored two loads of marijuana at Baker's place and arranged for Moscatiello to stash the lab equipment and chemicals in a concealed room built on the back of Baker's garage until the Ocasek house became available.

* * *

Squeak made a short trip up to Boston to help set up the lab, mentor Murray's new chemist, and buy some of the supplies. "This would be after Christmas of '89 or right around the time of the new year. January, probably. Chris was under considerable pressure, no surprise. He must have had a hundred thousand bucks in this thing—or his backers did—and had nothing to show for it."

Hemorrhaging more money every day as they accumulated materials, Moscatiello was anxious to produce something salable. This led to what Squeak called, "shortcutting."

"They just thought that they were going to get the minimum amount of equipment necessary to get the job done, and they apparently thought, 'Well, we can eliminate this step. We really don't need to do that step.' Based upon their non-existent understanding of organic chemistry," Squeak said.

Expecting this approach to fail, Squeak let them get on with it, and headed back to Wichita as soon as he could.

He'd be back.

CHAPTER 34

Cape Cod, Massachusetts, March-July 1990

"Fuck Squeak," one of the celebrants said.

"Yeah, fuck ol' Squeak," said the other.

Bobby Rubino said nothing. Fentanyl was hard, 3-methylfentanyl was harder, and Rubino was whipped. After three months of effort, he'd produced what everyone hoped—and Bobby prayed—would be a marketable quantity of fentanyl, the equivalent of at least one and possibly several kilograms of pure heroin.

But there was a massive problem.

With Martier and Moscatiello helping, Rubino worked his way three times through Squeak's nine-page outline of the process. He knew from his conversations with Squeak what the finished product was supposed to look like—a fine crystalline powder, white or off-white in color—thousands, maybe tens of thousands of lethal doses of one of the most potent narcotics ever developed.

It hadn't been easy; the last couple of months had been a stressful time of trial and error…mostly error, judging by the result.

Forty years earlier, Paul Janssen in Belgium had gone through a similar multi-year passage of experimentation before patenting the method that had resulted in fentanyl. Squeak had broken Janssen's method into a recipe that didn't require Janssen Pharmaceutica's world-class facilities in Turnhout. In theory, his scaled-down adaptation could be managed by a chemist with limited training from a laundry room in the basement of a rock star's house on Cape Cod.

In theory.

There had been moments of optimism, with Rubino close enough to success that a little gloating was called for. Squeak recalled, "They at one point determined that they were successful, and they were running back and forth and yelling, 'Fuck Squeak.' I was actually at dinner with them when they told me, 'Fuck Squeak.' They thought they could move ahead on their own without me."

Although he wasn't too concerned about his partners' doubts about his indispensability, there were real danger signs that Squeak took seriously. At the same dinner, he "got a couple of looks from Moscatiello's girlfriend, like *you don't know how close to getting killed you are.*

"What does surprise me is that they would expect someone they were basically trying to rip off for technology to just hand them this money and this work product and walk away. That astonished me. I couldn't believe they would think I was that gullible. They had unrealistic beliefs of the higher level of talent they had, as opposed to the rather mediocre level of talent they really had, and a belief that they could just step into anything and do what anybody else could do without any kind of an experience base," Squeak recalled, adding, "That will get you in quite a lot of trouble in organic chemistry. It could get you killed."

But fentanyl was hard, and Rubino wasn't nearly as confident as his celebrating sponsors that he'd got it right. Rubino had two jobs in the basement. First, he was responsible for making a "clean" batch of fentanyl or 3-methylfentanyl. His employers didn't expect much in terms of quantity; fifty or a hundred grams of pure fentanyl went a very long way, and 3-methyfentanyl went even farther.

His second job would be cutting that fentanyl into the equivalent of a kilo of pure heroin by mixing those fifty or a hundred grams of deadly white powder with multiple kilos of some inert but similar-looking powder.

After three tries, Rubino wasn't even close, because, even with Joe Martier's help, he lacked all of Paul Janssen's resources: a world-class laboratory, unlimited time, energy, and money…not to mention talent. This left him nowhere near the fluffy white crystals that would announce complete success.

Martier remembered the growing sense of frustration in the Ocasek basement. "We actually, because I was usually there most of the time, would work two or three days and a pump would go out. We'd disappear for two weeks, come back, work two or three more days, and something else would go wrong. It was a total disaster. Instead of getting a white crystalline powder, [Rubino] ended up with approximately half a quart of something that looked like dirty motor oil."

"Black gunk," Squeak said. No white powder in sight… because fentanyl is hard.

There was a problem stage, Rubino told his sponsors. He'd been unable to get through that stage at all on his first two attempts, and the third time, this one working with Martier, was not the advertised charm. The result was the black gunk.

"Right at the end of June, we took one run through the whole reaction sequence, which we had never done before, just to go to the end to see what happened. But it was pretty obvious in the intermediate stages that there was a huge mistake," Martier said.

Rubino thought he'd reached fentanyl, though. He believed that, according to Squeak's recipe, the motor oil held the elusive white crystals somewhere in its inky depths, and told Martier and Moscatiello that bringing the fentanyl out of solution was the next and final step. They were close, he thought, but Rubino proved unable to convert the black motor oil, which obviously had no market value.

Squeak, still consulting by phone from Kansas, thought that "at that point, what I understood is they were pouring the stuff that they should've saved down the toilet and saving the junk."

An exasperated Moscatiello fired Rubino, but that left them with no chemist, no fentanyl, and no prospects for any future success. Frustrations boiled over into a "lengthy argument" about Moscatiello's $100,000 investment, the rental of the beach house, and a "salary" for Martier that Moscatiello had paid for his work in the lab…not to mention all the glassware, chemicals, and equipment they had taken big risks as TX Green to purchase.

But the promise of fentanyl still beckoned, and Moscatiello wasn't ready to completely surrender.

He closed the lab in Falmouth, moved all of the chemicals and the lab setup back to Richard Baker's place in Pembroke, and stored everything in the concealed room behind the garage. Then, out of alternatives, he returned to the only person he knew who was confident he could produce the promised fentanyl.

Squeak was back in the picture.

"Joe had very poor intuition for how chemical reactions proceed. He seemed to think, basically, he had enough experience to get past the cookbook phase. He didn't," Squeak said of his partner.

"I liked their chemist; the poor fellow was scared to death. Tried to get Martier and Moscatiello to let him come down, spend a week with me and show him the art of high vacuum distillation. They didn't want him to know how to do this, wouldn't let him come. Worse yet, they micromanaged him. I didn't give very good odds on his chances, and then they fell flat on their tail."

"We were over a year and a half into this project. Chris was probably out a hundred thousand dollars, and absolutely nothing had been accomplished," Martier said. "He and I got in a huge argument, and what we ended up doing was getting Marquardt on the phone, telling him we were coming to see him, and he absolutely had to straighten this out."

Squeak laughed about getting the telephonic cry for help. "Yeah, 'fuck Squeak' turned rather quickly into 'we really need Squeak.'"

Gloating just a little, he told them to come on down.

They'd be going to Wichita, he said. That was the first time Martier and Moscatiello knew their wary partner wasn't living in Tulsa as he'd been saying, but in Kansas.

"The absolute next day," Martier said, "we poured the gunk into a bottle, I put it in my jacket, and we flew to Wichita."

Squeak picked them up at the airport, but didn't drive to the lab. Instead, Martier said, "He scooted us two hundred fifty miles south to a town called Duncan, Oklahoma."

They were going to see the Lodge Master.

CHAPTER 35

Duncan, Oklahoma, 1990

Squeak's long-standing contempt for credentials didn't extend to those of his PhD buddy, Keith Hollenbeak. An assistant professor at O.U.'s Chemistry Department in Norman when Squeak met him in 1976, Hollenbeak stayed in touch over the years since.

It was Hollenbeak who had turned Squeak onto TMA, which he'd billed as the "psychedelic of the future."

"We shared an interest in money," Squeak said.

By the time Squeak got back from Lewisburg, Hollenbeak had left the university. "Keith was very bitter because he was not offered some kind of tenure rank the University of Oklahoma, and ultimately had to go into industry. It's the whole story of every dissatisfied academic," Squeak said.

Hollenbeak got a job with Halliburton, which billed itself as "one of the world's largest providers of products and services for the ever-evolving needs of the energy industry." Working in the company's research laboratory in Duncan, he had access to the same type of world-class industrial facility that had employed 3-methylfentanyl chemist Michael Hovey.

Squeak said about his crime partner and friend, "Keith is a perfectly fine natural products chemist, and a decent organic chemist.

"But those guys, they give up on things when they find out they're not going to be given all the awards and honors and kudos and things like that. And I think this became discouraging to him. And gradually, he started to do seedy things at Halliburton."

Hollenbeak apparently had some free time, because he and Squeak were working together on another project, turning to another drug that had enjoyed great popularity in the 1970s and early 1980s.

Methaqualone, a hypnotic sedative, had been prescribed as a treatment for insomnia since its introduction in 1955. It had been sold in tablet form under the brand names Quaalude and Sopor, and known on the street as "Ludes." Methaqualone had become so popular as a street drug that by the early 1980s, counterfeit Quaalude tablets were being manufactured by the millions in South America and smuggled into the United States like cocaine and marijuana.

In 1984, the federal government moved methaqualone into Schedule I with other substances having no medical use, shutting down all legitimate production. There was still plenty of demand for recreational methaqualone, though. And that proven market for bootleg Quaaludes left an opening for clandestine chemists, one Squeak and Hollenbeak were exploring when Martier and Moscatiello called Squeak to say they wanted a word.

"Chris was down and distraught, apparently under quite a lot of pressure, and I said, 'Okay, Chris. I'll bring you out of this thing. We'll get this thing straightened out," Marquardt said, actually quite pleased at Martier and Moscatiello's distress. Their troubles—and the money they would spend to fix them—would power the creation of his sophisticated super lab.

To lock them in, providing definitive proof of his own indispensability, Squeak first needed to prove their failure. For that, he needed a mass spectrometer. Hollenbeak had one at Halliburton. "Keith was a Mason, maybe lifelong. I didn't tell Joe or Chris his name, just said he was the 'Lodge

Master' and he could run a mass spec. That was all they needed to know.

"They flew down with the product. I had Hollenbeak analyze it. Flop."

This wasn't a message either of Squeak's partners wanted to hear.

"Chris was obviously scared, probably of Murray. Martier had Erin sold on the idea that there was some product there, not wanting to be seen as a flop in the eyes of his lady."

Squeak took charge, saying that from here on out, he would be doing the chemistry. He immediately hit on his two partners for more cash.

"'Right,' I said. 'I'm going to need some additional equipment. We're going to have to do this thing right. You're not going to be able to operate from a footlocker in a laundry room. This stuff is not just going to fall together, but we can get it done.'"

Moscatiello still wanted the lab—and Squeak—in Massachusetts, so Squeak made plans to go up to Boston. Before going, though, Moscatiello filled him in on the silent partners in their deal…not naming them, but making it clear that his financial backers were heavily connected to organized crime in Boston and to the Irish Republican Army. Squeak read this as a not-so-subtle warning that Chris and his friends were not to be trifled with.

Moscatiello had another message: he and his backers wanted to focus on 3-methylfentanyl. Squeak had no doubts that he could make it the frighteningly lethal fentanyl analogue. "It involved some additional steps, and was beyond Joe or Bobby's abilities. I could produce it; I already had, and it had almost killed me, but that wasn't the issue."

The issue, he explained to Moscatiello, was 3-methylfentanyl's lethality. Fentanyl would be hard enough to cut to a dose that wouldn't kill its consumer. 3-methylfentanyl was an order of magnitude more difficult.

"I told him there was no absolutely safe way to dilute it. As I'd told Joe, if we make this stuff, we're going to kill people. He wasn't concerned. He just wanted something to give to his backers. It made me wonder whether these IRA terrorists intended to use it as a chemical weapon."

Maybe killing people was the whole point.

CHAPTER 36

Boston, Massachusetts, late 1990

Up in Boston, Squeak checked out Robert Baker's place—previously just used for storing the equipment and chemicals (and Murray's marijuana), but now holding everything from the Ocasek house in Falmouth. He found most of what he needed, but went shopping for more.

Unlike Moscatiello and Martier, Squeak had been in this situation hundreds of times before, and had used his "manipulative skills" and vast knowledge of chemistry to bond with the sellers to get the items he needed without drawing attention to himself. He'd always been able to fit in easily with others in his line of work, so he got along fine with the proprietors at the many Boston-area chemical supply places.

He also took the opportunity to pick up some items he didn't need for fentanyl production, but couldn't pass up since he was in the neighborhood. This included glassware handblown by an artisan at the Massachusetts Institute of Technology. It also included several instruments and some chemicals that he didn't want to be seen buying himself.

Having left explicit instructions on what else to get and how to get it, Squeak headed back to Wichita.

He did insist on two items he considered absolutely essential. Both would prove to be big trouble. "Benzene. Almost indispensable. You can go almost anywhere if you start with benzene. It is an immensely useful thing. That's the deeper solvent. It's impossible to conceive of running a chemical industry without benzene."

Highly toxic, flammable, and a known carcinogen—benzene is used in a wide variety of chemical processes, and Squeak already had safe suppliers for all of these chemicals in Oklahoma. He occasionally obtained fifty-five-gallon barrels of benzene from chemical companies supplying the petroleum industry in Texas and Oklahoma. Sometimes they even gave him these barrels as free samples.

Because it's so ubiquitous, there are lots of choices for a benzene supply. The DEA knew how valuable benzene was to clandestine chemists, so they asked suppliers to report unusual sales and losses to DEA-identified companies, but it wasn't a chemical on the watchlist. Due to its toxicity and danger to the environment, benzene also got extra scrutiny from the Environmental Protection Agency, so buying it for a clandestine lab definitely carried certain risks. Squeak let his partners know that benzene was vital, and told them to get a bunch of it.

The second item was useful in the fentanyl manufacturing process, but Squeak considered it essential for another key part of the scheme. There was no way to dilute something as lethal as 3-methylfentanyl and be 100 percent safe. Overdoses were inevitable, just as they had been with the China White in California some eight or nine years before and in Pittsburgh just a year earlier. In those cases, the fentanyl analogues had been cut so heavily that the forensic laboratories analyzing the white powder had initially found no narcotic at all, but it had still killed people.

"I saw dose controls as a problem, and I told Martier that," Squeak said.

When asked how Martier responded, he shrugged. "Didn't bother him any. Said that's what junkies expected is to be dead."

Squeak, wary of the heat deaths would undoubtedly bring, wasn't writing off the dose control problem. He emphasized that they would have to deal with it at their level, because those lower down the ladder weren't capable.

"I knew that the people close to the street level would try to cut it the same way they handled heroin or cocaine. Toss it in a mixing bowl, add a lot of mannitol or lactose, mix it all up with a spatula, and put it into little bags. There's no way to control the dose that way. No way to prevent hot shots. Which, it turned out, is exactly what happened."

To handle this dilution at their level, Squeak said, they needed a large capacity rotary evaporator, a machine capable of blending chemicals and efficiently removing solvents by evaporation under low pressure. "One of the problems with 3-methylfentanyl is you've got a little bit of product and a lot of cut. You find something that's 3-methylfentanyl soluble, and you put it in a rotary evaporator, and you tumble it with the cut. And the solvent evaporates off slowly. Under ideal conditions, that will serve as the first cut."

To check these items off Squeak's list, they started by ordering a 50-gallon barrel of benzene from J.T. Baker, a long-established chemical company. It didn't go well.

Squeak didn't go on this trip, but heard plenty about it later. "They looked like big city drug dealers. I understand they picked it up dressed up in their drug dealer finest with the sunglasses, deer skin jackets, things like that. It's just your average chemical purchase…guy drives up in a Range Rover, plops the barrel of benzene in the back. It naturally got the narcotic agents interested."

* * *

Martier and Moscatiello were convinced they'd picked up a DEA tail when they left J.T. Baker, driving south toward Pembroke and Falmouth, where they thought they were able to shake it. Still, this was bad, but Moscatiello had worse. His friend Michael Murray told him that a source in Boston's federal building had information about the benzene barrel, and for $150,000, would tell what he knew about the surveillance and the federal investigation of TX Green.

According to his source, the "feds" had an ongoing investigation of three individuals: Moscatiello, Martier, and a third unidentified person. The source also said there was surveillance on Martier's house, and a pen register installed on his phone.[4]

This was all uncomfortably close to the truth, and Moscatiello said he'd already paid. He wanted Martier and Marquardt to fork over $50,000 each to split the cost three ways.

Squeak, who was very glad to be 1,500 miles away in Kansas, thought it was all an extortion scheme. "I thought it was all bullshit."

Bullshit or not, the incident thoroughly spooked Martier and Moscatiello, who were ready to bail out on the fentanyl operation, at least until the heat died down.

Moscatiello, now into the scheme for $300,000 with nothing to show for it besides heat from the DEA, was going to lay low for a while. Martier said he was moving back to Pittsburgh.

So things went quiet in Boston.

---

4. A pen register or dialed number recorder (DNR) makes a record of all outgoing calls from a specific phone number. The recorder does not record conversations as a wiretap would, only the information about the number dialed and the length of the call. A "trap and trace" does the same for incoming calls.

CHAPTER 37

Wichita, Kansas, 1990 – 1991

In Wichita, Squeak had everything he needed to make fentanyl in quantities from a gram up to thirty pounds or more. He'd done quite a bit of research into 3-methylfentanyl and thought he could also produce that in quantity.

What he didn't have, with Moscatiello out of the picture, was a customer. Since he was pathologically opposed on principle to making drugs without payment, it looked like fentanyl was going nowhere fast.

Joe Martier had relocated back to Pittsburgh, giving up on fentanyl, at least for the time being. When Squeak completed his trial batch just after Thanksgiving 1990, he let Martier know he'd achieved some success. Martier was immediately back in, but wary about going back to Boston. Moscatiello wasn't the only person in America able to tap into the heroin market, so he called another former Danbury inmate acquaintance, Benito "Benny" Febre, in Los Angeles.

Febre jumped at the opportunity, and agreed to pay $100,000 for a kilogram of fentanyl that would be cut to be the equivalent of a kilo of pure heroin. Going by their original plan, this meant that Squeak, using a rotary evaporator, had to cut 50 grams of fentanyl with 950 grams of lactose or some other diluent. He was still shying from the heat that a lot of dead junkies might bring and said, "I might have erred a little on the cautious side," but he'd come up with a batch he thought was "acceptable."

An earlier sample for Moscatiello, thirty-five grams, had been a pale purple color distinctly different from the heroin it was supposed to impersonate. This batch was slightly reddish-brown, a color more common with the Mexican heroin on California streets. Squeak thought he could get the color right, close enough to pass for the heroin their customers hoped they were buying.

Shortly after Thanksgiving 1990, Martier flew down to Wichita and met Squeak, who took him to his new house at 600 Flora Street where he had his lab set up. Not much more than a shack, the house was set a safe distance away from nearby homes on a quarter-acre lot, so he wasn't concerned about detection. "I lived down the block from a police station. That didn't bother me in the slightest," he said later.

He took some precautions, storing all of the chemicals and lab equipment in his mini-storage units, bringing them to the house only when he was ready to make some fentanyl. When the lab was idle, he set out photographic paraphernalia, "rolling out the enlargers and print dryers, print paper, and other things that made it look like a darkroom in case someone was to break into the house."

When the lab was up and running, there could be no doubt of its purpose. "There's a lot of glassware set up, and a rotary evaporator spinning merrily around, and stirrers turning, and multi-neck flasks, and things refluxing, and the vacuum pump thumping away. This is not the time you want to bring around any visitors. When everything is safely stowed away or stuffed under benches and the flasks are neatly lined up in closets, and everything is stoppered up and put someplace, well, it's just an empty room with a lot of photographic development equipment to give it local color."

The darkroom cover also accounted for any stray smells.

Martier commuted from a nearby motel, and they got down to work. Using a pound of lactose, a half-pound of inositol, and a half-pound of fructose, they cut in the 50 grams of fentanyl, which Squeak said was about 80 percent pure, and packaged the powder into four quarter-kilo bags. Martier spent the night and then flew to Los Angeles, met Febre at his condominium, and handed over the fentanyl before heading back to Pittsburgh to await payment.

None was forthcoming, because Febre said the dope was too weak and couldn't be wholesaled or even retailed in Los Angeles. He also complained about the cut, saying it was "too sweet" for customers accustomed to heroin's normally bitter taste. Febre said he thought he might be able to sell some of the fentanyl in New York, but he tried and Martier said, "for whatever reason, he took it to New York and found out he couldn't sell it anywhere."

Martier gave up, told Febre to mail the remaining fentanyl back East, and went home to Pittsburgh. Once again, fentanyl had proved itself to be hard, and despite all their combined efforts over the previous twenty-four months, the conspirators hadn't managed to get any of their product out onto the street to paying customers.

When he received the package of "too sweet" fentanyl, a discouraged Joe Martier said, "I threw it in the Allegheny River."

* * *

Squeak wasn't nearly as discouraged as his partner. Now that his lab was up and running, he thought he almost had it. He worked through Christmas and into the new year, then he told Martier he was close. Martier flew up again, but the new batch wasn't finished yet. He stayed in Kansas for a week while Squeak completed the job. They were both pleased with the result.

"He worked over the holidays, and made an additional quantity of fentanyl. He made it right, too, I might add. It was white. For the first time, he'd really made a useable product," Martier said.

Febre had gone to Puerto Rico to visit family and then to New York, and told Martier that if he could produce a good batch of fentanyl, he would try to sell it there. In late January, Martier flew up to New York City carrying 165 grams of fentanyl—triple the size of the previous batch.

"It was higher in quality, too," Squeak remembered. Nobody wanted a repeat of the Los Angeles debacle or the complaints about how feeble the first batch had been.

That wouldn't be a problem this time.

Martier and Febre met and took the fentanyl up to the Bronx. "I had never been in the Bronx before or since, but we went into an apartment in the projects and we cut the stuff," Martier said. Using "over a kilogram of mannitol, rubber gloves, several strainers, two large plastic containers," and a triple-beam scale, they mixed in the fentanyl to produce about "a kilogram with three ounces," Martier said.[5]

When told about the process later, a disgusted Squeak said, "A couple of strainers and a goddamn bucket. We're actually very fortunate several hundred people weren't killed."

Martier left the now-diluted fentanyl with Febre, stayed in New York for "a few days," finally collected $42,000 of the promised $60,000, then got on a bus and headed for Pittsburgh. He told Febre to mail him the balance when he collected it from his distributors.

For better or for worse, and after two years of trying, Squeak's fentanyl was about to hit America's streets.

The impact would be worse than even he could have imagined.

---

5. Mannitol, a sugar alcohol, is commonly used as a cutting agent, particularly with drugs that are "snorted" or inhaled, like cocaine.

PART III

Marquardt – The Last Outlaw

CHAPTER 38

Brook Avenue, The Bronx, Friday afternoon, February 1, 1991

You pay your nickel and you take your chances, and people were chancing their nickels that Friday on Brook Avenue in the Bronx. The street was humming with the energy of high hopes, great expectations, and the proceeds of just-cashed welfare checks.

Out on the block, schoolchildren with colorful backpacks—Hello Kitty, Batman, Pokemon—wove between hustlers in hoodies hawking "Venom," "Mongrel," and "Prada," as they caught cars pulling up to the curbs. Runners in Air Jordans, Yankees caps, and athletic jackets dodged through the sidewalk crowds, turning heads but not slowing down for the passing of a patrol car from the 40th Precinct.

Brook Avenue was all about heroin that afternoon. Almost all of the hustlers, the runners, and the slingers were bundled up against the cold, working the block between 138th and 139th, moving smack instead of crack.

Business was good. The first-day-of-the-month welfare check money had come through right on time, and the street workers were going inside to get warm and re-up in their stash pads, picking up more of the little glassine packets, each with its colorful trademark label: Dynamite, Time Bomb, and Game Over, FIRE, LIFE, DOA, and one that had been a regular on the block for about six months, Tango & Cash.

Those small, square packets with the black lettering cost much more than a nickel; they were $10 each and called "dime bags." The Tango & Cash brand took its name from a 1989 Sylvester Stallone and Kurt Russell action movie about two cops trying to bring down a dangerous drug lord. Tonight, Tango & Cash would be taking out junkies by the score.

The dealers and the hypes from this Mott Haven neighborhood around Brook Avenue weren't the only ones on the street as the money flew and darkness gathered later that afternoon. Seekers from other boroughs drifted in by subway and bus and on foot to the block, which was known throughout the city as an open-air dope supermarket.

And Brook's reputation had spread even farther. Cars with Jersey plates and Connecticut's parked around the corners or idled at the curbs, huffing steam from their tailpipes as jumpy young men, most of them sitting on a pistol or with one close at hand, waited for someone to get back from the apartments upstairs where the real action was happening.

They had good reason to be nervous. Bad things happened on the avenue. Two blocks down on 138th Street, the 40th Precinct had checked off more than 1,000 aggravated assaults and shootings the previous year, and 2,100 robberies…and those were just the ones that got reported to the cops. And the precinct detectives had stood over 72 homicide victims in 1990. Most of them had been killed over some drug-related thing, and a goodly number of them had died on or within screaming distance of Brook Avenue.

So it paid for a person with a big wad of buy money in his jacket pocket to take a few extra precautions. Like sticking your Glock under your leg where you could get to it when you crossed into New York from Connecticut on I-95 southbound.

You pay your nickel, and you take your chances. But there's no point in being stupid about it.

Brook Avenue and 138th Street, The Bronx, Friday, 9:45 p.m.

His nickel paid, Angel Luis Morciglio, Jr., settled with the tools of his trade onto a shooting gallery sofa, pushed the plunger home, and felt the wave wash over him. This wave was like all the others for a moment, like all the other nickels and all the other chances…and then it was different. Then the blackness came, rushing in on him like a train plunging into a tunnel, and Angel flew from this world forever.

He'd been born in Mayaguez on the western end of Puerto Rico, but he'd come to New York with his father at seventeen. "He was a good boy," Angel, Sr., said. "He went to church and won the prizes at school for English. He drank some, later."

He did more than that, shooting heroin, though apparently not regularly. On welfare after being laid off from a supermarket job in September, he worked part time cleaning apartments and looking for a job, but he told his mother-in-law he "was having problems."

"He was trying to turn his life around," his father said. It's the standard scripted line for family members in this situation, and his father may have even believed it.

Married, at least common law, for three years, Angel's wife had given birth to a baby girl they named Angelica, two months earlier.

Angelica would carry her father's name but would never remember her daddy, because at 9:00 p.m., friends waved to Angel as he walked on 138th toward Brook with ten bucks he'd borrowed from his mother-in-law in his pocket, and determination to get something to start the weekend off right. He found it at Brook and 138th in a cluster of the corner boys calling out the names of a dozen different brands. One of them was Tango & Cash.

By 9:30 that Friday evening, the 911 calls started coming in and ambulances—"buses" in NYPD radio parlance—began rolling out into the Mott Haven neighborhood almost continuously. The police and paramedics could revive some people at the scene, but most of the junkies left unconscious—and frighteningly deep into the void on their ride to the hospital.

Back on Brook Avenue, patrol units were calling for buses at both ends of the block between 138th and 139th Streets at the same time. Junkies collapsed in apartments nearby and out on the street. Panicked so-called "friends" of a suddenly comatose addict, afraid of being caught with a dead body, dragged their unconscious amigo out onto the pavement and abandoned him (or her). It was a callous but common enough gesture that cops had a name for it: felony littering.

That's what happened to Angel Luis Morciglio, Jr. He passed out in an anonymous apartment, the blackness caved in around him, and he was gone at age thirty-two. Whoever was with him hauled his lifeless body down to the street where a couple of passersby found him propped against a wall next to a bodega and tried to revive him while an ambulance came. It took him to the hospital, but it was too late.

"His life had already been sucked away," his stepmother said later, and at 9:45 p.m., New York City had its first Tango & Cash fatality. It wouldn't be the last that weekend.

Two miles away, Lincoln Hospital's Emergency Room, the busiest in New York City even on a normal weekend, was swamped by these unusual poisoning cases. Overdoses weren't that uncommon; Lincoln treated them regularly. Most were novice heroin users getting a stronger dose than usual, or somebody getting a poorly diluted bag. If the victim got medical attention soon enough, a "hot shot" could be treated fairly easily with an injection of Narcan.

Though popular with the ER doctors and the paramedics who like doing miracles, Narcan was frequently less appreciated by junkies. A comatose (and dying) junkie given the dose of Narcan promptly awakened, often vomited, and sometimes began vehemently cursing the nurse, doctor, or paramedic for ruining the best high he'd had for months. The ungrateful addict typically then checked himself out of the hospital, and went looking for that same brand of heroin to get another shot.

At the Lincoln ER that Friday, the doctors administered Narcan and got the usual immediate results, which told them that whatever was poisoning these addicts and sending them into respiratory arrest out on Brook Avenue was some sort of narcotic drug. The police, who were talking to the junkies and others on the street, had narrowed the brand down to Tango & Cash, found at the scene of a couple of the overdoses. There hadn't been enough time to test the packets to find out what exactly was causing the overdoses— whether it was just extra-strong heroin or something else— but samples went to NYPD's crime lab, and they would be giving answers on that score soon.

By that time, more than fifty people had been treated in the emergency rooms at Lincoln and at Harlem Hospital, where a second overdose victim, Michelle Fox, age 35, died at 10:30 p.m. The detectives responding to Fox's Manhattan apartment with the paramedics found the little white packets with the Tango & Cash labels. They suspected she had been up to Brook Avenue to score, but her world got painted black before the ER doctors at Harlem could save her.

As Friday drew to a close, the weekend was just getting started. And there were still lots of people who wanted to take their chances on Tango & Cash.

130 Hampton Street, Hartford, Connecticut, Friday, 11:00 p.m.

They had gamblers with nickels up in Hartford, too. By 9 o'clock that evening, the driver of one of those Connecticut cars had gotten back from the Bronx with his big bundle of Tango & Cash packets, and set up shop in the Stowe Village housing project in Hartford's rough-edged North End.

Stowe Village, which sounds like it should be the name for an idyllic ski resort, was a complex of thirty-one multi-story apartment buildings that looked more like H-shaped cell blocks. It was one of those places built with government money, red bricks, and good intentions, and then filled up with poor people, heroin, crack cocaine, and crime.

Low-level dealers operated out of a couple dozen of the 598 apartments at any given time in the complex, moving around, keeping the customers satisfied and the Hartford cops guessing.

That's where Sam Jackson, looking to score his usual, picked up a dime bag of this Tango & Cash stuff, then took it to an apartment in the complex nearby at 130 Hampton. Sam Theodore Jackson was almost nobody. He'd never been married, and hadn't finished school. When he worked, which wasn't often, he did common laboring—most recently for Anthony D'Agostino and Son, a local construction company. He lived on Donald Street—a dead end, appropriately enough—hard by the Connecticut Southern tracks where the bang and rattle of the cars in the Conrail yard went on 24/7.

Nothing much distinguished Sam Jackson in life, and he lurched through twenty-seven years of it without leaving a mark. He didn't win any prizes or earn any honors, and when he died early on the morning of Saturday, February 2, 1991, his lonely passing flared brightly for a moment, blazing briefly on the pages of the *Hartford Courant* and the *New York Times* before history forgot him entirely.

The Hartford cops got a call to the Stowe Village apartment and were told there would be a body waiting for them, so detectives went to the scene, too. They found Sam Jackson, collapsed on a sofa, looking small and lost and alone. There was no obvious cause of death, but the detectives had their suspicions; those tracks on his arms and fresh injection marks were good clues about Jackson's hobby.

By the time they got around to Sam Jackson, his hobby was causing all kinds of problems for the Hartford police that Saturday morning. It had started the night before with a Friday evening surge of ambulance runs to the Mount Sinai and Saint Francis hospital emergency rooms, where overdose patients were arriving unconscious and barely breathing.

As they had down at Lincoln Hospital in New York City, the paramedics and the ER docs in Hartford had been batting a thousand with Narcan until the police got the call on Sam Jackson on Saturday morning.

Dr. Jesse Samuels, a Hartford emergency room physician, said the EMTs and Narcan had saved many lives. "Several of the victims were young mothers who would be dead young mothers if they hadn't been saved by the paramedics," he added.

Somebody at 130 Hampton had cleaned up after Sam, taking the syringe and the packet and all the other normal junkie paraphernalia before the cops came, so the detectives called it an "untimely death" for the time being and sent him to the morgue. The medical examiner would screen him for the true cause, but those tests take weeks, and by noon on Saturday, the police and everyone else had far too many other problems on their hands to worry about what exactly had killed Sam Jackson.

Saturday dawned clear and cold; the wind chill hovering around freezing. Conditions were not bad enough to keep the dealers out of the courtyards in Stowe Village, or off the corners on Brook Avenue. So the crack hustlers and the smack men—the ones handling this Tango & Cash—were on the street, meeting customers at car windows or off the benches in Stowe Village, sending happy buyers off with their morning wake-ups and their afternoon delights.

In empty buildings and stinking alleyways, in vacant stores and ratty apartments, in thousands of squalid little sepulchers from Hartford to Newark, junkies took their communion.

And the 911 calls started up again.

Hartford Police Headquarters, Saturday, February 2, 1991, 2:00 p.m.

By mid-afternoon on Saturday, the Hartford cops, who were talking to their counterparts in New York, had narrowed down the field. They'd finally identified the problem; the snitches and the woozy patients in the ER had described the small packets with the Tango & Cash brand name that were filling the ambulances this weekend.

Like the NYPD, the Hartford police seized some packets from some of the overdose scenes, getting enough powder from these samples to enable their forensic chemist to come in on a weekend and run a lab test.

It wasn't good news. They expected to find heavily adulterated heroin, as usual, but these contained another narcotic called fentanyl. The chemists warned the police that this drug, a painkiller that's also used by anesthesiologists to sedate patients for surgery, was more powerful than heroin.

How much more powerful? It depends. Ordinary fentanyl runs to about 40 to 50 times stronger than heroin and 80 to 100 times more powerful than morphine, which is a sobering enough thought. But fentanyl has what the chemists call "structural analogues," chemical compounds that have a similar molecular makeup but differ in one or more components. That little difference, that minute tweak, a very subtle alteration of the chemical structure could, the chemists said, produce fentanyl cousins far more potent than morphine or heroin.

How much of it did it take to kill people? The cops wanted to know.

Well, don't panic, the experts said, but take the analogue 3-methylfentanyl that might be in these packets…that one could be more than *3,000* times more powerful than heroin. A dose of 3-methylfentanyl the size of the dot on top of an "i" could easily be enough to kill an adult human being. Maybe a couple of them. If 3-methylfentanyl was in any of these packets, the problem got substantially more complicated.

The chemists added that police officers should use extreme caution processing any packages of Tango & Cash they encountered on the street. Even breathing around this stuff was risky. Oh yeah, and it absorbed through breaks in the skin, so you might want to think about wearing gloves to handle it, the chemists said.

Despite the breezy admonition that it was not necessary to panic, the Hartford police felt some emergency response very close to panic mode was called for at this point. Why? Because in Hartford, New York, and New Jersey, the word was out on the street about Tango & Cash, and junkies were doing what junkies always do in times like this.

One of them, a hype and dealer named Richie, summed it up perfectly. "When an addict hears that somebody OD'd, the first question they ask is: 'Where'd they get it?' Because they want to get some of it for themselves."

Frank Rudewicz from the Hartford PD saw the danger. "The users hear there is pure and potent stuff out there, and they flock to get it. It is an unbelievable high for them, or they can cut it up and get more for their money."

With the junkies and the dealers seeing Tango & Cash as a win-win situation, demand soared for the little dime bags that the police had just been told were too deadly to hold in their bare hands.

On Saturday afternoon, the police department brass and the city's public health authorities huddled to work out some sort of plan to alert Hartford's addicts to the danger. Out on the streets, the pace of the ambulance runs was picking up. The paramedics barely had time to restock their trucks with Narcan before heading back out, sirens screaming, into the North End for another OD, another junkie who'd just bet his life on the powder in the little white packet.

Hartford wasn't alone. The same scene was taking place that Saturday afternoon in New York City and across the Hudson River in Paterson and Newark, New Jersey. In fact, with dark and scary visions of mass felony littering taking place in their streets, the public health authorities and police administrators were all talking to each other, trying to work out a common solution as the ambulances kept rolling out.

Assuming the dealers weren't trying to deliberately poison their customers, which seemed unlikely, why would someone add something like this fentanyl analogue to these packets?

As always in the illegal drug business, the answer was "money."

The heroin in a normal Tango & Cash packet had been cut or diluted a half-dozen times before it reached a junkie on Brook Avenue. The solution finally injected into an addict's arm might be only 10 – 30% pure and sometimes worse; the rest of it might be milk sugar, the "baby laxative" mannitol, sorbitol, and sometimes quinine. Putting a little fentanyl or 3-methylfentanyl into the mix meant that the amount of heroin in the bag could be cut even more drastically, and the junkie would still get a kick.

True, some would be kicked right into the emergency room or the morgue, but everybody on the planet who sold heroin generally, and Tango & Cash in particular, lived by the "you pay your nickel, and you take your chances" principle. That's especially true as it applied to their completely expendable junkie customers.

Those customers who survived the Tango & Cash blackness described the experience. Jose from Mott Haven said, "Normally I feel a good rush. I feel nice. But when this came on, I blacked out completely."

A young woman had a similar experience, saying she "got a weird feeling from it. I started to go down, to go under, and felt really sick." She, too, passed out, came out of the darkness hours later, and wanted another fix.

Another addict said he passed out in the shower. After being retrieved by his family, he slept for twelve hours. When he awoke, like everyone else, he went straight back out again, looking for more.

Yet another shared a dime bag of Tango & Cash with a friend, saying he'd blacked out in a subway station at East 138th Street. "It's a good thing I shared the bag with somebody, because if I did the whole thing by myself, I'd be dead."

That was the common experience in the tri-state area, where hundreds of addicts rode Tango & Cash on deep dives into oblivion on Friday evening and the early hours of Saturday morning. Many of them had gone to the hospital, and a few were dead. When the effects wore off around noon on Saturday, February 2, addicts all over Hartford, the Bronx, and New Jersey climbed back out of the blackness and went looking for more Tango & Cash.

Frank Rudewicz remembered that Saturday well. "It was crazy. We were busy all afternoon. All night. The ambulances were going to Stowe Village nonstop." Rudewicz, a Hartford police sergeant at the time, was promoted to command the department's intelligence and organized crime unit the following year. "Stowe Village had narcotic activity in every building, and we were getting calls there about sales and junkies passed out. We thought there would be more deaths."

Hartford Police Lieutenant Frederick Lewis said, "We have overdoses all the time, but this has been an epidemic."

Dr. Woodrow Myers remembered the weekend, too. Myers, who was New York City's public health commissioner at the time, saw this crisis as a public health disease prevention issue. "These may have been addicts bringing this problem on themselves in a way, but it was still our responsibility to try to protect them from what was basically a poison. They were being poisoned, and we tried to stop it."

By late Saturday, everyone was forming a plan to do just that.

Brook Avenue, The Bronx, Saturday, 6:00 p.m.

Tango & Cash sales were still going strong Saturday night. In fact, they were picking up. The cops could tell because they could hear the ambulances screaming away from the fire stations and hospitals, heading out into Hartford's North End and into Mott Haven in the Bronx.

By Saturday afternoon, the 911 calls had started coming in to dispatchers in New Jersey, too. The story was the same: a junkie passed out on the pavement in the Broadway section in Paterson, or in an apartment or a vacant lot, sometimes with a needle in his arm and a surprised expression on his face.

Newark got two fatalities right off the bat: Willie Bryant, 33, and Donald Delossantos, 34, were both too deep into the black to revive. More were trickling into the hospitals, and there was a twist—the New Jersey packets included a new label, "Goodfella," another reference to a recent movie, this one the popular 1990 mob film *Goodfellas*.

In the emergency rooms, the doctors burned through their stocks of Narcan. Even the ambulance crews were working without letup, dropping off patients, grabbing handfuls of supplies, and pulling out on another call—headed back to the same block in Mott Haven for another passed-out junkie.

The bemused 40th Precinct cops reported two felony littering calls. Santiago Garcia, 28, and Dennis Rodriguez, 29, both came to Lincoln's ER as D.O.A.s. Rodriguez had traveled all the way to the Bronx from Perth-Amboy, New Jersey to score some Tango & Cash and die.

As Saturday night turned into Sunday, the police and public health officials in Hartford and New York, and now Paterson and Newark, finalized a plan to warn the addict population away from the "toxic heroin" hitting the streets. While they groped around for a strategy, the narcotics units in all four cities were hoping to get to the source. Undercover agents went out into the drug-scoring spots, trying to buy the Tango & Cash or Goodfella packets, and detectives from the narcotics and organized crime squads had their informants looking for the dealers who were selling those brands.

By midnight, everybody had agreed on a plan for Sunday, but it was too late for Joe Anthony Saunders and another unidentified junkie in Paterson, both of them D.O.A. at St. Joseph's Hospital, and Rueben Miller, 36, of Irvington.

Saturday ended as it had begun: cold and dark, and with the specter of more deaths looming.

Stowe Village, Hartford, Sunday, February 3, 1991, 9:00 a.m.

On Sunday morning, the police hit the streets with their new plan. In Hartford, squad cars with loudspeakers and officers with bullhorns read a prepared message in Stowe Village and on the streets nearby. The announcement, repeated in Spanish and English, said that a deadly "Toxic heroin was sold Friday in New York City! Use of this toxic heroin has resulted in overdoses and deaths! If you have used this drug, seek medical attention immediately!"

Frank Rudewicz described the decision-making behind the public service announcement. "We didn't want to call it some kind of super heroin, in case people got the idea that it was a better high." That was how the phrase "toxic heroin" came to be inserted into the announcement. "With an exclamation mark," Rudewicz pointed out. "It makes it sound like somebody was trying to poison junkies. But all the hypes were talking to each other, and they knew that these were OD's. As soon as we mentioned Tango & Cash, they all started looking for it."

In New York City, the police used sound trucks to cruise the drug spots, the scoring scenes, and all of the open-air drug marts, especially the ones in the Mott Haven neighborhood where the whole thing had started. Some of the announcements specifically mentioned Tango & Cash and Goodfella, and linked the poisonings to these brands. In the South Bronx and Harlem, people heard the same announcement which named Tango & Cash.

Newark and Paterson went a step past that, and named "Chinatown" and "Jackpot," two other brands on their streets. Undercover officers had reported that street dealers were changing brands and selling the Tango & Cash dope under the new labels. On the other hand, some enterprising dealers were printing up Tango & Cash labels, and selling ordinary dope under the now-notorious name that the police trucks were advertising out on the streets.

"We were aware of that reaction," Dr. Woodrow Myers said. "Addicts are risk-takers, and we knew that a certain percentage would seek out a brand that had a reputation for causing overdoses."

Quite a few were willing to gamble their lives on those labels that Sunday. After hearing the blame laid on Tango & Cash, junkies flocked from all over to Brook Avenue looking for that brand. Pretty soon the ambulances were running to Lincoln again, adding to walk-in traffic: people who had heard the loudspeakers and heeded the message.

"A lot of these people weren't sick or overdosing, but they came in and the ER staff checked them out," Dr. Myers said. "Lincoln and Harlem got hundreds. The other hospitals all got some."

There were no more fatalities in New York, but 22-year-old Dana Chaplin, an investigator for the Essex County Public Defender's office, became the youngest Tango & Cash victim in Newark; he was found dead on discovery by police in a vacant building on Chancellor Avenue.

The reaper wouldn't be denied in Hartford, either. Early Sunday morning, a patrol unit found Charles Matt Logan, 38, in a vacant store on Center Street, a few blocks south of Stowe Village. There wasn't much doubt about what had killed him. Logan, who was known to his friends as "Butch," was sitting in a discarded chair, his back to the wall, a syringe dangling from one arm and the other partially eaten by rats. An empty packet of Tango & Cash lay on the floor.

He'd scored sometime in the early morning hours, so he was dead before the squad cars started circulating with their warning about the "toxic heroin!" But Butch Logan, an unemployed custodian, was a junkie, and shooting heroin was what he did. So he probably would have fired up the packet of white powder even if he'd heard the cops on the loudspeaker.

"It's the risk you take, being on the street," said one resigned female addict who knew all about nickels and chances.

Sometime that weekend—there's some disagreement about how soon—a call went out to the dealers in Mott Haven: unload Tango & Cash.

Richie, the addict/dealer, said he got his orders quickly. "Not even ten hours later, we started getting the word to get rid of all the stuff we had left because it was killing people." Others heard the caution later. Few heeded the advice. Not when there was money to be made. So the sales went on, sometimes under a new brand name, until the supply of packets was all gone.

Michael Johnson and Edwardo Acevedo of Newark both continued selling Tango & Cash until Newark police arrested them, though Johnson had changed the label to "Goodfella" on the packages he sold to the undercover cop.

40th Precinct, NYPD, Monday, February 4, 1991, 9:00 a.m.

The long weekend was finally over, and things returned to their normal hectic pace in the 40th Precinct station house. The initial—but still incomplete—butcher's bill for Tango & Cash's weekend was in: twelve dead and 115 hospitalized, 68 of them in or near the 40th Precinct.

That total would be revised upward to seventeen dead a few days later. Hundreds more had been treated and released; maybe 1,000 all told had walked in or been transported to the emergency rooms in three states.

If not for Narcan, the death toll might have been in the scores, maybe the hundreds.

The ambulances had finally stopped running; like an out-of-control wildfire, only one thing could stop it. This thing died when it ran out of fuel.

The police still had some cleaning up to do. NYPD undercover officers had made some buys on Brook Avenue, and the low-level dealers would be arrested later. Those cases did not lead to anyone higher up, or yield any clues as to the source of the fentanyl in the Tango & Cash packets.

The New Jersey cops didn't do much better. In Paterson, their detectives busted Richard Cosme and Jose Mendez, and seized twenty packets that field-tested positive for heroin. Tests later at the crime lab also found fentanyl, which was just what everyone expected.

Undercover agents in Newark bought Tango & Cash from Michael Johnson, 33, and Edwardo Acevedo, 27, who were arrested on Sunday even as the sound trucks were circling through Newark's most notorious open-air drug marketplaces. Police said Acevedo had continued selling the packets even after hearing the trucks' warnings.

In Hartford, police detectives tracked down the man they believed sold the Tango & Cash packet to Charles Logan; they picked up James Duke, a 44-year-old junkie and alcoholic, and charged him with felony drug sales for the $10 per day that he made running heroin for dealers higher up the chain.

The next link up in that chain was William Little, age 23, known on the street as "Chill Will." The cops wanted to hang murder raps on both Duke and Little, reasoning that the fentanyl in the packet had killed Logan just as surely as if they'd stuck a gun in his ear and pulled the trigger. But the prosecutor demurred, saying that Connecticut law didn't allow that charge if Logan had other drugs in his system at the time of his death.

Logan, a heroin addict, had heroin in his blood, so the two men faced the narcotics charge and a manslaughter rap that the prosecutor would allow, since Duke told the cops that he'd warned Little how the Tango & Cash was killing people.

"If the people take it, that's their problem," Chill Will had said; this was exactly the chilly sort of attitude that dope dealers have toward drug sales generally, and Chill Will had toward his customers in particular.

For their roles in the death of Butch Logan, Duke received an 8-year suspended sentence and three years of probation. "Chill Will" Little got ten years in prison, and that was the end of the Tango & Cash Fentanyl Outbreak of February 1991 except for the paperwork. There's always paperwork.

The reports went out through NYPD's maze of commands to the Organized Crime Control Bureau's Narcotics Division, and the Narcotics Borough Bronx. More went to the Intelligence and Organized Crime detectives and the officers working on the federal task forces. The federal Drug Enforcement Administration offices in New York and New Jersey heard about it from NYPD, Hartford, Paterson, and Newark on Monday, and it was the kind of news that prompted a call to Washington, D.C., where it was routed to an office where they'd been waiting on that call for a long time.

The DEA people in Washington weren't any smarter or better informed than the police officers or public health officials in New York or Connecticut or New Jersey. They didn't have any special secret intelligence that would allow them to solve this fentanyl problem or, better yet, make the whole thing go away. What they did have was the ability to monitor "the big picture," which was made up of drug seizures all over the United States, even the world.

The DEA followed emergency room visits related to drugs and drug-related deaths, looking for trends, and it had programs that monitored the chemicals and equipment used to manufacture drugs like fentanyl in clandestine laboratories. Unlike Hartford or Paterson or even NYPD, the DEA could put all these pieces together, and maybe start narrowing down the search area. To revert to the hoary analogy, even if the DEA couldn't find the needle, it might be able to eliminate some of the thousands of haystacks out there.

Long Island's *Newsday* summarized the problem. "Gene Haislip, deputy assistant administrator of the Drug Enforcement Administration, said in a telephone interview that if the drug being sold is pharmaceutical fentanyl stolen from a hospital, the problem will be more 'manageable.' But if there is someone up there manufacturing this stuff, you have a much more serious problem because it's unknown how much is around.'"

But on Monday, February 4, 1991, the people at the DEA knew only that sometime recently, somewhere in America (or maybe the world), someone had opened the lid on Pandora's Box.

Now the DEA had to find that someone. They knew this wasn't going to be easy. It would take time, patience, old-fashioned detective work, and modern high technology. It would probably also require a lot of luck.

The DEA's own expert, John Maher, had been warning for years that this day would come, and now it had, and the lid was off. A dozen people were dead already, each of them somebody's son or somebody's daughter. Maher had seen that coming, too, and though he was gone, retired in 1985, he had made another sobering prediction before he left.

There would be a hell of a lot more than twelve people dead before anybody could get Pandora's lid back on the box.

CHAPTER 39

Wichita, Kansas, 1991

Those Brook Avenue dealers who had sparked a nationwide uproar wouldn't be getting any more Tango & Cash right away. Headlines like "Killer Smack Seized," "Tango Death Toll Hits 17," and "7 Drug Users Die on 'Super Smack'" had thoroughly spooked the people up the ladder. Their first venture had drawn far more heat than any of them expected…unwanted publicity about their "killer drug" blared on the front pages of the *New York Times* and several hundred other newspapers. It made the morning news on television and radio stations, and even filtered down through time zones and landed on KMUW, the National Public Radio affiliate in far-off Wichita, Kansas, where it prompted an angry telephone call from a key player in the scheme.

At the other end of the line, the phone rang in Pittsburgh, a thousand miles away.

"I guess you heard our competition put some bad dope on the street in New York," Joe Martier answered, getting to the bullshit right away.

In Kansas, the man everyone called "Squeak" knew bullshit when he heard it, and hated it. He wasn't buying into it now. "Hey, Joe, I didn't just fall off the goddamn train yesterday. I know that was our product that killed those people. And besides, I don't *have* any competition."

Erik Marquardt pulled the payphone's handset closer as cars buzzed past on U.S. Highway 54. "I'm the only one in the whole damn country making this shit. You and *your* friends are the only ones selling it. And you just made sure every narc in the U. S. of A. is looking for both of us."

He'd been saying from the very beginning that the dealers at the lower levels would be "utterly incapable" of cutting the fentanyl into anything resembling safe doses, and the proof was on every radio station and news outlet in the country that morning, so Marquardt ranted for a few minutes, venting a little steam, saying "I told you so," with feeling.

Martier came back, blaming as much as he could on the people below him who'd been unable to handle the powdered dynamite that Marquardt had provided them. He knew there was some truth in there amongst the bullshit, but wanted to make a point.

When he'd made it, they agreed to put off further work on fentanyl until some of the heat caused by dead junkies— something else Squeak had predicted—faded.

Marquardt slammed the phone down and climbed into his truck, heading back to the chemicals that, unlike people, didn't bullshit you and always reacted exactly the way they were supposed to react. And if the things in these bottles and beakers killed him, it would be because of a mistake *he* made, not one by some dumbass in Pennsylvania or a couple of mafia wannabes in Massachusetts and New York. He could live—or die—with that.

Clandestine chemists paid their nickels and took their chances, too.

Joe Martier remembered, "We already had the surveillance in Boston [the benzene barrel], and we already knew that we bought 'watched' chemicals. It seemed prudent to quit, because this was sure to kick up more of an investigation, a thing like this. So, we quit for a while."

Marquardt and Martier might have been bowing out for the time being, but Benito Febre wasn't ready to give up so easily, and wasn't happy that his partners were bailing out on him. Professing his innocence, he called Martier "insisting there was no reason to freak out because whatever happened here, it was totally not our responsibility." He told Martier that he hadn't sold the drug until the afternoon of Friday, February 1, and asked, "How in God's name could this be on the news Saturday morning?"

Although Febre continued to call Martier over the next few weeks, saying, "we were being idiots," Martier "just stayed buried until February, March, April, May," and the calls gradually trailed off…as did the Tango & Cash fentanyl and the deaths that went with it.

* * *

Hell's Kitchen, New York City, 1991

In the DEA's Northeast Regional Laboratory in New York City, Chemist Jack Fasanello wasn't quite ready to say, "I told you so," but he was thinking it. Now, with over a dozen people dead on the streets and more bodies piling up, Fasanello thought he knew exactly where to start looking for those responsible.

He remembered that first call. "I was waiting for fentanyl to hit the street. When it did, I was called to a meeting by the NYPD, and one of the captains asked me if I could think of any subjects that might have been producing the Tango & Cash fentanyl. At the time, I could think of three. One was a chemist at Ciba-Geigy who was found unconscious with a syringe of fentanyl in his arm; one was another chemist doing research for a company in Connecticut. The other one was TX Green."

Fasanello's instincts were spot on, but he and everyone else were playing catch-up in February 1991, and they were all six months behind the curve.

TX Green's August 1990 purchase of the benzene barrel had put Moscatiello and Martier on the DEA's scope, but Boston's blown surveillance meant Fasanello would only find out much later that TX Green had been the correct answer to the suddenly urgent fentanyl question all along.

Fasanello had worked on the Michael Hovey case in Delaware, and was familiar with the other fentanyl investigations the DEA had conducted since 1980. So he knew that previous chemists—Hovey, Daniel Hodes, Thomas Schaefers in Pittsburgh in 1988 and the earlier China White cases in California—had all been educated at the master's or PhD level, usually working in sophisticated university or industrial labs, or both. Two of his suspects this time fit that mold perfectly, and it was logical to assume that whoever was behind TX Green did, too, and when the DEA quickly investigated the industrial chemists and ruled both men out, that left TX Green as the only known possibility.

Fasanello was also pointing everyone in the right geographical direction, as he believed the fentanyl lab was located somewhere in New England and probably in the vicinity of Boston. In addition to the benzene barrel—now missing—TX Green had made a number of other suspicious purchases, most in the Boston area but some as far away as New Jersey. The DEA had gotten close: once with the benzene, and once with an order for a high-capacity rotary evaporator from Switzerland. Neither lead had panned out, but Fasanello was going to push for another look.

In the meantime, the lab in New York got Tango & Cash packets to test. Although they were alleged to contain Colombian heroin, Fasanello found something else he expected. "I was sent a package consisting of two glassine envelopes that were stamped 'Tango & Cash.' And my analysis concluded that they, in fact, contained fentanyl and no heroin."

He was able to make another important conclusion from his tests. "It was fentanyl hydrochloride, which indicated to me that it was clandestinely manufactured." This ruled out the possibility that the fentanyl had somehow been diverted from legitimate pharmaceutical sources. There was an underground chemist out there somewhere.

And there was more bad news. The heroin packets sold in New York—those dime bags—are ordinarily single-use; addicts consume all ten dollars of it in one injection. Dime bags normally contain between 50 and 100 milligrams of heavily adulterated heroin, but Fasanello said, "At the time I analyzed the Tango & Cash envelopes, they contained less powder— approximately forty milligrams—ten percent of which was fentanyl hydrochloride, and the rest mannitol, a common cut in heroin and coke."

This finding was important for two reasons. First, ten percent of 40 milligrams equals four milligrams, at least *twice the lethal dose* of fentanyl. With the addicts in the Bronx expecting their customary heroin in the Tango & Cash packets and firing it all up at once as usual, fatal overdoses were inevitable; that's exactly what occurred that first weekend. Further, the haphazard, even primitive way that Martier and Febre had cut the drug undoubtedly meant that some packets contained more than four milligrams of fentanyl, though some would have contained less. The luck of the draw meant the difference between a good high and sudden death—a hot shot—that afternoon on Brook Avenue.

It would take two years for Fasanello to appreciate the second key fact in his analysis. He didn't know it, but Martier and Febre had cut their 165 grams of pure fentanyl hydrochloride with a kilogram plus three ounces of mannitol. This would have resulted in almost exactly the proportion of fentanyl to mannitol that Fasanello discovered in his two samples. This is very strong evidence that the deaths on that first weekend can all be traced back directly through Febre and Martier to Marquardt's lab in Wichita.

By the end of February, the DEA in New York had opened a fentanyl case on TX Green, "although at that point we were calling it the Tango & Cash investigation," Fasanello said. To assist his forensic side of the case, the

DEA assigned a task force agent, New York State Police Detective Joanne Leoni.

Although no more Tango & Cash fentanyl hit the streets—no fentanyl at all because Marquardt and Martier were on hiatus—Fasanello and Leoni were on the right track, and would pursue the people behind TX Green to the bitter end.

That end was two years and 1,400 miles away.

CHAPTER 40

Wichita, Kansas, 1991

Marquardt's cooling-off pause didn't last because he'd finally got fentanyl right; the dead bodies still piling up on the East Coast were grim proof that his chemistry worked. As he had done with methamphetamine in Oklahoma years before, he'd found a product that would produce actual revenue. In fact, fentanyl was far more lucrative than meth; the six ounces in that first batch to Febre was supposed to fetch $60,000, half of which was Marquardt's. Even the $20,000 he actually received was much more than he would have made on a similar amount of meth. Meth precursors like P2P brought in even less.

And he needed more money. His dream of creating Prairie Lab included at least one mass spectrometer, plus some other instruments he thought belonged in such an exalted setting. In the past, he would have just raided another university, but he'd turned away from thieving. And there was the fact that some mass spectrometers were about as big and heavy as a Volkswagen, which made them quite a bit harder to subtly carry off.

He hadn't had a sudden epiphany or impulsively developed some moral scruples against stealing; his reasons were strictly practical. His record—which already included nine felony convictions, most of which were for stealing things like mass spectrometers—guaranteed that getting caught again in even a small theft would lead to long years behind bars. It made more sense to use his laboratory skills to make drugs, sell them, and use that money to buy the instruments he wanted.

He thought that with a little better luck and maybe some different partners, fentanyl could still make PrairieLab a reality.

And there was another factor in fentanyl's favor: he found it very, very interesting.

In 2019, the U.S. Department of Homeland Security estimated that "there are about 3,024 potential fentanyl derivatives that might be synthesized," but this may be just the tip of the iceberg. Some believe the number of these chemical cousins to Dr. Janssen's original creation might be far greater. "How many? Infinite," one pharmaceutical chemist told the author. [6]

"This was certainly intriguing," Marquardt said. "One can only do so much with amphetamine, although there are a few interesting variations. And of course, those and the other phenethylamine derivatives have been thoroughly explored by Gordon Alles and Alexander Shulgin and countless others."

With fentanyl, he could create analogues that were less potent—perhaps the equivalent of morphine or heroin. These would be easier to cut, safer to handle and sell, and probably just as profitable as real China White heroin, which sold for up to $200,000 per kilo wholesale in New York.

Even better, he wouldn't have to follow in the footsteps of other people like Alles and Shulgin. Fentanyl and its analogues provided Marquardt with exciting and virtually

---

6. In its *Technical Appendixes*, The Commission on Combatting Synthetic Opioid Trafficking reported in 2022 that one "pathway" or method could "theoretically produce more than 650,000 structurally unique fentanyl analogues that are highly similar to fentanyl." For all four of the identified pathways, a total of "3.7 billion structural analogues of fentanyl are feasible." www.rand.org/hsrd/hsoac/commission-combating-synthetic-opioid-trafficking.

limitless opportunities to boldly go where no man had gone before…to be not just the first to reach the summit, but the actual discoverer of a whole chain of chemical Everests. Fentanyl could allow this high school dropout to make the kinds of discoveries that had immortalized his idols: Haber, Bosch, Niemann, Alles, even Paul Janssen himself. The sheer number of potential analogues, or what the federal government would later call "fentanyl-related substances (FRS)" posed what Marquardt termed a "Goldilocks possibility."

"I believed it was possible to find, through experimentation, a fentanyl analogue that was neither too powerful—3-methylfentanyl, for example—or too weak, but one that would be just right, having real commercial opportunities without all the death that seems to accompany fentanyl itself. Consider the possibility that one could produce a variant that exactly mimicked heroin's effects and duration, or even improved on it. One could create that in a laboratory setting from common chemicals, and completely eliminate the entire poppy-opium-morphine-heroin production sequence," Marquardt said.

Viewed in this light, fentanyl had potential far beyond mere money. That money, though, would enable him to build PrairieLab where all the rest—more money, but more importantly, the acclaim one could expect to receive for a discovery that changes world history—would follow.

Getting there—making Louis Cirillo's Lewisburg dream of completely upending, then replacing the world's heroin trade—depended first on the money he could make from fentanyl right then. Marquardt retreated into his tiny house and began exploring fentanyl in earnest.

"It intrigued me. The major obstacles, it seemed to me, were potency and yield, but there were other aspects I needed to investigate," he said.

Marquardt began his fentanyl studies following the same process Paul Janssen had pioneered in the late 1950s and early 1960s. The so-called Janssen synthesis was well documented in the chemical literature, and so were the routes to 3-methylfentanyl and several other previously discovered analogues. He wondered, though, whether there was a different route to the same end. Because Janssen's fentanyl was hard.

It had another problem, too. The Janssen process used a lot of laboratory resources, including precursor chemicals, to achieve a relatively low yield. Again, this isn't a major concern for the pharmaceutical industry, but it's a distinct liability for the clandestine manufacturer who needs to get as much finished product as possible and whose resources are much more restricted.

Marquardt thought there might be an easier route that resulted in the same yield or better, and started experimenting to find out.

Using the same Janssen process in his fentanyl "darkroom" on Flora Street, he created a batch he considered to be the best yet. Selling it with Martier, Moscatiello, and Febre all out of the picture was a problem, and he was leery of all of them, anyway. Instead, he turned to others interested in mining the fentanyl gold.

"Larry Blakeslee from Leavenworth. He gets out from prison and prevails upon all his friends, including me, to get him started again. So I give him 75 or 80 grams of fentanyl, and he goes out to Los Angeles and overdoses.

"I call up looking for him and his roommate says, 'Oh, Larry's in the hospital, he got drunk,' or something like that. 'How do I cut this stuff?' His roommate tried to sell it and died of an overdose handling it.

"They did not tell me any of these tragedies that were occurring because they didn't want me to know they were having problems handling the product. 'Nope, we can cut it. No problem.' Yeah. Well, his roommate tried it, end of game, he hit stiff city."

If anybody needed further proof of fentanyl's lethal side, Marquardt's brief West Coast adventure, with both of his distributors hospitalized and one dead, certainly furnished it.

Sadly, none of these warning signs deterred anyone from forging ahead on the fentanyl train.

In April, Chris Moscatiello climbed back aboard. And he wanted something even deadlier.

"Chris still wanted 3-methylfentanyl, and although I was uneasy about it being sold on the street, I did solve the problem, did find out ways that I could crystallize enormous amounts of 3-methylfentanyl without much difficulty. It was a big, big project that I messed with for probably close to a year, off and on, because it was never certain we were going to have any real demand for this stuff. And I preferred to keep the operation running with either commercial fentanyl itself that would not attract any massive attention as designer drugs.

"Well, they attracted more than enough attention anyway, but that's just the nature of the business. But it was apparent that I now had an industrial method for fentanyl and thought I could develop it for 3-methylfentanyl."

He'd need a proper lab to do it, and his dream of PrairieLab was closer than ever.

CHAPTER 41

Wichita, August 1990

Acquiring a mass spectrometer had always been mostly a dream. Marquardt took a step closer to that reality in August 1990 at Dawson Sales, a surplus equipment dealer in Wichita. "I ran into Sam out at Dawson. Both of us were shopping for electrical equipment. He was going to build a Tesla coil or some such nonsense. We got to talking."

Philip "Sam" Houston was a Kansas native, an amateur astronomer, and part of an established family in Wichita. A part-time oil geologist with a degree in geology from Kansas State University, he collected meteorites and telescopes, and kept both in his Wichita home.

"Some money in his family," Marquardt said. "But he was running low on cash because he'd chopped through this inheritance he got from his uncle, about $80,000. Took him the better part of a year and a half to piss it away."

Houston wasn't employed at the time. "He used to watch oil wells. Nepotism. His father's a rather well-known person in the local oil industry, and got him his jobs, and Sam made himself so insufferable out on the job that finally all the nepotism in the world couldn't get him a job," Marquardt remembered.

"Sam is what you'd call a know-it-all. His own sister hates him. It's rather hard to get along with the guy."

Their first chat carried over to lunch at a nearby restaurant, and Houston invited Marquardt to his place—a ninety-year-old house on a tree-lined Wichita street that was distinctive for the astronomical observatory dome on the top story.

"We went through the house, and were wandering through the basement. He's a packrat, never throws anything out. I looked in a box and saw a gallon of ethyl acetate, a pint of acetonitrile, and a couple of cans of ether. Upstairs in the dark room on the second floor, he showed me a bottle of trifluoracetyl chloride concealed among darkroom reagents. And I said, 'Wow, look at you, Sam Houston! Amongst other things, apparently, you've been dabbling in organic chemistry. You're going to make a little LSD, huh?'"

Houston said he'd been "contemplating trying it about 15 years ago," which confirmed Marquardt's suspicion that the two of them were on the same page about drugs and drug manufacturing.

"We discussed drug-related adventures over lunch. He told me that while a student at K-State, he had harvested low-grade marijuana from the military reservation at Fort Riley and converted some to hash oil."

Marquardt was convinced that his new acquaintance had no obvious lab skills and wouldn't be much use on the drug manufacturing end, but he did have potential value. "I continued to tell him one drug adventure story after another, and admitted to having manufactured fentanyl at some time past. I also alleged I had available huge quantities of drug money—a million plus—and needed assistance in cleaning up the money. Houston was fascinated."

Their conversations continued through 1990 into 1991, and through the tense moments following the New York disaster in February, the two men got closer as Martier and Moscatiello both went on hiatus.

Marquardt was still experimenting with fentanyl, talking with Lawrence Blakeslee in California, and anticipating that the Pittsburgh and Boston end would come back online at some point. "We're going to start up again, and so at this point I get Houston onboard, and I tell him, 'If you do mechanical maintenance and electrical maintenance around the shop, and free me up so I can do organic chemistry, we can make a whole lot more money before the DEA gets us.'"

Houston was agreeable, and with him on board, Marquardt—always alert for someone he could manipulate or exploit—thought he could use his new buddy to reach two other goals. Houston had a solid reputation in Wichita, no criminal record and, best of all from Marquardt's perspective, he had a checking account and a somewhat legitimate explanation for having some cash.

"He had the inheritance story, which was a good one explaining where he got his money. In his case, it was true, there was an inheritance, but it was all bullshit because that money was gone."

But that checking account would be useful for the establishment of PrairieLab, and especially for the purchase of a mass spectrometer, because the places that sold them—manufacturers and universities—were likely to be skeptical of someone who walked in and plunked down $50,000 in cash.

"A few days after the New York incident in early February 1991, we discussed the possibility of getting a building," Marquardt said, and the two of them continued to explore their options. "Money laundering was first discussed covertly in respect to purchasing a new ($50,000) or used mass spectrometer from Hewlett-Packard. I offered to pay him a ten percent commission. Later in the spring, the possibility of a used V.G. high-resolution mass spectrometer from W.S.U. opened up."

V.G. Micromass, a British company, began specializing in mass spectrometry in 1974 with their then state-of-the-art VG 70-70 model, which retailed for $400,000. By 1991, newer and more sophisticated devices had appeared, but the 70-70 was still widely used in university, government, and corporate laboratories around the world. It is a massive machine with multiple modules and banks of controls that would look right at home in a 747 cockpit or a Bond villain's secret lair. W.S.U.'s chemistry department, only a few miles away, had a VG 70-70, and Marquardt wanted it.

"It wasn't functioning and would cost the university quite a bit to restore it to operating condition, but I advised Houston to pursue the deal after negotiations that lasted the summer."

With his lifelong dream of mass spectrometer ownership tantalizingly closer than ever before, money became a more urgent need…and at almost that exact moment, Chris Moscatiello stepped back into the picture.

* * *

The DEA's New York investigation of Tango & Cash was going nowhere. There were no more fentanyl deaths, although Joanne Leoni had established contacts with all of the medical examiners in New York City and the surrounding area, asking them to be on the alert for fentanyl ODs. That hadn't been easy; she'd telephoned, stopped by in person, and even resorted to giving out New York State Police coffee mugs, t-shirts, and other items along with her phone number at the DEA's regional lab. Nobody was calling because Tango & Cash had gone quiet.

Fasanello was still bitter years later, convinced that the people behind TX Green could have been arrested in late 1990 and fentanyl stopped before it ever hit New York's streets. He said, "Boston dropped the ball. [DEA-New England Special Agent in Charge] Carlo Boccia said, they were 'out of sight, but they weren't out of mind,'" Fasanello said.

Maybe. But whoever "they" were, they weren't in jail, either, and eight months later, Fasanello and Leoni were still working the few leads they had—but with no fentanyl on the streets, those had faded away along with the fatal overdoses.

All that was about to change, because the Boston connection was back.

CHAPTER 42

Wichita, Kansas to Pittsburgh, Pennsylvania, Summer of 1991

Chris Moscatiello didn't think things could get much worse, but he'd been wrong before and he was wrong this time, too. Into the fentanyl scheme for over $300,000, he had nothing to show for it besides a "fifty-liter barrel of black sludge"… but it got even worse.

Although this wasn't an immediate threat, Moscatiello was now the sole link in a chain that led from his fentanyl partners to Michael Murray, his racketeer brother Joe, and other menacing associates who included Boston mob kingpin James "Whitey" Bulger and the Irish Republican Army.

Before he'd blown town, Joe Martier had taken himself out of that same chain, and told Moscatiello to go directly to Marquardt for fentanyl in the future.

Moscatiello waited for about three months. But he still had all that debt, and in April 1991, he reached out to Martier, saying he wanted to take another run at fentanyl. Martier agreed to contact Marquardt, who was ready to go, and said if they were going to resume the operation, he needed some beta phenethylamine, a key 3-methylfentanyl precursor. TX Green had previously purchased a substantial quantity, and some of it was still stored in Pembroke at Baker's house.

In late April, Martier drove up to Boston to get it.

Back in Pittsburgh, Martier called Marquardt to find out how he wanted to get the beta phenethylamine. "I'll meet you halfway," Marquardt said, which worked out to be Effingham, Illinois. There at the Crossroads of America in early May, the two of them talked about life, death, and fentanyl—"a couple of goddamn killers" deciding what to do next.

The answer they agreed on was "full speed ahead."

Moscatiello still wanted 3-methylfentanyl, he wanted control, and he hadn't given up on getting Marquardt back to Massachusetts. In late June 1991, he let his chemist know he was coming to Kansas and wanted to talk. Marquardt, who had just finished a batch of fentanyl and was very pleased with the results, said to come on down.

This proved to be a key meeting for both of them.

They faced a daunting wall of mistrust and suspicion that needed to be overcome before reaching any kind of agreement. Marquardt, who had been insisting from the very beginning on getting payment on delivery and preferably before, strongly suspected that Moscatiello and the shadowy people behind him didn't intend to pay him at all, and might have a more sinister plan in mind. Many of their conversations up to that point had been tainted by the ill feelings spawned by the failure of the lab in Ric Ocasek's Falmouth basement. The memory of hearing his overconfident partners saying, "Fuck Squeak" to his face didn't ease the tensions.

Moscatiello, meanwhile, thought Marquardt owed him at least $300,000 and more like a million, which was their originally-agreed upon deal, and he didn't intend to pay Marquardt anything at all until he'd recouped his losses and climbed out of his hole. Marquardt had promised from the beginning to make the 3-methylfentanyl, or at least to mentor Rubino through the process, and hadn't done so, leaving Moscatiello holding a barrel of useless, but extremely expensive, black gunk. He had, he believed, substantial grounds to be upset with his chemist.

In this poisonous atmosphere in Kansas, they hashed out their various grievances for several days in June. They found some common ground, and each was ready to make some concessions to get their project back on track. Marquardt had 500 grams of fentanyl ready to sell. Moscatiello had a fully equipped laboratory and a substantial amount of what they believed might be recoverable 3-methylfentanyl, not to mention a barrel of benzene, glassware, chemical precursors, and other material that Marquardt could always use.

As usual, money was the prime sticking point, and Moscatiello confirmed Marquardt's suspicions that at least some of his $300,000 had come from others, namely Michael Murray.

"He told me his backers had some kind of affiliation with the Irish Republican Army, and one of them was in prison for running marijuana and a shipload of guns to Ireland," Marquardt said. "Whitey Bulger's name came up, and it was my impression that Bulger was taxing Moscatiello and Murray to allow them to sell their stuff in Boston."

Although it may not have felt like it to Moscatiello, he had the upper hand in these talks, which is why he ultimately flew back to Boston with a half-kilo of fine white powder—500 grams of fentanyl he could cut with nine and a half kilos of filler. The resulting mix would be the equivalent of ten kilograms—over twenty pounds—of pure heroin valued at a million dollars or more.

Marquardt caved on his demand to be paid up front because with the Martier/Febre end of the operation on hiatus thanks to the February New York fiasco, and with Larry Blakeslee still recovering from his near-death experience in May, Marquardt simply had nowhere else to sell his fentanyl. "You can say 'this is worth a million dollars' or whatever, but none of it's worth anything unless you can get paid for it," Marquardt said.

He was willing to take a chance on Moscatiello because, at this point in June, Sam Houston's negotiations with Wichita State University for its mass spectrometer were very close to fruition. If they succeeded, Marquardt would need some cash to close the deal and take possession of his cherished instrument. Having a reliable outlet for his fentanyl took him a big step closer to PrairieLab.

He was also making a point, demonstrating conclusively that in *his* lab, at least, he could come up with exactly the chemical compound he'd said he could make.

Rubino in Falmouth had flopped, but Squeak in Wichita had succeeded, and those 500 grams of pure fentanyl proved it beyond any doubt.

And finally, they agreed that the 500 grams were to be considered as payment in full for the $300,000 Moscatiello claimed to be owed.

That obligation had now been extinguished, future shipments were to be paid cash on delivery, and Marquardt "didn't want to hear another goddamn word about any past debts I allegedly owed." In fact, he wanted to be paid $300,000 for converting Rubino's black gunk into 3-methylfentanyl, but he postponed that discussion to a later date when he, not Moscatiello, would be holding the better hand.

They both got a win when Marquardt agreed to go up to Boston to work on the 3-methylfentanyl.

"I made it clear that I would be taking my pick of anything at Baker's house when that job was completed," Marquardt said, and expected to return to Wichita with enough raw materials to make fentanyl "by the ton"—only a slight exaggeration.

With everybody finally singing from the same page, Chris Moscatiello headed back east.

* * *

Everybody got busy in the summer of 1991 as their various plans came together. Marquardt had perfected his manufacturing process, and Martier flew down to Wichita in early July to help finish a load for Moscatiello. The two of them drove to Tulsa to pick up chemicals from Bob Fearon, then finished 500 grams of fentanyl and cut it to 800 grams, which they believe would be the equivalent of eight kilos of pure heroin.

On July 16, Martier took the fentanyl by train to Chicago and then flew on to Boston, handed the dope over to Moscatiello at Faneuil Hall, then continued to Pembroke to check on the lab stored in that secret underground room beneath Richard Baker's woodpile.

"I went over to the university with my newfound ill-gotten gains, paid Houston $6,600 for the mass spectrometer, and he gave WSU a check. I gave him the ten percent brokerage fee to handle the entire transaction." Then the two of them carefully wrestled the big machine into Marquardt's pickup and moved it to a storage unit in Wichita where it would stay until they found a more suitable place for it, meaning inside PrairieLab.

Marquardt had Houston looking for that spot, too. That search would end in September.

Some money had come down to Wichita from Boston, and despite the sniping back and forth over who owed what, Marquardt hit his stride on fentanyl production.

Leaving aside these worrying issues, the operation was finally running the way its creators had hoped. Marquardt had his process set up to regularly produce 300 to 500 grams of fentanyl, Moscatiello was starting to pay actual cash for it, and he indicated that he'd worked out a system for marketing the drug at the wholesale level.

In fact, Moscatiello had described the distribution side of the operation to Martier on his visit to Boston. He said that he and Murray were supplying the fentanyl to two different groups. The "A Team" consisted of Murray's associates in the Boston area, while the "B Team" consisted of black traffickers who would be selling the fentanyl in New York.

"The New York people were supposed to be connected to Colombia somehow," Marquardt said later. "They wanted to leave the impression that the fentanyl was coming from Colombia, and the people distributing it were all in New York. Not Boston, and definitely not Kansas."

With money filtering back down to Wichita, it looked like their scheme was finally working.

* * *

New York City, Summer of 1991

Back in New York City, Joanne Leoni and Jack Fasanello had been watching for fentanyl overdoses and other evidence that Tango & Cash was back, and in mid-1991, some of this evidence started turning up. Police and medical examiners began reporting fentanyl in seizures and in the toxicology screens of overdose victims.

"We started to see quite a number of them. I think we got up to something in the area of 180 overdose deaths," Fasanello said.

With stories of fentanyl deaths fading from the news, Marquardt was feeling pretty good about things. In Wichita, PrairieLab was almost a reality—and just in time, because while working on fentanyl in the Flora Street house, he had made what he called a "revolutionary discovery," one he would describe to an awed associate as "nation-wrecking."

That's because for thirty years, Paul Janssen's fentanyl had been exactly what the DEA described: "Difficult to perform and beyond the rudimentary skills of most clandestine laboratory operators. Only individuals who have acquired advanced chemistry knowledge and skills have successfully used this synthesis route."

As Martier, Moscatiello, and Bobby Rubino had learned, fentanyl was hard.

Not anymore.

CHAPTER 43

Wichita, Autumn 1992

Science fiction author, Isaac Asimov, once wrote, "The most exciting phrase to hear in science, the one that heralds new discoveries, is not 'Eureka!' but 'That's funny…'"

In late summer 1991, Erik Marquardt had one of those funny moments, and it heralded a change in our world.

When DEA Agent John Maher described the hypothetical chemist who would bring drugs like fentanyl to America, he emphasized how dangerously exceptional that person would be. He wouldn't be just extremely intelligent and a talented chemist like Michael Hovey, who had succeeded in producing a substance like fentanyl in a world-class laboratory like DuPont's. He would be someone who could master the process and do it in a clandestine setting in a 620 square foot house in Wichita, Kansas.

Maher never met Marquardt, but he had the full measure of the man. He might have added that this most dangerous chemist would also be constantly looking for a better, more efficient, cheaper, faster, and safer way to achieve his desired result.

And he would be good enough to find one.

Marquardt understood the Janssen method for producing fentanyl. He had the patent application and other literature, and could replicate the Belgian doctor's work in a far less sophisticated laboratory. What separated him from all of his clandestine peers was his ability to deviate from the "recipe," to improvise and innovate, and his willingness to invest as much time, resources, and effort as necessary to find a better route from raw materials to profit.

Although the profit part had taken almost two full years, Erik—following Janssen's recipe—had gotten there at last.

Now, having climbed fentanyl's summit, he could turn to its almost infinite number of variations, analogues, isomers, and chemical cousins that all posed intriguing questions. He spent the succeeding weeks in the Flora house investigating those questions.

He'd done this before, finding an obscure 1966 patent application on a completely unrelated subject, realizing it would allow him to "make P2P in unlimited quantities without ever going near a chemical on the watchlist."

Years later he sat back in his recliner chair, lit his pipe, and recalled the event as Mozart played softly in the background. "I wanted to go through this thing sequentially, building the molecule. I saw no possibility of ordering benzylfentanyl (a pharmacologically inactive, key Janssen precursor) or any of these compounds."

As he always did with methamphetamine, he needed to start a couple of steps lower down on the ladder. This was the kind of advanced chemistry that put fentanyl out of reach of the ordinary clandestine chemist. "It seemed to me from the onset to start out with some very simple compound like a phenethylamine and proceed through several steps from there. And indeed, it was sometime later before I found out that I could avoid much of that."

A 2008 patent application for "A method for preparation of fentanyl" describes the Janssen method's difficulties and shortcomings, saying "The main disadvantage associated with this process is a multi-step, hence requires more time and overall, appreciably reduced yield."

Marquardt obsessed on yield, but Janssen's other drawbacks included an extremely "energy extensive" and uneconomical process, and the need in all five steps to remove solvents—something that was "environmentally unsound and unsafe." It also requires chemicals that pose safety, fire, and environmental hazards, and the palladium carbon used in one of the steps was very expensive. Finally, researchers concluded that the Janssen route was "unfit for large scale (sic) production, i.e. industrially and commercially unviable."

Skipping some of the more problematic steps on the road to fentanyl made the whole process easier, safer, and cheaper, and resulted in a higher yield and a more profitable product.

Omitting those steps began with a ruined batch and a "that's funny…" moment in the autumn of 1992. It started with a flask full of "red gunk."

"I had a small quantity of a compound in a 100-milliliter flask and hadn't had much luck at crystallizing this compound. A couple of times, I got it to go with a spin in the rotary evaporator, and I got some crystals and maybe I can get this thing to crystallize, but it's going to be laborious.

"So I want to get that red gunk out of my poor little flask, just readily dissolve it so I could throw it in the waste bucket and start over. Pour some plain old muriatic acid in the flask, and it smoked up the room. I go to pour it into the waste crock, and it doesn't pour! Solid as a rock. Hold it up to the light and I see little crystals. And just on impulse, I went to the refrigerator and got some cold acetone, and came back in and busted this stuff up. When I poured acetone into it, the red gum readily went into solution, and I busted up the mass with a stick and held it up to the light. The whole flask was filled with crystals with a small layer of acetone containing the unreactive side-products present. I've got a little pot full of pretty white crystals in my hand: the immediate precursor to fentanyl."

"I was tremendously excited, because here I had a simple technique by methods that, without chromatography or elaborate crystallization schemes, could bring down that product out of solution. It was a very convenient and fast workup. I could proceed from there directly to the next stage.

"Anyway, you do this, you're going to spend a lot of time on it, but I got the operation so that it would work beginning to end in about five or six days or something like that, depending how hard I decided to push it, and with substantial yields of fentanyl. Then later I had a similar lengthy adventure with 3-methylfentanyl."

Marquardt's accidental discovery allowed him to move quickly, safely, and efficiently to both fentanyl and its analogues. "You had to pay some dues to do it. In the case of the 3-methylfentanyl, I had to construct a special piece of equipment that made some features of the process easier and carried on two functions necessary for crystallization successfully. It was sort of a Rube Goldberg device, but it worked extremely well.

"If you wanted to make a lot of 3-methylfentanyl, this would be the way to do it. You could use relatively crude reaction processes, and then without resorting to chromatography, crystallize massive amounts of 3-methylfentanyl.

"Simply put, with this process, one can make nation-wrecking quantities of dope. A friend who actually read the process called it 'real Darth Vader stuff,'" Marquardt remembered.

Quite a bit of the fentanyl now killing 70,000 Americans every year is manufactured using the same process that Marquardt "stumbled upon" in a "that's funny" moment and a flask full of red gunk.

His assessment in 1992 that this method could produce "nation wrecking (sic) quantities of dope" seems rather prescient: a very grim prediction fulfilled.

There is nothing even remotely funny about that.

CHAPTER 44

Goddard, Kansas, September 1991

At the beginning of September 1991, a couple of unresolved issues still lay simmering; Moscatiello had a fully stocked lab at Richard Baker's Pembroke house, plus a barrel full of what everyone hoped was 3-methylfentanyl. And Benito Febre, whose batch of poorly diluted fentanyl had killed thirty-odd people back in February, wanted to try again, getting the potency right this time.

In early September, Marquardt finished a 500-gram batch of fentanyl for Moscatiello. Martier drove down to Wichita and stayed a week, helping to produce the equivalent of four kilograms of pure heroin. With the fentanyl concealed in a whiskey bottle, Martier went home on September 6, ready to meet Moscatiello, who flew in from Boston.

At a Pittsburgh hotel, Moscatiello saw the fentanyl but instructed Martier to give it to a truck driver for transport to Boston. Moscatiello said that the fentanyl would be concealed in a secret compartment in a tractor-trailer truck that Michael Murray used to transport marijuana from Texas.

Paying Martier $58,000, Moscatiello headed for home.

Marquardt flew up to Pittsburgh to collect his split, returning to Wichita with enough cash to make his next move, a literal one.

Houston had been looking for a suitable building and found one in the Goddard Industrial Park, twelve miles west of Wichita. Goddard (population 1,800) had some attractive features. The wide-open farm fields surrounding the industrial park made survcillance difficult. With only a handful of officers, Goddard's Police Department didn't seem like much of a threat. The neighbors—all light industry: auto body and paint shops, and a day care center—provided a little cover.

PrairieLab occupied half of a sturdy steel building with a decorative stone front. Ed Loibl ran a body shop in the other half of the building.

"The industrial park in Goddard had several other businesses," Loibl said. "Kimple Mold right across the street, Ameri-Kart across the street. He maybe purposely surrounded himself with companies that had a lot of smell coming off them. My body shop had its share of smells between the paints, primers, and thinners and cleaners and waxes and different things like that."

Stray smells from a clan lab were always a concern, but Marquardt wasn't worried about PrairieLab. He quickly installed his non-functioning mass spectrometer and some other equipment he'd purchased, but he kept most of the chemicals and lab equipment (such as glassware that would draw attention) back at Flora Street or in the storage unit. "I didn't plan on running a lot of reactions at PrairieLab," he said. He kept his pipe lit anyway.

Loibl remembered the smell. "George always smoked a pipe in his office, and it always smelled real good in there. Reminded me of my grandpa… he smoked a pipe that always (sic) some cherry flavor."

Loibl commented on his new acquaintance. "George was laid back, always just smoked his pipe, sat and read books, and watched his machine. Kept a close eye on his mass spectrometer. He was a heavyweight guy, dressed in coveralls mostly, probably because of his weight. Drove an old junk truck and always went somewhere with his dog."

Marquardt didn't mind Loibl's interest, and he made friends with one of the local police officers who jogged in the area and would stop by to chat. "There was never any drug manufacturing going on at PrairieLab, although several batches of fentanyl were finished there. None of that would have caused anyone to suspect anything illegal was taking place."

Loibl did wonder, though. "He always had a big fat wad of money. I don't think he meant to show it off or anything, but when he would pay for anything, it would come out at the restaurant or whatever and I would see it. I asked him one day how he made his money, and he said 'making drugs.' And I kind of laughed. I seriously thought he was joking, telling me it was none of my business."

Ultimately, PrairieLab wasn't about manufacturing fentanyl or any other illegal drugs. It was a ticket to a different life. Erik Marquardt planned to go legit.

* * *

Not totally legit; he's still Squeak, after all. But mostly legal. Twenty years before it became a thing, he planned to become a patent troll.

When people talk about patents, they usually mean a new invention, like Edison's lightbulb, Bell's telephone, or Paul Janssen's fentanyl. But the government also issues patents for processes—new and different sets of steps that lead to a new or existing product. These processes need to be both useful and novel; they can't be obvious to someone skilled in the field, and they must change at least one step.

Marquardt saw an opportunity… and now that he had a real laboratory rather than the bedroom of a Wichita shack, he thought he could seize it.

By 1992, he certainly had the ability to synthesize some of those thousands of possible fentanyl analogues, and even had a new and improved process for doing so, but for the first time since he'd been a high school freshman, Marquardt wanted to move away from drugs like fentanyl or methamphetamine.

He planned to use PrairieLab to do it, using drug profits to get the operation started, then phase out the drug end by 1995. After that, he expected that all his future revenues would come from two schemes that would today be characterized as "patent trolling."

According to Investopedia, "A patent troll is a derogatory term used to describe a company that uses patent infringement claims to win court judgments for profit or to stifle competition."

Marquardt would use two approaches. In the first, he would do the chemistry and develop a different method for making a drug. Robert Fearon would obtain a patent for this process. Then, Marquardt said, when a "big commercial operator develops an idea in conflict with our PrairieLab patent, we squawk and settle out of court." He said he used this scheme to obtain another mass spectrometer "very quietly from 3M."

Although this isn't illegal, Marquardt described it as "essentially a flim-flam." His second approach aimed to "develop a better (as in lots better) synthetic method for the manufacture of an existing commercial product."

As he described this scheme, "a company, (say Burroughs Wellcome) makes a product (say AZT). PrairieLab develops a more efficient process, then either sells the data directly to the manufacturer—who quietly uses it—or enters into a nondisclosure agreement for a fee as Burroughs Wellcome continues with its existing process."

He didn't randomly choose AZT as an example; he'd already synthesized it back in Norman by following the same process originally developed by the National Cancer Institute in 1964. Now, he concentrated on finding that "better (as in lots better) synthetic method" to make AZT at PrairieLab.

After about six months of hard work and "serious chemistry," he found one. As Fearon sought a way to financially exploit the new process, Marquardt turned to another, even more challenging drug called Taxol.

In the early 1960s, scientists searching for compounds effective in chemotherapy for metastatic cancers discovered one that worked brilliantly on breast and ovarian cancers. Paclitaxel or Taxol was a cytotoxin, a substance that kills human cells by preventing cell division. Johns Hopkins University described it as "a unique plant-derived substance that stops tumor growth."

Since its original discovery, it's been used with success on cancers of the lung, pancreas, esophagus, and cervix, and AIDS-related Kaposi sarcoma. Taxol worked so well that some were calling it a "miracle," and doctors found it dramatically increased survival rates in women with early breast cancer. Other cancers "responded well" and demand for Taxol exploded.

That caused problems that Marquardt thought he could solve with chemistry.

Like morphine and cocaine, Taxol is an alkaloid, a naturally occurring chemical compound extracted from its plant source…in this case, the bark of the Pacific yew trees, the sole source for the drug. These trees only grow in limited areas of the Pacific Northwest, and they grow very slowly, taking many years to mature.

Harvesting the bark killed the tree, and worst of all, it took a lot of bark to produce a little bit of Taxol; one kilo of dried bark produced only 100 mg of Taxol. In one year, harvesters killed 6,000-7,000 trees to get four kilos of Taxol from 27,700 kilos of bark. Demand was so strong that the government listed the Pacific yew as a "near-threatened species," and finding an alternative source for the drug—preferably a total synthesis method like fentanyl's—became a very high priority for researchers around the world.

The first to get there would hit the Taxol jackpot. Bristol Myers Squibb licensed the rights to the drug from the National Institutes of Health was charging almost $1,000 per dose for ten dose treatments and within ten years, sales would top $9 billion.

But Taxol had another appeal. In the late 1980s and early 1990s, Taxol became what one researcher called, "the holy grail of synthesis." Whoever got there first would achieve "the single most important milestone of complex molecular construction in recent decades."

Marquardt thought that sounded like his kind of challenge.

"Very, very complicated chemistry. Serious business," he said.

Starting as he had with AZT, he obtained a sample of Taxol and, this time using his own—now functioning—mass spectrometer, broke the extremely complex molecule down and began working through a lengthy multi-stage process to recreate the compound. Since he didn't have any Pacific yew trees handy, he needed to identify the chemical precursors necessary to the synthesis, settling on several that seemed to lead in a positive direction.

This quest had another benefit. "It was quite a pleasant change to purchase a chemical that wasn't on DEA or OBN's watchlist."

He made good progress, ran reactions with chemicals he'd never used before, and spent fentanyl proceeds to purchase more electronic equipment and glassware—including a very expensive falling film distillation apparatus that wasn't absolutely necessary for fentanyl or meth, but could apply to his Taxol project, which hummed along through 1992 and into the new year.

Years later, he read in the scientific literature that in 1994, Robert Holton and a group of his researchers at Florida State University published the first complete process that did not require any material from the Pacific yew. The

"Holton Taxol total synthesis" employs all of the chemicals Marquardt had been using at PrairieLab.

"So, I read that with considerable satisfaction. I was on the right path. Well on the way with Taxol. I'd have succeeded eventually.

"And of course, I can see several ways to improve on it."

Close was as far as he would get with Taxol, but he still mourned the lost chance at the "Holy Grail of Synthesis."

CHAPTER 45

Boston, a year before

DEA Special Agent Gerald "Jerry" Graves watched from the J.T. Baker loading dock as the sharply dressed man in the green Range Rover drove away. Graves, playing the part of a Baker employee today, had chatted briefly with his "customer" and quizzed him about the barrel of benzene that was now riding off to parts unknown.

Benzene isn't the sort of thing one normally wants to transport in the back of one's SUV. It's highly flammable, toxic in even small quantities, and a known carcinogen. Any exposure over one part of benzene per million parts of air (1ppm) for eight hours, or five ppm over a fifteen-minute period, is considered hazardous to your health. Getting it on your skin is bad news. Respirators and protective clothing, including eye and face coverings, are required for those working with benzene.

But the man from TX Green took none of these precautions. The DEA agents now carefully following his Range Rover kept a healthy distance back.

Graves remembered his brief encounter with the mysterious Mr. Green. "I don't know what role he plays in it, but he was certainly very clean-cut, very articulate, seemed knowledgeable and intelligent enough to respond to questions…but ignorant with regard to what exactly he intended to do with this barrel of benzene."

It was a puzzle, but at least Graves had answered one question. They finally knew the mysterious TX Green's true identity; the license plate on the Range Rover came back to Christopher Moscatiello of Charlestown. An investigation that had been going nowhere now seemed to have somewhere to go.

Jerry Graves was a former U.S. Marine who had worked on security and intelligence matters at American embassies in the Vietnam era. He'd been with the DEA for just over three years, assigned out of the academy to the Boston office.

It wasn't his first law enforcement job. He had been a Special Investigator with the New York City Department of Investigation where the native New Yorker had worked cases on "official corruption, theft, misconduct, bribery, and corrupt activity" within the NYPD and other city departments.

He followed those four years with four more as a patrol officer with the Houston Police Department in Texas before going to the DEA.

He hadn't wanted the fentanyl case; he had just closed a major investigation, and was fairly deep into two others.

"I was like, 'Oh boy, that's all I need is another case.'"

But his Assistant Special Agent in Charge, apparently following Ben Franklin's adage that "If you want something done, ask a busy person," called him in and said he didn't have a choice in the matter. Graves had been certified by the DEA as a clandestine laboratory safety officer, he was trained to seize labs, and he had been issued all the necessary safety gear.

He was the most qualified agent in Boston for the assignment, and he quickly learned that the DEA didn't have much to work with.

A couple of unidentified men calling themselves TX Green who had a mail drop in Harvard Square were buying glassware and chemicals. Jack Fasanello in New York assured Boston that whoever these two were, they were setting up a fentanyl lab, and it was most likely located somewhere in the Boston area. Fasanello also said that whoever was running this lab would be a cut above the average clandestine chemist the DEA routinely encountered.

Graves didn't think Moscatiello fit that description.

"The chemists and the laboratory operators we've arrested, we've always found them to be somewhat on an amateur level," Graves said. Moscatiello seemed more amateurish than usual. "He was unable to really answer basic questions. I said, 'Are you aware of how to store this chemical? Are you aware of basic safety measures?' And he seemed wary and coy with regard to his answers."

Moscatiello didn't head for anyplace that looked like a suitable lab site. Instead, he drove into a Charlestown "parking garage where he got out of the car, leaving the barrel." The surveillance agents couldn't see where he'd gone from there, but still had the Range Rover and its benzene in sight. "That, in turn, generated another surveillance, now of the parking garage, that lasted all night long to the early morning hours of the next day. There were issues of whether or not it was safe to leave the barrel in there, and we had to get some professional advice on this. We certainly didn't want any danger to the public," Graves recalled.

The following morning, Moscatiello returned to his car, started it up, picked up a second man, drove out of town, and headed south toward Cape Cod. Graves didn't accompany the other agents; Moscatiello was sure to remember the J.T. Baker employee who asked all those hard questions. But he heard about it later.

"That part of Eastern Massachusetts, just above Cape Cod, is the cranberry center of America. It's full of cranberry bogs, it's a flat area. The roadways only go between these cranberry bogs, and it's quite easy to see other cars if there are other cars following you," Graves said. Moscatiello drove erratically, making turns and doubling back, and he "determined that he was indeed being followed."

The DEA didn't have a tracking device planted in the barrel, so when Moscatiello burned the surveillance and disappeared, the barrel vanished with him. Only later would the DEA learn that Moscatiello took it to Richard Baker's place in Pembroke where he stored it underground.

Graves immediately made the connection between Moscatiello and Michael Murray, learning that both men had been busted in a 1983 case in which the DEA and FBI seized over 30,000 pounds of marijuana in a South Boston warehouse and a couple of cars. Moscatiello had pled guilty to those charges and received an eighteen-month sentence. Murray had been convicted in a jury trial in January 1984.

* * *

When Chris Moscatiello disappeared with the benzene, the DEA lost him, too. "We didn't know where he was living; just assumed it was somewhere near the parking garage in Charlestown," Graves said.

He was on parole, however, and required to provide their home address, but Graves suspected Moscatiello might lie about that.

But Moscatiello would have to report to the courthouse regularly, and Graves decided to set up another surveillance to follow him after his next scheduled meeting.

"We approached the probation officer, Frederick Ford. He also happened to be the probation officer of Joseph Murray and Michael Murray. We found that out later. Our sole interest at that time was just to ask, 'When is Mr. Moscatiello coming in?' 'He'll be in at 9:30 on such and such a date.' 'Thank you very much.'"

The DEA set up the surveillance on the appointed date, and agents saw Moscatiello enter the courthouse and go to the probation office. He didn't come out.

"We wait, and finally go in and say, 'Hey,' to Mr. Ford. 'Where's Moscatiello?' 'Oh, he left an hour ago.' 'Well, how did he leave? There was only one office door.'

"On the contrary, it seemed that there was a back door, and Mr. Moscatiello used that back door. We readily recognized that we may have made an error in contacting Mr. Ford."

At almost this exact moment, Chris Moscatiello was making a panicked phone call to Joe Martier, saying Michael Murray's source in the federal courthouse wanted $150,000 to fill them in on a DEA investigation of their activities. Within days, Martier would be shutting down the lab at the Ocasek house in Falmouth, shifting everything to Richard Baker's place in Pembroke, and moving his wife to Pittsburgh. Martier himself would stay in Boston until November, when his probationary period expired. Moscatiello was out altogether.

The DEA's fentanyl conspiracy case shut down before it ever got started.

Boston, Autumn 1990

Jerry Graves got one more bite at the fentanyl apple before his investigation went completely cold. He'd obtained a mail cover on TX Green's box in Harvard Square.

When law enforcement arranges for mail covers with the U.S. Postal Inspection Service, the post office provides details about the mail received at the suspect location. The tool only furnishes information about the outside of letters and packages, any information that's in open view. A search warrant is normally required to open the mail and examine the contents, and Graves didn't have enough information for one of those.

But the mail cover paid off.

Graves learned that TX Green "had been ordering chemicals from various other chemical companies in the area, as well as glassware from a custom glassblower at the Massachusetts Institute of Technology. So this in turn leads us to strongly suspect that a clandestine laboratory is now being assembled somewhere."

The M.I.T. lead seemed promising: orders for large-capacity, custom-made items that would have raised eyebrows if purchased from established laboratory supply companies. Best of all, the orders included a name other than TX Green. "One of our leads took us to Joseph Martier, who we determined was an associate of Moscatiello and also TX Green," Graves said. Learning that "he was on his way to pick up glassware from MIT," the DEA set up a surveillance on the glassblower in Cambridge. "Martier showed up, accompanied by his wife with a baby carriage. They went to the glassblower, picked up their glassware, put it in the carriage, and then wheeled it through Cambridge, Massachusetts to their home.

"It was pretty simple, but it was just surreal. We said, 'What are these guys doing?' I mean, this is amateur hour."

Martier's involvement raised some questions. Graves quickly discovered that Martier had been convicted before for manufacturing drugs in his home state, Pennsylvania. What was he doing in Boston? How was he linked to Moscatiello?

The agents thought that though they hadn't found the lab yet, they might have found the chemist.

Then another piece of mail put Martier and Moscatiello together.

That piece came from the American Instrument Exchange, and a call there established that TX Green had purchased a high-volume rotary evaporator, one that had been specially ordered from the manufacturer in Switzerland. Graves asked the company to let him know when the equipment arrived, as both he and Fasanello thought this device provided an even better opportunity to locate the lab.

Fasanello said, "We decided to put two beacons in the rotary evaporator. One that would be on all the time so we could track where it went, and one that would turn on when it was connected to the electrical supply, so we (sic) know when it's being used."

With both beacons installed, they let the instrument company call TX Green's answering service/phone drop and say, "Okay, it's ready."

Moscatiello didn't bring his Range Rover this time, renting a truck, but DEA, relying on the transmitter and keeping a "loose tail," immediately lost sight of the vehicle and its bugged contents.

Unfortunately, the tracking device went dead and the second one, activated when the machine was plugged in, never turned on. "I heard later from one of the agents that they dumped the rotary evaporator in Boston Harbor," Fasanello said. "So, they made surveillance, and we lost them. And a couple of weeks later, I called for a status, and I was told that the case was closed. I was very surprised that it was."

In Boston, Graves took stock of his investigation. He was fairly sure that Martier and Moscatiello were at least participants, if not principals, in a scheme to manufacture fentanyl. Their front company made a series of suspicious purchases, behaving exactly like criminals up to no good. His two suspects had track records and criminal histories that added up to very reasonable suspicion.

It wasn't enough. Management closed the case, subject to re-opening if anything further developed.

There was one final nail. Nobody in Boston or anywhere else was seeing fentanyl on the street. No overdoses; no fentanyl in DEA seizures or undercover purchases. Moscatiello and Martier had burned DEA's surveillance at least once, and maybe twice. From all available evidence, it appeared to DEA management that even if there had been a lab, someone got spooked and shut it down before it ever put any fentanyl out into the market.

And that's where matters stood for the rest of 1990: the lid to Pandora's Box firmly in place.

Three months later, Tango & Cash blew the lid off with a bang heard from coast to coast.

* * *

Awash in Tango & Cash deaths, Jack Fasanello pointed the finger straight at TX Green—known to be Chris Moscatiello and Joseph Martier—and New York opened a case file on both of them.

Boston DEA admitted that Fasanello could be on the right track. Moscatiello, still living in Charlestown, was probably dirty. Graves said, "Drug money is big money, and these guys are greedy. Christopher Moscatiello, we believed, would continue his criminal activities. He was just going to wait it out a little bit, let things cool down, and reengage."

But at the moment, although he reopened the TX Green case, Graves couldn't see Moscatiello doing much of anything. "We kept tabs on him, periodic surveillance of him, in the hopes of finding their laboratory; who were they in contact with? What kind of communications?"

He also pointed out that there might be bunches of overdose deaths down in New York City, but nobody seemed to be dying of fentanyl in Boston.

In June, though, someone turned the fentanyl tap back on, and the DEA kicked its investigation into high gear. Fentanyl had returned and started racking up the body count again.

CHAPTER 46

Wichita, Summer-Fall, 1991

"I never saw anything like it in my entire career. Headquarters told me, 'Whatever you need, just ask.' Money, people, resources, whatever. Just pick up the phone. They said it was the highest priority investigation in the entire country." Barry Jamison, resident agent in charge of the DEA's Wichita, Kansas office in 1991 still shakes his head in wonder at his agency's "all hands on deck" approach to the fentanyl outbreak that began in June of that year. By the end of the month, DEA had open cases in New York City, Boston, Philadelphia, Los Angeles, and Pittsburgh.

Field offices fed fentanyl intelligence from around the country into New York, where Joanne Leoni became the nation's leading authority on bootleg fentanyl, and her partner, Jack Fasanello, the expert on the chemistry side. Their goal was always to find some clue that would lead to the lab.

The DEA used every available resource in its search. Conspirators must communicate, records from the telephones of anyone suspected in the case, including Martier and Moscatiello, went to Leoni in New York. None of it pointed directly at the lab, but as Leoni's files piled up, she kept looking.

When he wasn't analyzing fentanyl seizures, Fasanello focused on chemical and laboratory suppliers, and he had diversion investigators, the staff that monitored DEA's regulated industries, looking nationwide at chemical sales. Reports of suspicious purchases of the key fentanyl precursors—methyl acrylate, methyl methacrylate, and aniline—were all routed to Fasanello.

He didn't know that he was playing a game with someone who knew many of the DEA's potential tricks and had plans to deal with them. For example, Marquardt knew that the DEA could intercept an order for chemicals (like a barrel of benzene) and insert a tracer, an isotope like Carbon-14 that would filter through the manufacturing process and show up later in a batch of finished product. "Any simple solvent or precursor can be labeled. They'll hang an isotopic label on it and if it turns up as residuals in the finished product they'll say, 'Well look here. There's our little tag,'" Marquardt said.

Three devices could detect these labels: a mass spectrometer, an infrared spectrophotometer, and a nuclear magnetic resonance spectrometer. Using the money from fentanyl sales, Marquardt bought all three and installed them at PrairieLab. "Indeed, that was one of the reasons I had mass spectrometry around was to locate their tags."

He used his equipment to play another game with the outgoing fentanyl, subtly altering each batch, including his own tags or labels he knew the DEA lab would detect in its analyses. If they were trying to establish a signature or fingerprint for his product, (which Fasanello and his partner, chemist Charles Cusamano, were doing), he would give them a different finger for each load of fentanyl shipped. He had another goal for this ploy. "I wanted anybody looking to believe that the fentanyl was produced in multiple labs, not just mine."

Back in New York, Fasanello's monitoring of chemical purchases generated stacks of reports from all across America. Almost all of them were useless, unrelated to the Tango & Cash investigation, but there was gold in the growing stack of paper. It would take Fasanello almost two years to find it.

Marquardt also knew that the DEA would be zeroing in on certain purchases. With Bob Fearon, a very well-established chemical purchaser, he created a dummy or front company, Professional Engineering Associates, which operated from Fearon's Tulsa business. As "George Martin," he purchased his chemicals on Fearon's accounts. And because he knew someone like Fasanello was somewhere on his back trail, he spread those orders out all over the country. He also counted on Fearon to alert him if the DEA started asking questions about the "George Martin" end of his operation.

In New York, organizing all of this information, putting it together, weeding out the irrelevant dross and homing in on the hidden gold outgrew the three-person task force, Fasanello saying, "I would get printouts on a weekly basis, and we all waited for the printouts to come because that night we would have a meeting. Joanne would go over phone calls. Charles would talk about the analysis of the material, because he did a lot of the analysis after the original Tango and Cash, and I would check precursor purchases, and sometimes we were in the lab until 2:00 a.m."

Fasanello and his crew were already swamped and the more information that came in, the more he and Leoni thought the problem was bigger than anybody at the DEA realized. "It was a puzzle and it seemed to me we were close to solving it," he said. But part of the problem was that each field office only had a small part of a puzzle that was beginning to look like it reached from coast to coast. Nobody—Fasanello and Leoni included—could really see the whole picture.

"We started to see that it was mostly East Coast," Fasanello said. "There were a lot more deaths than we thought." Each time a medical examiner reported a fentanyl death, the DEA office in that city opened a case file; Baltimore, Newark, and Norfolk, Virginia joined in.

Fasanello decided to ask for help. "I had a friend, Tony Seneca, who was the head of the dangerous drug desk in Washington. I called him and said, "Tony, this is very important and nobody's looking into any of this stuff. So, he called a meeting of all agents involved in the fentanyl case and their supervisors."

Their presentation in New York brought in agents from across the country for the first time, unifying the effort and clarifying the fentanyl picture. "After that, we started to get a lot more information from all over, about more deaths and chemical orders," Fasanello said.

* * *

Barry Jamison and Wichita weren't yet a part of this effort in June 1991, because apart from the conspirators, nobody in America knew that the only fentanyl lab in the country was operating in a small house four miles from Jamison's office. By September 1991, Marquardt had that lab operating full-bore and over the next eighteen months he produced over four kilos of pure fentanyl—more than two million lethal doses—shipping almost all of it to Moscatiello in Boston.

Martier and Marquardt worked out a routine. In Wichita, Marquardt would finish a 500-gram batch. Using payphones, he contacted Martier in Pittsburgh, who came down to pick up the product and take it to Boston. Moscatiello would pay for the shipment in cash, which Martier took back to Pittsburgh, split, and sent Marquardt's share to Wichita. They started this routine with a 500-gram shipment in June, another in September, and six more followed through October 1992.

Before they got there, though, Moscatiello wanted to resolve some unfinished business back in Boston. There was the matter of their other lab, now inactive and stored at Richard Baker's house in Pembroke. And a barrel of black gunk.

* * *

Boston – Wichita, November 1991

Marquardt had told his partners that he thought he could get some 3-methylfentanyl out of that barrel.

"Do it, then," Moscatiello said, adding that he wanted it done there at the Pembroke lab. Surprisingly, Marquardt agreed.

Martier, who had been in Pembroke, "starting reactions, evaporating the solvent off of some reagents," headed down to Wichita to watch the Flora house while Marquardt was gone. He expected to be there a while; Marquardt thought it might take a few weeks. But suddenly, Marquardt showed up back at home, and let Martier know that he was "Really pissed off," which might have been putting it mildly.

Martier described the reason for the unexpected move. "He [Marquardt] was working in the lab one night and Baker and Moscatiello came out to get him and said they had to close the place down. Michael Murray had just been busted for marijuana in Texas."

Marquardt recalled receiving this unsettling news, saying, "Chris came in and said that the boss of bosses, some big-time gangster, had said they were hot, and now we had to close down the whole operation, and it was all my fault for not doing it sooner. And I told him to eat shit, and we had a lot of harsh words."

The news got worse. Marquardt, pressing Moscatiello hard, learned that Murray had used Baker's place to store three truckloads of marijuana, including a 2,000-pound load earlier in 1991, bringing it in a tractor-trailer truck that the DEA now held in a Texas impound lot.

Even worse, this was the same truck—the one with a secret compartment—and possibly the same driver (who turned out to be a DEA informant) that ferried a half-kilo of Marquardt's fentanyl from Pittsburgh to Boston only two months earlier.

Marquardt reacted in fury, but the instinct for self-preservation quickly kicked in. "I felt as if I was sitting in the electric chair wondering when someone was going to turn the current on."

He wasn't alone. "Chris was scared to death that he was going to be busted right now," Marquardt said.

So was Baker, and Marquardt, who knew from long and mostly painful experience how drug agents operated, figured (correctly) that Baker, and probably Moscatiello, would flip as soon as the DEA got around to them. Knowing the identity of the country's only fentanyl chemist and the location of the lab would be priceless information and anyone offering it would get a very good deal in the trade. It was time to go.

He left hastily, but didn't go emptyhanded. "I said, 'Well I won't escape from this thing with any money, but maybe I can escape with the pots and pans.' So, I loaded up all the glassware and the chemicals in my truck and set off across the country in my pick-up truck, a 10 liter (glass flask) and some other stuff riding with me in the cab. Out of Massachusetts, and drove across on the interstate, without incident, past many policemen, and a couple of traffic checks. And with the back of a pickup truck reeking of ethyl acrylate, which is kind of a hard smell to hide."

Unsurprisingly, Moscatiello didn't want the barrel of 3-methylfentanyl. Marquardt didn't want it either, but he also didn't want it there when the feds showed up. The barrel went into the back of the pickup, but everything he didn't want, "like anything with a serial number," he left behind. Baker buried some of it and took the rest, including the DEA's bugged rotary evaporator, and dumped it in the ocean.

Alone in the cab and safely away from the "hot" lab, Marquardt had some time for reflection. Although it's never cheering news to hear that someone in your conspiracy has just been arrested, Marquardt started to see some plusses in

Michael Murray's misfortune. First, he didn't know Murray, never met him, didn't want to, and wasn't threatened by this perfect stranger's new legal problems, especially since they involved marijuana in Texas and not fentanyl in Kansas. He wouldn't always be so sanguine about the potential danger from Murray, but for today, the threat seemed safely remote.

Second, the Pembroke lab had been extremely well equipped; he knew this since he'd been responsible for picking everything out and then spending other peoples' money (probably including Murray's) to buy it all. Now stocked with free equipment and chemicals that he could use for his own projects down in Kansas, he was happy to pack up as much of this windfall as he could carry and wave goodbye to New England forever.

Finally, having all of Martier and Moscatiello's former stuff in his lab down in Wichita meant he controlled production, giving him full control of the entire operation. He had never trusted Moscatiello or the shadowy, IRA-connected people behind him, believing that "the organized crime types had absolutely no intention of paying for the product" and might be planning to kill him after delivery.

"Chris had an evil little laugh, 'hee, hee, hee,' which you usually heard when he was talking about hurting somebody or pulling something that put him on top of someone else. Not an entirely pleasant person, and not someone who inspired a lot of trust."

Now in command, he "turned it into a pay-as-you-go situation, parceling the product out at about a pound at a time—no money, no product," he said.

If anybody wanted any more fentanyl—or anything else—from this point forward, they were going to have go through Erik Marquardt.

There's no place like home.

CHAPTER 47

McAllen, Texas, November 1991

Unlike Marquardt, Michael Murray saw almost nothing positive about his arrest on November 6, 1991 in McAllen, Texas. The DEA had jumped a little early, believing he'd already collected the thousands of pounds of marijuana he'd gone to the Texas border town to pick up, but that was all the good news.

The bad news was that they did find $1,149,650 "*hidden in a compartment in the tractor cab*" of the semi-truck Murray had planned on using to carry the marijuana back to Massachusetts. [Emphasis added]

Agents got another $100,000 from Michael's brother, James, which put Murray's smuggling operation at least temporarily out of business.

The indictment in the case, unsealed the following March, charged that between 1987 and November 1991, Murray headed a conspiracy to smuggle multiple truckloads with many tons of marijuana from Texas to Massachusetts. That indictment named six people, including Mike and James Murray, Richard Baker, Murray's two partners, and his Texas supplier—a top-to-bottom clean sweep.

Clearly, DEA Agent James O'Hara had a strong case, and he made it even stronger by squeezing underlings like, to roll over and testify against everybody else.

Murray could rely on his brother to keep his mouth shut. He had no illusions, however, about Roberto López,

Murray's truck driver, Baker, or those others in the conspiracy. They knew a lot and, facing long prison terms, would probably yield to the government's pressure sooner or later. Murray fully expected to go to prison over the deal.

The key question was, for how long?

When it came to sentencing in federal drug cases, the "good old days" of shorter terms and release on parole were gone. New laws had brought changes, and none of those worked to Murray's advantage. Now, he could expect to serve at least 85 percent of his sentence. And that sentence was likely to be somewhere between two and four decades long.

That raised another worrying issue. This wasn't Murray's first trip to federal court. A 1983 case with his older brother Joe cost him four years in federal prison (although under the old rules, he'd served much less).

In 1983, Joseph Murray was the biggest marijuana smuggler in Massachusetts, regularly bringing shiploads of weed from Colombia up the East Coast to New England. In early April 1983, Joe's ship had literally just come in with a 15-ton load of Colombian pot. Michael and Joe stashed it in a South Boston warehouse until it could be moved out of Boston by truck.

When Whitey Bulger learned that the Murrays were storing marijuana in "Southie" without notifying Bulger or paying their "tax," he called his FBI contact to report Murray's activity.

The feds already knew about Joe Murray, who had been under periodic DEA surveillance since the previous summer, so Bulger's information wasn't a surprise. On April 6, agents stopped and searched a green Dodge camper and a white Ford truck that had just driven away from the warehouse. They got bales of marijuana from both cars, and arrested the drivers, and then searched the warehouse, seizing over 30,000 pounds altogether.

Bulger's associate, Kevin Weeks, said later that he and Bulger had been sitting in a car down the street, watching the arrests, and that afterwards, Bulger "reached out and had someone bring Joe Murray in for a meeting. At the meeting, he fined Murray $90,000 for storing the marijuana in Southie and putting the heat on us."

Joe Murray hadn't been present when the arrests went down, but the agents snapped up five other men—including brother Michael—and charged them all with "possessing and conspiring to possess more than one thousand pounds of marijuana."

A July indictment added Joe Murray and he and Michael took their case to jury trial in January 1984. Although Joe was acquitted, Michael lost, receiving a four-year sentence. Now, almost eight years later, the 1983 case came back to haunt Michael Murray.

The DEA didn't know about Murray's links to the fentanyl scheme, but Murray's $150,000 source in the federal courthouse said the drug agents did know about Chris Moscatiello, recent purchaser of a barrel of benzene and proprietor of TX Green. And that was an even bigger problem for Murray, because in 1983, Moscatiello pled guilty to being the driver of the green camper full of Michael Murray's marijuana.

Moscatiello, who called Murray his "best friend," could be counted on to keep silent for a while, at least; he'd held up fine in the 1983 case, going to prison without talking. But Murray knew that if Moscatiello got busted in the fentanyl conspiracy with all its dead bodies, his friend would be facing the weight of those same decades in prison that now smoldered ominously in front of Murray. The pressure on Moscatiello to roll would be immense—and probably irresistible.

Throughout the conspiracy, Murray had deliberately held himself apart from Marquardt and Martier, keeping Moscatiello as a buffer between himself and strangers, going so far as to have Baker lock Martier in a shed when Murray came down to Pembroke to meet with Moscatiello.

Apart from Moscatiello, only chemist Bobby Rubino and Richard Baker could implicate Murray. Rubino was gone, but Baker was potential trouble; he was involved in both the marijuana and fentanyl operations, and the feds either already knew—or would soon find out—that Murray had stored marijuana from recent smuggling runs at Baker's place in Pembroke.

Unless something changed, Murray faced at least twenty years. For somebody who had just turned forty a few months earlier, this was a daunting prospect.

So, Mike Murray had a problem: one that wasn't going away, and promised to only get more acute as time went on and DEA rolled up more of his people.

For now, he pinned his slimming hopes on the Code of Silence…while he looked for a "Get Out of Jail Free" card.

CHAPTER 48

Belgrade Lakes, Maine, September 16, 1992

If Joe Murray had ever been a part of the fentanyl conspiracy, he checked out of it for good on September 16, 1992. Joseph Paul Murray, Jr. was 46 that year: he was from Charlestown—a townie, born and raised. He was the son of a Boston firefighter who'd brought up a family of four boys and three girls in Charlestown. Joseph and two of his brothers, Michael and James, had gravitated toward crime.

Joe, the oldest, climbed highest on the organized crime ladder in Charlestown, and did so with a surefire moneymaker. Beginning in the late 1970s, he'd made millions of dollars transporting tons of Colombian marijuana on oceangoing ships, offloading the cargoes onto smaller vessels offshore. It had been Joe Murray's marijuana in that South Boston warehouse in 1983, although Joe wasn't present when the DEA and the FBI arrived.

One of Murray's freighters, the 213-foot 1,300-ton British-registered *MV Ramsland*, had served as a mother ship until its seizure by the U.S. Coast Guard and Customs Service in November 1984. Customs found the *Ramsland* to be carrying more than 36 tons of marijuana concealed "in every nook and cranny" of the ship.

Customs had been tipped to the *Ramsland* by John McIntyre, a marine engineer who had previously crewed on other marijuana ships owned or controlled by Murray—including a fishing trawler, the *Valhalla*, which was even more notorious than the *Ramsland*, but not for a cargo of weed. When *Valhalla* had sailed from Gloucester in September 1984, she'd been carrying a million-dollar cargo of guns and ammunition, bound not for the Grand Banks, but for the coast of Ireland.

Valhalla's trip was the product of a year's work by the Irish Republican Army and a group of fervent supporters in Massachusetts that included Whitey Bulger and Joseph Murray. Murray is supposed to have spent a half million dollars of his own money, and Bulger and other IRA backers in Boston raised another half million to purchase the weapons. Murray also found a Gloucester trawler, renamed it *Valhalla,* and got one of his captains to agree to take it to Ireland.

Valhalla had sailed on September 14, 1984, and met the fishing boat *Marita Ann* two weeks later, shifting the weapons. Everything had been going exactly as planned... at which point it all fell apart. The Irish Coast Guard, which had been tipped by an informant inside the IRA, intercepted the *Marita Ann*, seized the guns, arrested the crewmen, and notified its American counterparts that the *Valhalla* was headed back to Boston, where the U.S. Coast Guard was waiting.

Indicted in 1986 for his role in the IRA arms smuggling case, and for the *Ramsland* marijuana, Murray was convicted with five others and sentenced in July 1987 to ten years. He went to prison without talking about Bulger or his partners in the *Valhalla* scheme.

But now he was thinking about it, trying to find a way out.

Murray's name came up in connection with the March 18, 1990, armed robbery of the Isabella Stewart Gardner Museum in Boston, in which two bandits made off with more than $500 million in art, including a Rembrandt and a Vermeer. The *Guinness Book of World Records* lists the Gardner heist as the greatest art robbery of all time and despite the issuance of a $10 million reward, the stolen paintings and other artwork have never been recovered.

Still serving his *Valhalla* sentence at the time, Murray wasn't a suspect in the actual robbery, but author and journalist Stephen Kurkjian speculated that "Paintings stolen like this are a 'Get Out of Jail Free' card.'"

Kurkjian theorized that criminals took the Gardner artwork in order to trade it later to get someone off a legal hook. If so, the priceless artwork—something everyone from the FBI to art lovers around the world desperately wanted to get back—would make the Gardner loot the biggest "Get Out of Jail Free" card in the history of American crime.

Joe Murray had played such a card before while in prison for the *Valhalla* case, contacting the FBI in 1988 to allege that Boston FBI agents John Connolly and John Newton were "selling information about electronic surveillance to Bulger and [associate Steve] Flemmi." The agents interviewing Murray said he was "willing to furnish information and wants nothing in return. The information he furnished now will help save the life of a friend or a loved one in the future."

Although one agent said Murray "would make a terrific informant," FBI did not follow up.

In Wichita, Marquardt didn't know any of this, and didn't hear about Joe Murray until much later. He'd heard about the IRA, though: he'd had these "Boston gangsters with Irish terrorist connections waved in my face, an unstated threat." In one conversation in Wichita, Moscatiello mentioned that one of his backers had sent a shipload of guns to Ireland, "Something that was supposed to scare me."

Chris Moscatiello and Joe Murray's brother Mike were seemingly fixed on getting a large batch of 3-methyfentanyl, and Marquardt wondered why. "It would make a decent terrorist weapon. The thought crossed my mind that perhaps these Irish revolutionaries wanted something lethal. I obviously didn't want any part of that. The heat would be beyond anything any criminal had ever seen," Marquardt said later.

* * *

He needn't have worried. Joe Murray took himself out of the picture permanently. After his release from prison in June 1990, he returned to Charlestown and resumed his criminal activities, reconnected with Bulger, and paid for protection on a much smaller scale.

He and his wife had some problems, however, and Suzanne Murray filed for a restraining order against him, moving with their three children to the family vacation home in Belgrade Lakes, Maine, intending to divorce Joe.

On September 16, 1992, Murray came to the house and confronted Suzanne. Their verbal altercation escalated when Murray armed himself with a fileting knife. Suzanne, however, had a .357 magnum revolver, and she emptied it, hitting Murray with five shots. Responding police found his body at the foot of the stairs, still clutching the knife.

After taking his knife to a gunfight in Maine, Joe Murray could no longer cash in the Gardner artwork card, if he ever had it.

Joe's brothers, Michael and James, however, faced decades in prison on marijuana charges. They needed such a card in the worst possible way.

In November 1992, Michael found one.

It was called 3-methylfentanyl.

CHAPTER 49

PrairieLab, Goddard, Kansas, August 13, 1992

"I knew the minute I saw him that we were going to be arrested," Marquardt said much later. "Didn't know when. It might be the next day or the next month, but sooner or later, it was inevitable."

On August 13, 1992, Joe Martier died in a toilet in Goddard, Kansas. It wasn't his first time dying and wouldn't be the last. He'd come to Goddard to pick up 300 grams of fentanyl for Benito Febre, helped Marquardt finish the batch, and then packed up the shipment to take to L.A.

"I found him in the bathroom of the facility. He had his dress shirt off, an undershirt on, one of his sleeves rolled up. He had his hand stuck in the toilet bowl, like he was either trying to shove something down or recover it. And he was sitting upright right next to the bowl, eyes wide open, nobody home.

"Well, this wouldn't do. So I hauled him out into the office, laid him down on the floor, and tried to bring him around. That wasn't working."

Marquardt said much later that he'd "thought seriously for a moment" about moving Martier somewhere else, to try and prevent the authorities from connecting the overdose victim to PrairieLab. But he finally decided, "I didn't think that he needed to die, but I knew this was going to be trouble either way." He called for an ambulance.

This wasn't Martier's first brush with that ultra-fine line between fentanyl's effective dose and its lethal one. He'd OD'd before back in Pittsburgh, and Marquardt had heard about that incident, one that had also involved fellow Lewisburg inmate Chris Jastrzebski.

"I understand they were sitting around in the living room, bored, and they thought, 'Let's do some dope.' So Joe went out to his private stash out in the garage, and they did some fentanyl. And Joe's little girl came into the living room to get some attention from her father, found him and his friend sitting there turning blue, and ran screaming to her mother.

"Mother came in, hid the dope in a flowerpot, and called the emergency medical people, who gave them some Narcan, and brought them around."

These two incidents were undoubtedly just the tip of the fentanyl iceberg, because in 1991 and 1992, American medical examiners weren't all looking for fentanyl in their overdose victims, so even the DEA's conservative estimate of 126 is certainly far too low. Jack Fasanello and Joanne Leoni recorded over 180 in New York City alone. At least 21 died in Pittsburgh, just in the month of August 1992.

That same month, Pittsburgher Joe Martier almost added his name to that list.

* * *

Back in Goddard, Marquardt met the ambulance crew and a couple of Goddard cops. "I didn't admit to knowing what was wrong with him, but suggested that they call his family. And they called his wife, and she was quite distraught: 'Oh my God, it's something like heroin. I don't know what it is. He did this before in my living room.' She volunteered that information. And the local policeman, Dyer, just turned from the phone and he said, 'Drug overdose.' And the EMTs brought in the Narcan."

As it would for thousands of overdose victims in 1991-1993, and for hundreds of thousands in our current fentanyl crisis, Narcan saved the day and the OD victim. "He was talking before he came out the door: 'Where am I? Where am I? Am I in Pittsburgh? What's wrong with me?' And he seemed to have no idea of where he was.

"It was much similar to that over in the hospital. He would alternate between fits of being perfectly reasonable and asking, 'Am I in Pittsburgh?' It seemed like his short-term memory was completely destroyed, or at least for the duration of the action of the drug. Interesting phenomenon."

Martier didn't remember much about the incident that would be so pivotal in the conspiracy, saying later, "I went into the back room, and I did, like, a whole list of dumb things. First of all, I was probably drinking about five beers. One of the first things I did was shut the vacuum off in the oven, and opened up and peeked inside, and I wanted to make sure it looked like enough to me; I didn't bother putting on proper equipment, no gloves or mask, and to make a long story short, I ended up overdosing on it. [Marquardt] told me that he found me with the filter paper in my hands, with it stuck on my hand in the toilet. It must have touched my eyes or hands or—I have no idea. I woke up in a hospital in Wichita."

Still seeing a lot of risk in the situation, Marquardt accompanied Martier to the St. Joseph's Medical Center's Emergency Department in Wichita, mainly to try and prevent him from blurting out any information about PrairieLab or its chemist. "About 4:00 in the morning, he'd finally become such a nuisance to me, I dumped him out at his motel and said, 'Call me up when you get yourself straightened around.' And went out to the lab and sat there and fumed.

"Finally, he calls me up about 5:00 in the morning and asks, 'Could you come over and talk to me, just as a friend?' And I says, 'Well, sure.' So I drove over there, and I talked to him. He asked me, sitting next to his bed, he said, 'What do you think's going to happen?' I said, 'I think we're going to get busted. If we make it through today, I think that this incident has generated enough information that it will be noted by the authorities, and they'll come for us.'"

Understandably, this news didn't cheer the still-recovering Martier. "He asks, 'Well, how long do you think we've got left?' And I said, 'If they don't get us today, I think we might last into the early months of the year.' Turned out we lasted to February 2nd or 3rd."

Marquardt told Martier the Febre deal was off. "I killed it," Marquardt said. "I didn't know what Joe did, but I was allowing him to go nowhere with any drugs at that point."

He wanted Martier out of Wichita, too. "I put him back on the plane in the morning."

The incident wasn't completely over. They still had a sizable quantity of fentanyl in Wichita, and another customer in Boston. Martier reached out to Moscatiello, making a routine but fateful telephone call, one that changed everything for everyone involved.

"The morning that he left Wichita on the airplane, the very morning of the drug overdose, Joe had gotten on the phone and explained to Chris Moscatiello what had happened, that we had some difficulties and he had overdosed in the lab on the product, and would Chris be willing to buy the product, and yes, Chris would," Marquardt said.

"By the time I got back to Pittsburgh, Moscatiello had sold whatever his inventory was, and he wanted four more, which was exactly how many Marquardt had, so we sold the next four to him," Martier said.

Marquardt drove up to Pittsburgh with the 500 grams of fentanyl he and Martier had been working on, and cut it to 800 grams, which Moscatiello anticipated would be the equivalent of four kilograms of heroin. Martier and Marquardt drove up to Boston, met Moscatiello at a restaurant, gave him the fentanyl in the parking lot, and received $40,000 in exchange.

They would do one final deal with Chris Moscatiello before the roof caved in on all of them, but there remained one other unresolved issue: 3-methylfentanyl.

CHAPTER 50

PrairieLab, Goddard, Kansas, early December 1992

"If I told them once, I told them fifty times, there is absolutely no safe way to cut this stuff, especially 3-methylfentanyl," Marquardt said.

And yet, for some reason he didn't understand, 3-methylfentanyl was what Chris Moscatiello wanted. Marquardt had promised that when he got back to Wichita after Michael Murray's 1991 arrest in Texas, he'd make a run at getting some 3-methylfentanyl out of the barrel from the Pembroke lab. That conversion, he predicted, would be harder than making it from scratch, and so it proved.

He'd made sample batches several times already, giving them to Martier for Moscatiello and getting positive reviews. Although he ultimately produced, "not more than 100 grams of 3-methylfentanyl, because of the difficult stereochemistry," he'd succeeded in creating a process that enabled him to manufacture the drug "in unlimited amounts. I could fill a dump truck with the stuff if I wanted to," he said.

But he didn't want to. He never saw 3-methylfentanyl as a solid—or safe—revenue source, no matter how much easier it was to make. "No, if you've got 3-methylfentanyl, man, that's a barrel of snakes. I didn't want to deal with the cutting, because there was too much bulk involved. And the down-the-line-dealers simply couldn't handle it."

3-methylfentanyl was a killer.

Moscatiello still wanted it, so as Marquardt hit his stride on fentanyl production, working through 1992 and getting multiple batches out for both Moscatiello and Febre (and getting paid for them), he also continued to work on 3-methylfentanyl. "Trying to solve the isomer problem."

Isomers are compounds—like 3-methylfentanyl—that have identical chemical formulas but a different arrangement of those atoms within the molecule. Isomers may have drastically different pharmaceutical effects. Dextro or d-methamphetamine, for example, an optical isomer of methamphetamine, is the active ingredient that attracts people to "meth" or "speed." The Levo or l-methamphetamine isomer has none of those properties and is sold over the counter in Vicks Inhalers.

3-methylfentanyl has stereoisomers, of which the cis arrangement is by far the most potent, 6,600 times the power of morphine. The trans isomer is still strong, about four times the strength of fentanyl, but Moscatiello and his backers wanted the cis version, which Marquardt noted was, "A full order of magnitude bump up from fentanyl, and in theory, a more desirable product."

Getting there, especially as he would be working from the "barrel of black gunk," was very challenging chemistry. "By the time you get done resolving the isomers, and fractional crystallization, you take a God-awful beating in the yield. So, you've done a lot of serious chemistry, a lot of complicated stereochemistry for precious little product."

In words non-chemists can appreciate, he faced a trade-off between a little bit of something that was extraordinarily powerful and more of something only marginally different from fentanyl itself. Both of them still took a lot of time and effort to produce, time he would rather spend on his increasingly reliable moneymaker, fentanyl.

He wasn't sure why his customers wanted the cis version, but he knew which one he preferred to make. Having already overdosed himself once just on accidental exposure to 3-methylfentanyl, he greatly favored the much less potent, less lethal version.

"Bulk 3-methylfentanyl was going to be a problem. You could see that right off. You might be able to dilute small quantities of it, but to prepare a large amount of it, and then to dilute it… you'll kill yourselves and half the people downstream."

He had the ability to dilute even cis-3-methylfentanyl, but he knew with certainty that Moscatiello no longer did. "It could be done somewhat safely using a rotary evaporator," which he had at PrairieLab. "But Chris dumped his rotary evaporator into Boston Harbor." And he doubted that Moscatiello's customers could cut the drug into anything like a semi-safe form. He even suspected that they might not want to.

"In that form and in a large quantity it's only really useful as a chemical weapon," Marquardt said, and he wondered again whether Moscatiello's Irish Republican Army backers might have other plans for 3-methylfentanyl.

He would find out later that they did.

* * *

Marquardt finished the batch of 3-methylfentanyl for Chris Moscatiello. He diluted the thirty grams of slightly reddish-brown powder with 220 grams of sugar giving Martier a quarter-kilo of "very crude 3-methylfentanyl. I didn't have any intention of purifying this stuff. They would have to find out how to do this themselves if indeed they wanted to. I had the means to purify it, but they did not have the means or the desire to pay me."

But it was 3-methylfentanyl, and Martier headed for Massachusetts with enough of it to kill 600,000 people or about every man, woman, and child in the city of Boston.

Moscatiello did want to dilute it, Marquardt telling him since they no longer had a rotary evaporator, he needed to buy a ball mill, purchasing one "at a place in Fall River, Mass, paid some outrageous price and milled the product down in the process of which Chris overdosed, I guess," Marquardt said.

Moscatiello recovered and succeeded in cutting the drug with almost fifteen kilograms or thirty-seven pounds of filler. "I never was aware of that. I just gave the junk 3-methylfentanyl to Martier, told him he and Chris could do what they wanted with it, and they diluted it. They decided that figure arbitrarily and made up this 30-pound dilution in the ball mill. And I don't even know what they diluted it with. I assume the mannitol that they obtained from New York. They had quite a lot of it around."

Although it was still highly lethal, neither the quality nor the level of dilution mattered, because none of this stuff would ever hit America's streets.

It was all going straight into the official custody of the Drug Enforcement Administration.

CHAPTER 51

Boston, November 1992

It took him a whole year, but in November 1992, Michael Murray finally hit on a possible solution to his dilemma. He didn't have the stolen Isabella Stewart Gardner artwork (which probably means his brother Joe never had it either), but he thought he had something the DEA might want just as badly. So, in the language of the Charlestown townies, Murray "turned rat."

He did this without telling his own attorney in the marijuana case. Instead, he reached out directly to the DEA case agent, James O'Hara, offering to provide information in exchange for leniency for himself and his brother, James.

DEA Agent Jerry Graves remembered the initial negotiations in which Murray angled for the best possible deal while giving up the least amount of information. "Michael Murray gives us nothing that is helpful because he was reluctant to cooperate to begin with, until he realized how strong of a case we had. And when he saw how tight the case that Agent O'Hara had made, he said that he would cooperate."

Murray didn't show his fentanyl hole card right away. "The agreement he signed said he will cooperate fully in *all* investigations. But Michael Murray at an initial briefing was coy," Graves said, especially after he mentioned fentanyl.

This isn't unusual; informants frequently minimize their own roles or involvement in the criminal activity they're describing. "A cooperating source will speak ad nauseum (sic) about anyone and anything, as long as *he's* not explicitly implicated. He's just a totally innocent guy who happens to have all this inside criminal information that he's happy to share with the government. But no, he was never directly involved," Graves said.

Another retired agent agreed. "An informant never tells you everything; they always tell you just as much as *they* think you need to know. The agent's job is to get him to tell you all the stuff he's leaving out."

"We understood exactly what his motivation was. Michael Murray's agreement hinged upon his full cooperation—a good report card, so to speak—to the prosecuting attorney's office at federal court, which would lessen his sentence in jail," Graves said.

Talking about his marijuana case didn't give Murray much leverage. O'Hara didn't need him for that; he already had everybody in the organization locked in tightly. O'Hara pushed Murray—the top man in that organization—harder by telling him, "You got to roll up. I don't care what your buddy down the street is doing. You got to roll up and give us something bigger."

"And that was when it came together, when Michael Murray says, 'Hey guys, I think I can help you with the fentanyl case,'" Graves remembered. "Murray finally said to him, 'Okay, Christopher Moscatiello is the guy financing this.'"

O'Hara didn't know Moscatiello. He wrote the unfamiliar name down and took it to Graves, who told him, "Yes, exactly right." Now sure they were on the right track, they listened as Murray told them that "Christopher Moscatiello is involved in the fentanyl laboratory and is the guy that's providing the money for the lab." Murray also said that the lab had been in Massachusetts, but the operators had moved it out of the state.

This information matched what Graves suspected in his investigation of TX Green. With Murray sounding more credible every minute, Graves and O'Hara were ready to move to the next phase of their investigation.

"The informant's job is to give you the information," an agent said. "The agent confirms or corroborates it. You *never* just take their word for it. Especially not a career criminal like Murray or Marquardt."

Graves questioned whether Murray was being completely forthcoming. "I suspected that perhaps Michael Murray was downplaying his involvement in any other criminal activity. I always wondered whether or not he might have been part of the financing with Christopher Moscatiello with regard to the laboratory, and whether he was benefiting financially from that."

But Murray brought the DEA closer to the lab than it had been for the past two years. Getting even closer meant exploiting Murray's connection to Moscatiello. "He had to be an active participant in the case," Graves said. "We had to send him in to speak to Christopher Moscatiello."

Again, the DEA wasn't going to take Murray at his word about these meetings; he'd have to wear a wire—a recording device—to document the conversation.

A DEA tech agent constructed a "specially made jacket for him in which we had microphones sewed into the collars," Graves said.

In a series of meetings between the two friends, the DEA listened as Moscatiello talked about problems with the laboratory. "We learned, for example, that they're having product problems with getting the chemicals, quality control, that they're still trying to increase production. They're not having good success with mixing it. They have issues," Graves said.

" But they don't seem to be concerned about the drug killing people."

The DEA wanted these recorded conversations between Moscatiello and the wired-up Murray to lead to the next phase of the investigation. "We wanted Murray to introduce an undercover agent to Moscatiello to help with his distribution problems," Graves said.

An opportunity to do this came when Moscatiello broached a new topic in the meetings, a question about Quaalude tablets. Marquardt and Keith Hollenbeak had been interested in methaqualone, with Hollenbeak making a sample batch of powder in his Halliburton lab in Oklahoma. Selling the methaqualone as counterfeit Quaalude meant converting the powder into tablet form. It was a process that required a tableting machine or "pill press," plus the punches and dies that counterfeited the Quaalude tablet.

Nobody in the conspiracy had access to such equipment, and the DEA regulates the "distribution, importation, or exportation of tableting machine or encapsulating machines," so acquiring one posed the same problems as key precursor chemicals.

The DEA agents, however, saw an opening. Their undercover agent could offer "to help their chemist in the manufacturing of these pills," which Graves hoped would get closer to locating the laboratory."

Graves and O'Hara even had a rough idea about the lab's location. "We knew that Moscatiello was making phone calls to payphones along Highway 54 leading into Wichita, Kansas. This led us to conclude that the laboratory was probably in Wichita somewhere."

They needed more than that. Wichita had over a half million people in the metropolitan area, but the agents were hopeful that Moscatiello would narrow it down for them, either in a recorded conversation with Murray or with the undercover agent Murray introduced.

In the meantime, Murray gave Moscatiello a phone number of someone he said had some expertise in tablet manufacturing and access to a pill press and told him to have his chemist call with any questions. The number was Jerry Graves' undercover line.

Hoping the unknown Kansas chemist would call, Graves instead "received a call from Joseph Martier. He was in Pittsburgh, and we talked about chemical processes; what their needs were. They wanted to make pills, a very popular pill called Quaalude."

"Martier made a couple of references to a third person, saying, 'The chemist, yeah, he needs more of this, always asking me for that. Needs more chemicals. It's hard to get the chemicals, and we're thinking of kind of slowing down. We can make more money with pills.'"

"I told him that I could provide him with a pill press, but what do you want to do with it? Do you know how to handle it? Do you know what you're doing? And it was clear to me, as we got deeper in this conversation, that he was *not* the chemist. His basic knowledge was lacking. So I offered him several possibilities. I said, 'I can get you a pill press. Ideally you can send me some of your product and I can make the pills for you, and I'll take a percentage of the pills,' or, 'I can go down and meet you at your laboratory with the pill press, and we could set up business together.'"

Graves tried to leave Martier with the impression that he was "associated with a New York crime organization. I gave him a postal box in New York City that I would use for undercover purposes to receive packages and asked him to ship me some of the raw powder so that I can analyze it and see what the problems were with it."

This effort to reach the chemist had failed. Graves knew Martier wasn't the man and said, "This was definitely beyond his particular field of expertise. Martier, his ignorance was incredible on it."

The agents turned back to Moscatiello, who had a fentanyl problem. Maybe the agents could help him out, Mike Murray said, finally playing his "Get Out of Jail Free" card.

* * *

The subject came up in one of the many meetings between Murray and Moscatiello, which were all recorded by Murray's wired jacket.

Graves recalled that, "Moscatiello said that they have about fifteen kilos of product already made, and they're having distribution problems." With fentanyl headlines on the national news, "They're afraid of bringing too much heat on themselves because of the deaths."

Murray said he knew where Moscatiello kept the drugs, telling O'Hara that if he wanted to get this fentanyl and take it off the street, he could find it at a storage unit outside Boston. Jerry Graves remembered the call. He was attending a conference in New York: another meeting of the fentanyl groups from different DEA offices.

"I receive a call from Jim O'Hara basically saying, 'Jerry, we have the fifteen kilos here.' And I notified the conference members, and as I am in New York, I go to Jack Fasanello and I said, 'Hop in my car. We'll go up to Boston.' We worked that night. Fasanello verifies quickly that it looks like fentanyl. And now we have to transport it down to the New York lab."

Jack Fasanello remembered the night he took charge of the biggest fentanyl seizure in DEA history. By the time he and Graves got there, the agents had moved it from the storage unit to the Boston office. "There's a large green garbage can, plastic. I didn't open it at the time. One of the agents had, and said, 'It's full of gallon bags of off-white powder.' We put it in a large trash bag and took it down to the parking lot, where we put it in a U-Haul and started back to New York."

They were taking no chances with this shipment. Nobody wanted to drive over 200 miles with the package on the seat next to them, or even in their car. So they rented a trailer, hitched it up behind a government car, and with a

DEA car in front and another following behind, the convoy set out for New York City.

Fasanello used the drive time to prepare. "On the way back, I called Charles [Cusamano] at the lab, and he was waiting with the mass spectrometer warmed up, ready to analyze it. I take the trash can into my lab with an agent and a powered air purifying (sic) respirator. I opened the garbage can and there are double gallon sized (sic) baggies, Ziploc baggies. And I read on the top of one in pen, '3-MF.' So I say, 'Jerry, it's almost like this guy is saying, 'It's 3-methylfentanyl.' And Jerry says, 'Oh, yeah, he said something like that.' And I said, 'Shit. That calls for a whole 'nother level of protection. In order for me to be exposed to this, I should be in a spacesuit.'"

The mass spec quickly gave an answer. "It was 3-methylfentanyl. I never got the percentage of it, but I could tell you this. When I saw that, I said, 'You know, Jerry, you could finance a war with this amount of stuff.' Because don't forget: Michael Hovey had three ounces of it and that was equivalent, he said, to 188 pounds of pure heroin. That's a lot of heroin."

With the 3-methylfentanyl safely in the lab's hands and back in Boston, Graves and O'Hara set up another meeting between Murray and Moscatiello. This one completely changed the direction of the DEA's case.

The agents instructed Murray to challenge his friend over the call from Martier to Jerry Graves. Murray did exactly that. "He says, 'Who the hell was the guy that the New York wise-guy was speaking with? These New York guys are upset. They don't know what you're doing. They want to know if I'm setting them up.'"

The recorder caught an off-balance Moscatiello trying to placate his friend. He talked about the problems in the "operations of the laboratory in Kansas and then said, 'Well, the actual chemist is a guy named Squeak.' And that is the first time we hear the name Squeak."

The DEA's Narcotics and Dangerous Drugs Information System (NADDIS) contains information from all of the DEA's investigations and intelligence activity: millions of names, addresses, businesses, phone numbers, airplanes, and vessels. And aliases or nicknames.

Graves checked NADDIS, looking for people called Squeak. He got a hit right away: a man arrested in January 1978 by the Oklahoma Bureau of Narcotics for running a clandestine methamphetamine laboratory in Beggs, Oklahoma.

To find out if he had the right Squeak, Graves called OBN, and quickly connected with an agent who told him that Squeak was the most sophisticated clandestine chemist OBN had ever encountered, and perfectly capable of doing the chemistry necessary to produce fentanyl, or anything else for that matter.

"If Squeak is your man, you've got big, big problems," the agent warned. Knowing how dangerous he was, OBN tried to keep tabs on him. At present, they thought he was operating outside Oklahoma, but not too far outside, because OBN agents and chemists saw him occasionally at oilfield auctions where he was buying equipment.

Wichita, only fifty miles from the Oklahoma state line, would be a perfect fit.

After hundreds of fentanyl deaths, dozens of false leads, immense frustration, and two full years of looking, the DEA finally had the name of the man behind fentanyl.

He was George Erik Marquardt.

CHAPTER 52

Boston, December 1992

Chris Moscatiello bragged a little about fentanyl to his new friend, stretching things slightly, and Rico was paying close attention. "I had told him that I was concerned that the stuff that he was giving me was very strong. That's when he opened up. He said, 'My cook, my chemist, we had an incident in the lab... One of his workers was overdosed with the stuff.' And I said 'Wow, really?'" Rico was impressed.

DEA Special Agent German Blanco had a unique background. "I was born in Colombia, and I grew up in the City of Medellín, pretty much when Pablo Escobar came to power with the Medellín Cartel. I grew up in one of the poorest neighborhoods in Medellín, the barrio San Javier, the *colonia*, which is the neighborhood where you saw a lot of the drug activity that Pablo Escobar was basically associated with."

Unlike many of his peers from the neighborhood who were seduced by Escobar's money and power, joining the cartel boss in his "*officina*," Blanco developed "a strong feeling of hate towards the cartels because of the way they carry themselves, that they could just do anything and get away with anything, and they were above and beyond the law."

And unlike his peers in barrio San Javier, Blanco was able to escape, joining his mother in New York in 1976. After school and "all different kinds of odd work in New York

City," a marriage and two children, Blanco was recruited at a job fair by the DEA which was looking for people with a Colombian background.

Assigned to the New York City office, the DEA's largest, he was working on Colombian cocaine cartels like Escobar's when he got a call from another office for an undercover job. Boston needed some help with a fentanyl case.

"I heard through the news, that there was an emergency going on in the city because a lot of the heroin users were dying almost instantly from the use of this new heroin that was being introduced into the market. With this new drug, the fentanyl, people were dropping like flies."

At the DEA's Boston office, Blanco met the case agents for the investigation, Jerry Graves and Jim O'Hara. This was a major case, Graves told him, and they had an informant who was close to the subject, Christopher Moscatiello. The informant, "Mike," would introduce Blanco as a Colombian trafficker from New York who wanted to buy fentanyl.

One of Moscatiello's associates was a chemist who was running a clandestine lab. Who was this person, and where was the lab? Blanco's "most important key objective" was to answer those questions.

On December 8, O'Hara's informant, Michael Murray, set up a meeting with Moscatiello at a bar in downtown Boston. After introducing Blanco as "Rico," Murray left, and Blanco, who had been told that Moscatiello had mob connections, was surprised that he seemed like a "regular guy, a yuppie." He wasn't flashy or especially menacing. "I didn't see any gold necklaces or any gold bracelets or any rings on his fingers." Blanco relaxed a little, even though Moscatiello took him to a second restaurant, something traffickers do to try to detect surveillance and sometimes, to rob or kill their customers.

Their conversation went very smoothly, Moscatiello "lighting up" when Blanco told him he was from Colombia and had connections in New York City to sell heroin or cocaine. This drug wasn't exactly either, Moscatiello said, but it had heroin-like effects. Blanco balked, saying he didn't know whether his customers would want it and asked for a sample he could take back to New York to test.

"And he says, 'How would you test it out?'"

Blanco told him, "I have somebody that can just give it to basically an addict and let him shoot it up and see how the addict likes it. If the addict likes it and comes back for more, that means that it's a good product and I'll definitely sell it."

Not missing a beat, Moscatiello handed it over, a small packet wrapped in aluminum foil. Blanco said he'd be in touch once he heard back from his test subject, the two exchanging beeper numbers.

The sample consisted of three grams of whitish powder, and Jack Fasanello, DEA's semi-official fentanyl chemist in New York confirmed that they had a winner, "100 percent fentanyl," Blanco said.

Convinced that Murray had connected the DEA with one of the key players in the fentanyl ring, Graves and O'Hara slowed the case down, giving "Rico" time to have the fentanyl tested out on his addict customers.

About a week later, Graves had Blanco reach out to Moscatiello. Blanco told him, "Listen, everything looks good, so let me come up to Boston on this day, and then I'll let you know when we get there so we can meet."

"And he said, 'Okay. Not a problem.'"

On December 15, they met again at the same bar, moving as before to a nearby restaurant. Moscatiello carried a mailing tube, leaning it against the bar while the two men talked. Blanco said he was concerned because the fentanyl "is very strong, very potent. So how do I deal with this? And then that's when he pretty much said that I needed to cut it down more because of the purity was very strong… that if I was going to sell it and that I needed to add a different agent to it."

Moscatiello recommended cutting the fentanyl "three or four times" and they discussed payment, Blanco, offering to exchange "kilograms of cocaine," for the fentanyl. "He said they were having problems selling the fentanyl because of its strength and he thought he could sell the cocaine more easily in Boston."

Then, speaking of fentanyl's potency, Moscatiello "opened up," telling Blanco about an incident in the lab.

"And I said, 'Where was this?' And he mentioned, 'Wichita.'"

DEA Special Agent German Blanco was delighted to hear this, but Rico Rodriguez, the cocaine and heroin dealer from New York, now sitting with his new friend, didn't react at all. "After all, what do I care about somebody who's overdosed? Millions of people are overdosing, so it's not my problem," Rico would say. But Blanco said, "Inside of me, I just wanted to jump up and down with joy because he just told me the city, and I just basically just wanted to get up and hug him and give him a strong heart for giving up that information. But of course, I just ignore, this doesn't mean anything to me."

They talked some more about heroin and cocaine and a pill press for making Quaalude tablets. Moscatiello also asked whether Blanco might be interested in buying some guns, saying he had "connections with the Irish people, and I didn't know what he meant by the Irish people, but later on I think that he was meaning the Irish Republican Army.

"He was saying, 'Listen, if you help me out with getting me a pill press, I can help you out with getting guns.' Kind of like you wash my hand, I wash your hand."

Finally, Moscatiello told Blanco to take the mailing tube, which contained a pound of fentanyl that could be cut to be the equivalent of ten pounds of pure heroin, Blanco promising to be in touch about payment.

Back at the DEA office, Blanco, "decided to play a little game" with Jerry Graves.

"We went back to the office, the group was there, and he goes, 'What happened?'

"'Nothing. Here's the tube, there's the fentanyl. What else do you need me to do?' He said, we were going to meet again because obviously I've got to 'pay him.'"

"And I waited a couple minutes and they just started to process the evidence or whatever. And I said, 'Oh, by the way, I forgot to tell you something. He did mention that one of the guys – a lab assistant – overdosed in Wichita.' And when I said 'Wichita,' there was silence in the group. Everybody was like, 'Huh?' And nobody said anything for a couple seconds.

"And then somebody said, 'What did you just say?' I said, 'Yeah, that somebody overdosed in the lab in Wichita. That's exactly what he said.'"

They still had that third meeting planned, but now hot on the trail of the lab in Wichita and following Graves' lead to the chemist called "Squeak," DEA put this meeting off, first to January and then into February. In their telephone discussions, Moscatiello agreed to take payment for the December 15th transaction in cocaine, as much as fifty kilos, depending on how much more fentanyl he received from the lab.

It was finally set for early February, timed to coincide with Wichita's bust of the lab. Blanco had his airline ticket and was set to go when he received a call from Boston.

The Moscatiello end of the deal was dead. Very, very dead.

CHAPTER 53

Goddard, Kansas, November 1992 – January 1993

Jerry Graves thought he had everything he needed to find the elusive fentanyl lab and its even more elusive operator, the mysterious "Squeak." Now, he and Jim O'Hara headed down to Wichita to let the DEA office there know that they had a problem in their backyard.

Almost two years after people began dying in New York and Graves started looking at TX Green in Boston, he thought they might be in the home stretch of the race to stop fentanyl...

But when he got to Wichita, they didn't believe him.

Fentanyl didn't come as a complete surprise to Wichita's Resident Agent in Charge, Barry Jamison; he'd been getting inquiries from back East for a while. "Initially, it was just [requests for] background information; telephone numbers, addresses," Jamison said. He had sent the information back to New York and Boston, none of it connecting to anyone Jamison or the task force agents knew.

With only 310,000 people in 1993, Wichita wasn't a huge city, and the agents, all locals, knew their territory. They weren't seizing any fentanyl, weren't buying any undercover, and most significantly, nobody knew about any fentanyl overdoses. "We weren't seeing any fentanyl on the streets at the time," Jamison said. So, he was skeptical.

Despite Jamison's doubts, Graves was confident he'd come to the right place. "Barry Jamison told us, 'I don't know what the heck you guys are doing here, but there is no drug laboratory in Wichita.'

"And I said, 'Well, we definitely could find the laboratory. Give me 45 minutes and we'll find it.'"

That's about how long it took.

Jamison assigned Troy Derby to help. "I worked with Troy and the local police officers, because I knew it was just a question of making a few phone calls to emergency services. We knew the approximate date, we knew it was recent, and we got all the drug calls from the emergency services as to where they responded to overdoses. And we were able to find PrairieLab in Goddard, Kansas," Graves said. Even better, the ambulance service and the Goddard police identified the overdose victim; he was Joseph Martier. A very happy Graves thought this cemented the link between Boston and Moscatiello and Wichita and Marquardt.

News of the lab did surprise the formerly skeptical Jamison. "My entire time in Wichita, I don't think we ever had a case in Goddard. It's kind of a sleepy little town just west of Wichita. I hate to say, I don't think a whole lot goes on there."

Graves wanted to have a look. "Agent Derby, O'Hara, and I checked out the address, looked it over. It was a bittersweet moment, I have to say, for myself. And then I called up my office to speak to the Assistant Special Agent in Charge and basically said, 'Yes, we have the laboratory, or a laboratory, but the bad news is that it was not operational.'"

The place didn't look deserted, although no one was inside. "We were able to peek through the windows and see the laboratory equipment. And we saw the waste left behind around the building that indicated that it was being used for drug manufacture," Graves said.

They also saw two large pieces of electronic equipment in the driveway. Graves contacted Jack Fasanello who told him both could be used to manufacture fentanyl. And there was a laboratory-type ventilation system, but it seemed clear that nobody was manufacturing fentanyl on the premises at that moment and maybe for a while before that. Bittersweet.

Jamison opened an investigation, assigning Derby as case agent. Troy Derby had been an agent for two years, assigned to the Wichita office after leaving DEA's academy. He'd been a Wichita police officer, working patrol and as a narcotics detective assigned to DEA task force for nine years before that. He'd attended DEA's training for clandestine laboratory investigators. This wasn't his first experience with underground chemistry.

First, he needed to answer two key questions. If the fentanyl manufacturing operation wasn't at PrairieLab, where was it? And where was George Marquardt?

Since he only knew about one location, Derby started a surveillance on PrairieLab and ran all the usual checks on their prime suspect. Marquardt hadn't made it easy for the agents. He had no driver's license, no vehicles registered to him, and no phones in his name. PrairieLab itself had been rented by a Phillip Sam Houston, so Derby assigned people to watch Houston's house on Larimer Street in Wichita.

Jamison said, "Once we identified the lab, we threw just about every resource we had at it, whether it was electronic surveillance, putting agents watching it around the clock. We were able to identify some of the records associated with that business. We started looking at those individuals. It really started opening up."

Derby's surveillance at PrairieLab paid off the next day, the agents seeing Marquardt and his battered pickup for the first time. Graves remembered the first time he saw the shadowy character he'd been chasing for two years. Marquardt left the lab and drove to a nearby convenience store. "It was a 7-Eleven that he came out of wearing his overalls, his flannel shirt, and he had his Pittsburgh Steelers knit cap on, I guess he was a big fan of Pittsburgh Steelers."

Marquardt led the agents to Flora Street and more agents were assigned to watch the house there, only 150 yards from a Wichita police sub-station.

Now, Derby had Marquardt's residence, and it, too, had possibilities as a lab site. Kimberly Tietsort rented the house and also paid the utilities, and Oklahoma identified her as Marquardt's stepdaughter. The Postal Service said that nobody named Marquardt received mail there, but "George Martin," a Marquardt alias, did.

Agents also followed Marquardt and Houston to two storage units nearby, both rented by Tietsort's boyfriend, Kevin Donovan, watching them move equipment from PrairieLab to the two units.

To get around town, Marquardt drove an older model pickup registered to Keith Hollenbeak, a chemist at the Halliburton Company lab in Duncan, Oklahoma. Telephone records, a key DEA tool in conspiracy cases, showed calls between the phone at PrairieLab—billed to Houston—and Hollenbeak.

Jamison had his entire office assigned to the case. "The investigations back east had been going on for a long, long time. They had a lot invested. It was a national priority. From the moment we identified the lab there, our real role was to coordinate everything with all the other offices. Making sure that everyone was aware of everything we did, trying to figure out exactly who was involved, because now we were focusing in on the lab, while all the investigations back East continued."

Jerry Graves headed back to Boston before Derby's investigation got underway, but he went satisfied that "We finally identified who we believed to be the chemist in the fentanyl case." Based on his conversations with the OBN agents who knew Marquardt very well, Graves was confident that whenever Marquardt "was confronted and arrested, he would cooperate" with the DEA.

He still needed to answer some important questions. How was the organization linked to New York, where most of the overdose deaths were happening? Who were the fentanyl distributors? How was Martier involved?

One other question bothered the agents. These people had been at this for two years, an operation that had generated at least hundreds of thousands of dollars in profits and maybe a lot more. Where was that money? It didn't look to Jerry Graves or Troy Derby like Marquardt, in his overalls and flannel shirt, his beat-up truck and tiny rented house, had it.

It puzzled Barry Jamison, too. "If George was making a lot of money off manufacturing fentanyl, it certainly didn't show."

Everybody figured that sooner or later as the investigation went on, the money question and all the others would be answered. The agents all thought they had some time.

They were wrong.

CHAPTER 54

Wichita, February 3, 1993

In the end, it was the wind that decided.

The DEA had been looking for the fentanyl lab and its clandestine operator for over two years, and late in 1992, they had finally found it. Two unlikely words—"Wichita" and "Squeak"—had suddenly focused the agency's entire attention on the investigation that was its highest national priority.

By this time, the DEA had open case files in Boston, New York City, Philadelphia, Pittsburgh, Los Angeles and, most recently, Wichita. In each office, management followed progress and any new developments closely. The regional laboratories in New York and Chicago were both involved.

Now everything came down to timing: fixing the sequence that would lead to arrests, search warrants, and hopefully seizures. Here the going got a little harder.

Three offices had good arguments for doing things their way and on their schedule. Boston had Michael Murray, the informant who had provided the link to Moscatiello and the key lead that had broken the case open. Boston also had undercover agent German Blanco, who was in direct contact with Moscatiello and in the middle of negotiations for more fentanyl.

Boston had another important concern. When Murray agreed to cooperate with the DEA, he'd committed to giving up five million dollars' worth of bearer bonds...the proceeds of the Joe and Mike Murray marijuana operation… plus any other assets that Murray had acquired from selling marijuana. That agreement also said he had to disclose everything he knew about other crimes and criminals in Boston. This included Winter Hill kingpin Whitey Bulger, and the "reputed head of organized crime in Charlestown," Robert "Bobby" Smith.

With open cases against both men, O'Hara and Graves thought Murray was stalling. They wanted time to push him harder. They knew that busting Moscatiello would undoubtedly "burn" Murray, outing him as an informant, and scaring off anyone else—especially Bulger and Smith—Murray might contact. Boston voted to wait a little longer.

Pittsburgh had Joe Martier, the middleman between the lab in Wichita and the distributors in Boston and New York. Pittsburgh agents Alex Schiraj and Frank Schmotzer knew Martier from his previous PCP case and felt very confident that they could turn him no matter when they arrested him.

Martier faced decades in prison. Literally and geographically in the middle, he seemed positioned to have the most information about the whole picture—plus a strong incentive to share it with Schiraj. Pittsburgh was neutral on the timing.

Wichita had Marquardt and the labs. Derby had drawn up search warrants for the Marquardt and Houston's houses, PrairieLab, and Marquardt's storage unit. He was ready to go, and Wichita voted for going as soon as possible.

That left a 1-1 tie.

"There are always going to be conflicts in these cases," a DEA agent said. "DEA is one agency, but there are dozens of offices all over the country, and whenever there's an investigation that involves more than one office there are going to be disagreements about how to run or close out the case."

That was especially true this time; people were dying, and fentanyl had been in national headlines for two years.

Stopping it was urgently important and stopping it would undoubtedly generate many more national headlines.

DEA agents call these investigations "career cases," because being the case agent on one could make your entire career. That worked for those above the agent: a career case could boost supervisors and special agents in charge, too.

"There can be a lot of politics in these situations," a retired agent said. "Every SAC would want the lead, would want the case run where he's got control. There can be squabbles."

Tensions now crept into those formerly relaxed meetings between the fentanyl case agents and chemists in New York where everybody had pulled together and shared intelligence over coffee, donuts, and slide presentations. Now they included group supervisors, RACs, and SACs—people with turf to protect and careers to promote, and a very shiny brass ring in sight.

In Wichita, Derby's boss, Barry Jamison, and Jamison's boss, Assistant Special Agent in Charge for the Kansas City district, and the ASAC's boss, the SAC for the Saint Louis Division, joined Derby on the calls. Graves and O'Hara in Boston had Carlo Boccia, the SAC for the New England Division, on the line, and the same was true for Pittsburgh and the other offices.

The key issue for all concerned, aside from who would be running things, was to set a time for the takedown: a delicate and sensitive decision that required the weighing of several factors.

"You always want the best evidence, and that's catching the lab in operation, hopefully with completed product on hand," an agent explained. "You also want to have tabs on all the key players. Don't want to start arrests when somebody important is out of the country or just in the wind."

And everybody wanted as airtight a case as possible. That becomes critical in an investigation like this because watching your career case implode due to your screwup, or just bad luck, will also affect your future career, and not in a good way.

"You can be the agent who got Pablo Escobar. Everybody in DEA will know you for that. You *don't* want to be the agent who blew the case on Pablo Escobar. Everybody in DEA will know that, too," an agent said. Losing this case in court later because of some mistake or lack of evidence would be worse than never busting them at all. "So there's a lot riding on it." And the stakes were even higher with fentanyl.

Barry Jamison had another worry. He and his small office had come into the case very late; Boston had been working it for two years when Marquardt and PrairieLab unexpectedly dropped into Jamison's lap. He had total confidence in Troy Derby and his task force agents, but was concerned that, "We could jeopardize not only the lab and its location there in Wichita, but we could adversely affect all the cases, and all the investments they had made back on the East Coast, and all the other offices that had been working on this for a long, long time."

If Marquardt, who everybody said was a very experienced criminal and familiar with how law enforcement worked, somehow burned Derby's surveillance now going around the clock at PrairieLab, the case could fall apart and Wichita—and Jamison and Derby—would be blamed.

The longer things went on, the better the chances that something would go wrong. Jamison wanted to move as quickly as possible, before Marquardt got spooked.

Too late: Marquardt had already been spooked.

* * *

"We were about to get busted," Erik said. He'd received a strange phone call from an old friend, "my tripwire down in Tulsa, Bob Fearon."

Fearon's cryptic message said, "He'd had a very interesting encounter, and I must know about it immediately." Marquardt called back and Fearon said, "Oh, it was nothing."

This didn't reassure Marquardt. "It didn't make any difference. I believed him the first time. I thought we were busted."

It wasn't Wichita's fault. Troy Derby had installed a pen register on the phone at PrairieLab and saw that on January 8, someone at that number placed three calls to the Eastman Kodak Company, a chemical supplier in Rochester, New York. The caller pressed the number 1 after being connected, which Derby found out was the procedure for placing an order. Earlier, on December 29th someone had made a similar call. Up until now, nobody knew of any deliveries to PrairieLab or to Marquardt or Houston's homes. Where had these orders gone?

The DEA subpoenaed Eastman Kodak, attached a list of fentanyl precursors, and asked if the company had sold any of these recently. Kodak said they'd made four sales for a total of 15 kilos of methyl acrylate and 6 kilos of phenethylamine to either a "Bob" or "George Martin" of Professional Engineering Associates in Tulsa.

The telephone number Kodak had for George Martin came back to Robert Fearon, and Derby found ten more calls between PrairieLab and Fearon. Running Fearon's number through NADDIS, Derby found a record that in 1985, someone named "Erik" had made two suspicious chemical purchases from Fearon's business.

He asked the Tulsa office to check it out.

An agent visited Fearon's complex and spoke to the manager, who said Fearon and Electro Chemical Discoveries was now operating as Professional Engineering Associates. A FedEx driver confirmed that he'd delivered packages to Fearon for Professional Engineering.

The inquiries caused some confusion back in New York. Jack Fasanello said, "Phone calls were going to a place in Oklahoma. We were trying to fit what was going on at this place, why that many calls were made to this company. So now we started looking for chemicals going there.

"Finally, we get a printout, and it's late at night. Charles and Joanne asked me, 'Well, anything going to Professional Engineering?'

"And I say, 'No. In Oklahoma, the only person ordering stuff is a Chinese professor.'

"And they said, 'What's his name?'

"And I says, 'Professor Eng.' And they said, 'Professor Eng is Professional Engineering abbreviated.'"

Phone calls from their suspected chemist and fentanyl precursors both going to the same place tightened up their case. With that cleared up, Fasanello told Derby that the methyl acrylate and phenethylamine ordered would be enough to make between five and ten kilos of fentanyl. PrairieLab was the pot of gold at the end of the long, dark fentanyl rainbow.

* * *

At PrairieLab, Marquardt sat next to the mass spectrometer, smoking his pipe and debating his options with himself. He'd known this day was coming. He'd even prepared for it by purchasing land, concealing the ownership, and arranging for it to remain secure in case he went off to prison for a while.

He'd bought a lot of equipment, more analytical instruments, and enough glassware and chemicals to put himself back on his feet and in a well-equipped lab the day after the government cut him loose. All of it was stored on his secret property.

Setting all this up had been difficult and expensive, consuming most of his fentanyl profits. He said, "It probably would have been easier and cheaper to build an atomic bomb," but he felt good about his "Little House on the Prairie," saying, "At this point, there isn't one hell of a lot anyone can do to steal it from me. Though I wouldn't want anyone to know where it is, or how I got it. I was never foolish enough to take my co-defendants (or anyone) there."

Erik's old dream of living out his life under prairie skies, leaving chemistry and physics and the old Squeak behind forever wasn't happening.

"Becoming a fugitive didn't appeal to me much. That's a short and kind of paranoid and unhappy life unless you have huge amounts of money and could afford to lay low. Otherwise you have to involve your friends, and that puts them in a real difficult position. I could go stay with friends of mine in Europe, for instance. Well, eventually, I would be tracked down, and they would get in a great deal of trouble with their home governments, too. So we don't do that."

This left him with two stark choices. Staying put probably meant a long stretch in prison, which didn't hold many fears; he'd been there before. That didn't mean he wanted to go back. Or, hoping he had some time, he could try to shut down the lab and get rid of anything related to fentanyl, methaqualone, or any other controlled drug. "Sit back and wait and tell the arriving policemen, 'Fentanyl? Never heard of it.'"

In the cloud of fragrant pipe smoke, the mass spectrometer hummed and his dog, Polly, slept in a corner. "No, at that point, we're too far into it. The train, if you will, has picked up far too much speed. And you're not going to leap off of it."

* * *

Another meeting, this one a conference call with all of the management people pushing their preferred choice on timing. Boston's Carlo Boccia argued for more time, others saying the plug needed to be pulled sooner rather than later.

Nobody knew where Marquardt was in his manufacturing process. Derby's surveillance of PrairieLab didn't show that kind of activity, mostly because Marquardt had just finished a batch, so not much was happening in Goddard or at the house.

They should wait until they were more confident they'd find fentanyl on the premises, someone argued, and this is always the DEA's default position. "Catch him 'holding'" had been the narcotic agent's mantra for ninety years.

Barry Jamison recalled the moment everything changed. "I remember that conference call, I distinctly remember it, where we were talking about waiting and trying to coordinate until they were manufacturing the fentanyl. And Jack Fasanello weighed in, saying this drug was so potent that if just the fumes got in the wind or the airstream…it could cause death or serious harm to people.

"And I remember asking him, what do you mean, 'if it gets in the airstream?'

"And Jack says, 'This stuff can blow and…'

"I remember interrupting and saying, 'Jack, this is Kansas. The wind blows every single day in Kansas. There's never a day the wind doesn't blow in Kansas.'

"And Jack says, 'Well, that could be a huge, huge concern.'

"And then, I interjected again and said, 'Jack, just a couple hundred feet away is a daycare center.'

"And when I said that, to this day, I still remember the silence. Just dead silence. Despite having 6, 7, 8, 9 offices on the conference call, nobody said a word for five or six seconds. It seemed like half an hour. But everything changed."

Fasanello outlined the various scenarios: all bad. "Hazardous chemicals, possible explosion, vapors, and actually the drug itself that's being manufactured."

Generally, laboratories using or producing hazardous chemicals utilize a fume hood. Unless the hood has a scrubber at the end of it, it just vents outside the building. "If the winds go in the wrong way, these could blow into the window of the school. I said we should get on this before there's an accident," Fasanello said.

Jamison said, "Once Jack said that stuff about these fumes in the airstream, suddenly we could no longer wait for them to manufacture the fentanyl. We had to move before they started doing that.

"I hate to say it, we had undercover agents, we had cooperating witnesses, we had sources, we had all kinds of intelligence. Every resource we had, we were throwing at this investigation, and suddenly, it came down to a daycare center just a couple hundred feet away. Not only in Wichita, but in all the offices back east, everyone's priorities changed because of that daycare center."

With everybody signed onto the now-expedited plan, Jamison hung up with another wry observation. "We'd been having some back and forth about who was in charge of the case, who'd be making the decisions. Boston's SAC was pretty insistent on calling the shots.

"But I noticed after the daycare center came up, everybody was perfectly fine with letting Wichita run things. Seems nobody wanted the responsibility if a bunch of kids got killed. So I got it."

In the end, it was the wind that decided.

CHAPTER 55

Wichita, Kansas, February 3, 1993, 9:00 a.m.

With the decision made to take down PrairieLab as soon as possible, every DEA office involved in the case turned to making it happen. This meant arrests, seizures, the execution of search warrants, a highly choreographed, tightly managed, and often exquisitely timed event in the case.

That's because the "takedown" is potentially *the* pivotal moment in any investigation and even more so in major cases like this one. The takedown may make a case, generating evidence that locks in the people agents already know about and opening doors onto new players. Searches and arrests generate leads to more locations and more potential defendants. It's important to get this right.

Coordinating this activity across three states and two time zones, synchronizing all the action with four DEA field offices and two laboratories fell to the smallest office, Wichita, where Jamison and his task force had at least four locations to search, two people to arrest, and not nearly enough agents to do it all.

The DEA sent help. "We figured out what day we were going to hit the lab, and days before that, we had people coming from St. Louis and Kansas City and New York and Boston. Heaven only knows how many other offices, because everything was going to hitchhike off what we did," Jamison said.

He had his own people too, task force agents from the Kansas Bureau of Investigation, Wichita PD, and the Sedgewick County Sheriff, all familiar with the territory. "There was a lot riding on what we were doing in Wichita, so we had an awful lot of people involved. You're obviously dealing with some toxic chemicals, toxic locations. We didn't know exactly what we were getting into, so we had to proceed cautiously," Jamison said.

That caution included bringing agents trained for the seizure of clandestine drug labs and several forensic chemists from the Chicago laboratory and Jack Fasanello from New York. With him was Detective Joanne Leoni, the two of them on Tango & Cash from the beginning and in Wichita for the end.

Jerry Graves and Jim O'Hara split up for this visit; Graves going to Kansas and O'Hara managing Boston's takedown of Moscatiello.

Supported by information from Boston, Pittsburgh, and New York, Troy Derby prepared an affidavit that described the DEA's case against Marquardt, Martier, and Moscatiello, identifying the key locations, the places where he hoped to find evidence. There was PrairieLab, of course, and Marquardt's house on Flora Street. He also thought he had probable cause for Sam Houston's house and a pair of units in a mini-storage facility nearby.

On February 2, U.S. Magistrate John Wooley agreed, signing off on the four warrants.

As this was going on in Wichita, Alex Schiraj was doing the same thing in Pittsburgh, getting warrants for Martier's house and a storage unit nearby. Still confident that Martier would roll over after his arrest, he planned to arrest him and execute the search warrants after Wichita arrested Marquardt and Houston.

"One of the main things you want to know before the takedown is everybody's location. Are they at home? Are they at the lab? Are they somewhere you can find them?" a retired agent said. "It's not always possible, but you don't want to have somebody out of sight where he might be able to warn other players, flee, or hide evidence."

In Boston, O'Hara didn't know Moscatiello's whereabouts, but the DEA had a locator beacon on his Range Rover, which was parked near the townhouse in Charlestown, so that would be where O'Hara and his team would start their search.

In Wichita, Jamison had people on Marquardt's house, at PrairieLab, and on Houston's house. Jerry Graves, who had been helping coordinate all the input from other offices all day on February 2nd, drew a stakeout assignment. "I did surveillance from midnight to 8:00 a.m. on Philip Houston's home," Graves said. On the morning of the 3rd, already up for 24 hours and not assigned to one of the raid teams, he headed for the DEA office when a team arrived with the search warrant.

The raid teams had started early, too. "We all gathered together very early that morning, I think three o'clock in the morning," Jamison said. The briefings took several hours, Derby making team assignments and parceling out the chemists and clan lab to locations where he thought their expertise would be needed, which today, was all of them.

"We had teams at a lot of different locations. Each team operated independently. Once we started moving forward with all of our search warrants, offices back on the East Coast began their operations," Jamison said.

A little before nine, Marquardt left his house, driving in his battered pickup truck through Wichita toward Houston's place. Derby decided to stop him before he got there, and four DEA cars surrounded him on the edge of North Riverside Park, about a half-block from Houston's home.

"I looked out the window and saw a whole lot of policemen out there. And I knew it wasn't going to be a very good day," Marquardt said.

On the morning of February 3, 1993, surrounded by cars full of narcotic agents, Marquardt stepped into the street, waiting patiently for the first agent to reach him. "Well, this doesn't look good," he said to Barry Jamison.

"What took you fellows so long?"

CHAPTER 56

Wichita, Kansas, February 3, 1993, 9:30 a.m.

Jamison and Derby didn't arrest Marquardt right away, although they definitely detained him. Jamison explained. "The first thing we had to do with George was to read him his rights, because George kept saying, 'I'm going to plead guilty.' And 'you got me. I knew you guys were going to catch up with me sooner or later.'"

They couldn't shut him up, and didn't want to, so they stood and talked at the side of Marquardt's pickup for thirty minutes before finally bundling him into a DEA car.

Marquardt's detention had been the signal to start at the other locations, but the teams held off while Marquardt told Derby what he could expect at each place, what hazards they might face, where the evidence could be found.

Deciding to take him home so he could show as well as tell, they headed back to Flora Street, Marquardt telling Jamison, "'Look, I told every one of these guys, there's no way we're ever going to get away with this. They're going to catch us, and we're going to go to jail for a long time. I told them that over and over and over.'

"And he told *us* that over and over and over," Jamison said.

The team at Flora waited for Marquardt to arrive, then the agents entered and secured the house, followed by the chemist Jack Fasanello, who got his first look at Marquardt.

"He was already in the kitchen and I went in and assisted with questioning him."

Fasanello described him as "a heavyset fellow, kind of happy. He wanted to know what took us so long to get him and he didn't seem to worry about anything."

Very pleased to meet fellow chemist Fasanello, a helpful Marquardt directed him to the bedroom where he would find "two infrared spectra of product that had been manufactured at the lab."

"An infrared spectrum is kind of a fingerprint of a molecule and it's a standard way to identify compounds," Fasanello explained. "Each is unique to that drug, and his infrared spectra matched our standard of fentanyl hydrochloride."

In this surreal scene, one that none of the DEA people had ever seen before, a clandestine chemist openly bragged about his illegal activity, providing exactly the same printed documentation of his guilt that DEA chemists like Fasanello would bring to the chemist's trial.

"He wanted me to have the spectra to show me how lousy the 'gangster stuff,' what he called it, was compared to how pure his product was," Fasanello said. "And I was impressed with the quality of the fentanyl that was in the product. It was very good fentanyl, maybe 95 percent. The material that came out of the chemical process was very, very good."

It was beginning to dawn on everybody that Erik Marquardt was completely different from anyone they'd ever encountered before. But now they were off to PrairieLab… where things would get even more eye-opening.

* * *

In Goddard, the team secured the premises, which were unoccupied.

Fasanello said, "It was loaded with chemical equipment. There was so much stuff there that I walked in and said, 'Oh my God, we're going to be here for a week.'"

And again, Marquardt had plenty to say about what had been his lifelong dream, proudly showing off his instruments to the bemused crowd. He had the machine he'd used to create the two spectra prints he'd given to Fasanello. "Some very sophisticated equipment. There was an NMR – Nuclear Magnetic Resonance instrument and an infrared spectrophotometer he used to analyze the drugs that were being produced. The analytical equipment was as sophisticated as the equipment in our lab in DEA and the synthesis apparatus was larger than our stuff," Fasanello said, still marveling a little forty years later.

And of course, there was the VG-70-70, Marquardt emphasizing that he'd bought the mass spectrometer in non-working condition and had made it fully functional all by himself.

Trying to get an idea about the size and scope of the operation, and its capabilities, the chemists took stock of the lab's contents. "The synthetic equipment that he had was essentially pilot plant size. Which means large batch, whereas my equipment was laboratory size, like 500 milliliters or a liter. His was five or ten liters," Fasanello said.

It wasn't the largest clandestine lab Fasanello had ever seen; he'd been in one in Boston so big he could stand on one of the stirring devices. This one had by far the most sophisticated equipment for analyzing the lab's output, though. Nobody at the DEA had ever seen a clan lab with even a fraction of the electronic gear Marquardt had assembled. The thought of a meth cook or a biker lab with a functioning mass spectrometer was so outlandish that no one had ever even considered it.

Much of Marquardt's equipment wasn't strictly necessary. "He could have made the fentanyl—or anything else—with a much more basic setup," an agent said. "But he just loved doing the chemistry."

"He had a lot of pride in what he made. And I think if he wasn't rushed, he possibly could have done a much better job. He gave me a piece of glassware called a falling film distillation apparatus, which is a very sophisticated piece of equipment. And he had just purchased it and it was brand new and it was wonderful to watch," Fasanello said.

Those devices sell today for $35,000 to $140,000 and more. Marquardt spent over $10,000 for his, using it on the black "motor oil" retrieved from the Massachusetts lab. "The operation to purify 3-methylfentanyl without a falling film distillation turned out to be a horrible mess. The [precursor] would not readily crystallize initially, and you had to do a falling film distillation to obtain that pure crystal. Otherwise, you were stuck with a red gummy mess."

Sometime later, standing and happily talking shop with Fasanello and chemist Sandy Angelo from the DEA's Chicago lab, Marquardt was pleased to hear that Fasanello had tried to make fentanyl under the conditions a clandestine chemist would experience, and more pleased when Angelo said, "Yeah, and he couldn't get anything but red gum, trying to make fentanyl."

Marquardt, very familiar with the red gum that had led to his accidental discovery of a shortcut of the Janssen process, told the DEA men how to get past this apparent dead end. "They described Jack's series of failures and that's when I brought up, I said, 'Well, the trick is this falling film distillation.' And you need to get some of that equipment that's laying around here."

With agents and chemists starting the tedious process of gathering up the evidence at PrairieLab, Fasanello and his group went to the storage units back in Wichita. One contained more chemicals and equipment, all of the materials Marquardt used at the Flora Street house and stored in these units when, as it was that morning, the Flora lab wasn't running. The other stored the chemical waste from the lab.

Fasanello said, "We were there for two days, and then I went back to New York, and I think the Chicago chemists worked another couple of days on it. There was so much stuff."

They found plenty of evidence of fentanyl manufacturing at both locations. This included precursors and reaction byproducts, and numerous empty precursor and chemical containers, but no fentanyl at PrairieLab and only a small quantity of "intermediate and final (crude) product/fentanyl (less than 250ml) at the house." The DEA agents asked Marquardt about the finished product, and he said he would be glad to tell them where they could find some. They should start at Philip Houston's house, where they would find a package containing three videocassettes, with 150 grams of fentanyl concealed in the middle cassette. That package, Marquardt said, was his latest batch, ready for shipping to Joseph Martier's Los Angeles connection, Benny Febre.

The agents at Houston's house found a place absolutely crammed with stuff of every kind and description, from telescopes to space rocks. When Fasanello got there, he saw that Houston, "had an observatory on the roof and wonderful antiques. Antique binocular cards that you look through and see 3D, but they were antiques and he had thousands of them."

The videocassettes, exactly as Marquardt described them, were right where he said they'd be. The agents arrested Sam Houston.

* * *

Wichita, Kansas, February 3, 1993, 4:07 p.m.

While the search teams worked on Houston's house, agents took Marquardt to the DEA office in Wichita, where the investigation would continue. Jerry Graves had been manning the telephones, communicating with Pittsburgh and Boston and keeping the other offices up to date on the activity in Wichita.

"Fielding inquiries from the other officers around the country; what's the status of the case? Is the laboratory secured? There was a lot of higher up DEA interest in the investigation. There were a lot of balls in the air, so to speak."

Graves met the man he'd been chasing for two years in DEA's holding cell, a task force agent telling him, "'Here's George.'

"They brought him in, he was in his overalls, it reeked of chemicals. And I immediately had them strip him of all of his clothes, secure those clothes, put him in what's known as a Tyvek suit, which is a chemical resistant (sic) suit, and my first question was about whether he had been advised of his rights by the task force officers earlier."

Marquardt said he had been saying, "'I'll cooperate, and I'll do whatever you want to do.' I said, 'Well then you know why you're here.' He said, 'I've actually been waiting for you guys. I'm guilty, I'm going to plead guilty tomorrow.'"

With the formalities out of the way, Graves turned the conversation away from Marquardt, asking about other people involved in the conspiracy. Marquardt immediately identified Joe Martier and described his role, saying the 150 grams of fentanyl at Houston's house was supposed to be mailed to Martier's friend, a distributor in Los Angeles called "Benny."

But before Graves could get any further into the interview, he was shunted aside. "The Wichita office agents would handle any further investigation, which is DEA protocol. They didn't want to be put in a situation where an agent from another region would have to be flown in all the time to testify in a local case," Graves said. He went back to coordinating with Boston, where O'Hara was dealing with a problem with Chris Moscatiello.

The team that would be working with Marquardt from this point forward consisted of Troy Derby and a task force agent coincidentally named Sam Houston. They also included Joanne Leoni, the fentanyl expert from New York. This group began the tedious process of extracting every bit of information as possible from Marquardt, now their "cooperating source," or CS. They began with his partners in the operation, asking whether Marquardt would be willing to call Martier and discuss this shipment while the DEA recorded the call.

"No problem," Marquardt said.

In a series of recorded calls to Martier at his residence and then to a supposedly more secure Pittsburgh payphone, Marquardt got an address in the Los Angeles area to send the package, along with statements from Martier implicating him in previous shipments.

After the final call, Alex Schiraj and other agents arrested Martier, moving on to execute search warrants at his house and business. The following day, Martier said, his attorney told him that "Marquardt had set me up the whole previous day, that all the conversations were taped and there was absolutely no way that we could go to trial with this." Martier rolled, following his now-former partner's path to cooperation with the government, just as Alex Schiraj had predicted.

Back in Wichita, the DEA explored possible avenues with others Marquardt identified as participants in the scheme. Sam Houston wasn't talking at the moment, but Marquardt had plenty to say about him.

He also implicated Keith Hollenbeak, and Troy Derby and DEA agents from Oklahoma would go down to Duncan and arrest Hollenbeak in Halliburton Company's lab. But on the evening of February 3rd, as things wound down, Derby put Marquardt, still not technically under arrest, into a local motel for the night, agents outside for everyone's security.

Jerry Graves, who had been up for over thirty-six hours and busy for most of them, went back to his own hotel room and passed out on the bed, half-in and half-out of his Tyvek suit. "And that was the end of the Wichita adventure," he said.

The adventure was over in Boston, too.

CHAPTER 57

10 Blueberry Lane, Wilmington, Massachusetts, February 3, 1993, 9:30 a.m.

The footprints led through the snow straight to the body… the last of the fentanyl deaths that had begun with the lonely passing of Angel Luis Morciglio on Brook Avenue in the Bronx, two years and two days before.

The DEA said the fentanyl conspiracy left dozens, even hundreds of bodies strewn in its toxic path that stretched from 1991 to 1993…fatal overdoses in cities from Boston to Norfolk, Virginia and as far away as Los Angeles.

With fentanyl, there's always room for one more. On the morning of February 3, 1993, a contractor's crew, straggling into work on Blueberry Lane in Wilmington, Massachusetts came to their construction site to find a man's body.

Wilmington Police Detective Mark Jepson, who responded to the scene, said, "It's all residential up there. All the houses, they were being built at the time this guy was murdered. It was just a road. All the infrastructure was there, but there were no homes yet. He was taking a leak, and someone shot him in the back over the edge into somewhere below. It was a couple of feet down, over far enough so we couldn't see him from the road."

Christopher Moscatiello was dead at age 40. He'd been murdered, killed "execution style" by someone he trusted. Someone who stood behind him in the sub-freezing darkness of a February night. A friend, perhaps…a partner…a co-conspirator…but a betrayer for sure.

"According to the state troopers at the scene, he was found shot twice in the back, and then three closeup shots to the back of his head, effectively killing him," Jerry Graves said.

Moscatiello's body was only a short distance away from a car he'd rented in Boston the afternoon before: the last time Chris had been seen alive.

The detectives had many questions, and no easy answers. Who was this person? What was he doing in this isolated, lonely area eighteen miles north of his Charlestown home in the middle of the night? Who was with him in the car? Was he meeting someone?

There were footprints in the snow from another man in Saucony sneakers. Where had this man gone, and how did he go? Who was the booze in the rental's backseat for? And the really big questions: Who wanted this man dead bad enough to shoot him five times "gangland style"…and, of course, why?

As they worked the crime scene, the detectives started with their victim, trying to get to know Chris Moscatiello. He had a record; they found that out right away…a previous arrest for armed assault and possession of cocaine in Weston, Massachusetts in December 1987.

That incident had begun with a party, then turned into a hostage drama with a barricaded suspect "waving a gun," pointing it at his own head, and threatening three others in the house. It had ended when the hostage-taker, a thoroughly intoxicated Moscatiello, passed out. This had allowed two of the partygoers/hostages to flee, the last one taking the gun and giving it to the state police SWAT team outside.

Guns and drugs, the detectives thought, were not exactly a rare combination in a murder victim.

His rap sheet also showed an arrest and conviction in federal court on marijuana charges in 1983-4, and time in federal prison. That case linked him decisively to organized crime in Boston, to Joe Murray's crew in Charlestown.

Those kinds of connections also piqued the curiosity of homicide investigators, who understood that random coincidences do exist, just not so often in murder cases.

As they would learn when they dispatched someone to notify Moscatiello's next of kin that morning, this wasn't the only coincidence that might not be so coincidental.

The officers arriving at the townhouse on Monument Square were surprised to find more cops already on the scene as DEA agents executed a search warrant on the house and tried to locate the owner so they could arrest him. Well, that wasn't happening, the state police detectives said, because Moscatiello was lying in a snowbank in Wilmington, as dead as the DEA's case against him.

Soon afterward, Moscatiello's wife drove up to find a crowd of police on her doorstep. "I went to work that morning and didn't hear anything from him at all, and I said to my boss, who was actually my dad, 'You know, I'm kind of worried that that maybe Chris fell off the wagon,' so I went home. As soon as I parked the car in front of my house, I was surrounded by all kinds of agents. And I remember going in the house. I didn't know what was going on. I mean, I wasn't really part of that world and never had been, and I just remember sitting down on a settee in the foyer of the house, and they told me that Chris was dead."

The news broke Maryann Moscatiello. She'd told people that Chris was "the love of her life," and now he was gone. "I don't think they gave me any details. I ultimately called my dad. He came to get me, found me outside on the sidewalk in my bare feet. I mean, I was in shock at that point, and he took me home. I was in shock for months. I mean, I didn't eat. I lived with my parents. Didn't shower. Yeah. It was incredibly traumatic."

The DEA agents at the scene, now hoping they could answer some of the homicide detectives' questions along with some of their own, went forward with their search. They had explanations for the alcohol found in the rental car: Maryann told them Chris had stopped drinking, "been sober for years." She was very surprised to hear he had anything alcoholic in the car. She and the agents thought the booze had been for someone else, someone he was meeting in the sub-freezing weather up in Wilmington that night.

Jerry Graves thought he could explain why Moscatiello hadn't taken one of his own cars, the BMW or the Range Rover, to Wilmington that night. "One of the things that always intrigued us is that Moscatiello was found dead driving a rental car. He somehow knew that the DEA had put a tracking device on his car, and we were electronically tracking him. We don't know where that information came from, but Moscatiello ended up meeting someone."

The DEA had a couple of candidates for the leak. One of the agents executing the search warrant at Moscatiello's house "located a floorboard that they pulled up and pulled out $10,000 of cash with the business card of a lawyer named Frederick Ford," Jerry Graves remembered. "Ford was [Moscatiello, Joe and Michael Murray's] former parole officer at the federal courthouse who had become an attorney and was now practicing law in Massachusetts."

The agents strongly suspected that Ford had tipped Moscatiello to the DEA surveillance two years before, and although he had left the federal probation office, Ford continued to have shady underworld associates.

The best candidate was someone who knew with absolute certainty that DEA had Moscatiello under surveillance. He also knew that the DEA planned to arrest Moscatiello in the fentanyl conspiracy case very soon, possibly that day or the next.

That person was Chris Moscatiello's "best friend" and the DEA's informant in the case, Michael Murray.

* * *

"Michael Murray is—was—Chris's best friend, and I'm pretty sure Michael killed him."

Cynthia Moscatiello, Chris' sister, seemed very confident on that point. She'd never met Murray before Chris died or heard about him from Chris and Maryann. She met Murray for the first time the day after the murder.

"When Chris died and Maryann called my parents, they called me. My husband and I drove up with our young daughter. I went into Boston the next day to meet Maryann at the funeral home.

"I got there before Maryann, and I walked in and there were two men sitting in the room, and I didn't know who they were. One was the funeral home director, and the other one was Michael Murray. And I looked at the funeral home director, and then I looked at Michael, and I had this overwhelming sense that that man had killed my brother. And I didn't even know who he was. And then I found all this out later, and I thought, *huh, all right, little psychic stuff going on there*. I was sure he'd killed him."

Cynthia met with the police investigating the homicide, DEA agents, and the Assistant U.S. Attorney handling Murray's marijuana conspiracy case. She learned that others shared her belief. "They couldn't prove the case against Michael because they just didn't have any evidence. They all think he did it. The cops I've talked to and the federal prosecutor, George Vien, they all think he did it. But him personally, or did he hire someone to do it?"

What really bothered her was motive. Why would someone so close to Chris turn on him in such a drastic way? She knew Chris' criminal history; knew he'd done time, and done it in a drug case that also involved Murray. What in their past together had brought these two friends and fellow townies to this fatal junction?

Cynthia also knew the darker corners of Chris' earlier life because they'd lived in those places together—both of them trapped in a family situation and a childhood she described as "awful, just awful."

Chris and Cynthia were both raised 25 miles north in a comfortable home in Wenham, Massachusetts. Outwardly, the Moscatiellos lived the stereotypical 1950s middle-class, suburban lifestyle: a World War II and Korean War veteran father, a stay-at-home mother, and two children. The older child, a son, played hockey and "showed promise in leadership" in school before going on to Boston University.

This clichéd picture was, by Cynthia's recollection—and her brother's—a cruel façade and illusion, one hiding instead a dysfunctional family, broken and twisted by a mother's relentless contempt and scorn for her two children.

"My parents were Depression-era people. Both of them were damaged from their childhood. My mother especially," Cynthia recalled. Cecile Moscatiello had released her own demons on her children, especially Chris. "He was so smart, and he was very emotional. She was really hard on him, and Chris was really sensitive. And my mother just wrecked Chris, and he never recovered."

Looking back, Cynthia could be a little more detached. "It's interesting. You have two kids growing up in the same home, and one is destroyed, and the other one survives. He was destroyed. But I was able to let a lot more roll off than Chris was. I was the survivor."

Chris's destruction came in some of the usual forms in these situations. "He started drinking at a very early age. He had an alcohol problem in high school. He tried to kill himself and he ended up in a hospital. I can't remember which one. And of course, he had to undergo psychiatric counseling before they would let him out."

They went as a family to counseling, which was "also a disaster." Chris challenged his mother's treatment of him. "My mother looked at him and said something like, 'You're screwed up. You've always been screwed up. You'll always be screwed up.' What kind of mother does that? So cold and critical. She had no capability to be a mother at all."

That was the end of family counseling.

Maryann, the woman he would marry, told a similar story she'd heard from Chris. "He had a pretty hard childhood. A mom that was very abusive. I remember him telling me that his mom would say to him, 'You know, you're a bum. You're never going to be anything but a bum.' Who says that to her child?" Maryann was quiet for a moment. "But I think he believed her."

He drifted after high school, unfocused and directionless, leaving home and his parents behind. He let his hair grow past his shoulders and took to the road. Cynthia said, "He didn't go right to college. He hitchhiked across the country for a year; just wanted to see the country. And that's what he did. Took odd jobs here and there. He was gone for a year, and then he came home. And that was when he went to BU.

"He also went to Woodstock, and actually had a ticket. He went with friends, and he said the music was great, but it was 'wet and miserable.' He slept in the trunk of a car. He was a little more realistic about how it was."

At Boston University he majored in philosophy, driving a cab in Boston to pay his way through college, but there were signs of trouble. A friend said he was paying people to drive cars from Florida to Boston, cars that carried marijuana or cocaine. And then he dropped out of school completely just before graduation, apparently on a new path.

Maryann joined Cynthia in blaming Chris's mom for his descent onto a dark path that led him into alcoholism, suicide attempts, and, ultimately, drug trafficking and criminal conspiracies.

"I think he was stunted by his mom. I think that's one of the reasons he dropped out of college," Maryann said. "I mean, who drops out of college in your last year? Right before your last semester. That's weird. He never grew up inside.

"Anyway, I think that's pretty much why he ended up the way he ended up. He was so smart, but I think he wasn't able to use his intellect for good because he was so damaged. So making a quick buck was easier."

Making a quick buck in Charlestown, where he settled, meant crime. Neither his wife nor his sister was quite sure how or exactly when he took that step, but by the early 1980s, he'd connected with Michael Murray and was a trusted member of Joe Murray's crew.

Maryann Moscatiello first met Chris in 1984. They both lived in the same building in Charlestown and met through Maryann's roommate who'd invited Chris to a party at the women's apartment. The two grew closer, and by the time Moscatiello had been pulled into the fentanyl conspiracy, they were living together.

Maryann knew his history, about the marijuana and his 1983 bust. "Chris did, I think, six months on the pot thing. I met him after he was arrested with all that, and honestly, the pot was no big deal to me." She did think prison might have been one way Chris got deeper into crime. "Allenwood. That's where he was for the six months, and I swear to God, that's where people meet people."

But Chris didn't need to meet people in prison; he'd been convicted with Michael Murray, and those were all the contacts he needed for a career in drug trafficking.

Murray had been there for Maryann after the murder. "He came over. He changed the locks on the house after I went back there. I believe he paid for Chris's cremation. I couldn't... I was kind of a vegetable. So, it was like, 'yeah, all right, go ahead and do that.'" Chris had told her he trusted Michael; they were friends, and she could count on Mike. In the immediate aftermath of the murder, she did what Chris had told her.

Her view of Chris's benefactor changed over time.

After meeting with Assistant U.S. Attorney George Vien, she said, "He explained to me that Michael Murray had been working with the government. He was the one that told them about Chris, and they were about to arrest Chris. Yeah, I mean, wouldn't you think that maybe he's the one that could have killed him? Because he would have a lot to lose, too, you know, worrying maybe about what Chris knew about him."

Cynthia didn't share her own suspicions. "I didn't say anything to Maryann right away because Chris had told Maryann, 'If anything happens to me, if you need anything, you can trust Michael.' Yeah, there's some irony for you. And Michael was helping her out after Chris died. So, I didn't say anything until a few years later. Then I said, 'I think Michael killed Chris,' and she said, 'I do, too.' So she had come around to that at that point."

Chris's lonely death in the snow that night still haunts his sister, whose questions still hover around her, unanswered and probably unanswerable. "Chris trusted him. And then Michael ratted on him and killed him. I want to know if Chris knew before he died, or if Michael came up behind him and shot him, and Chris never knew. I actually wanted to drive up to Charlestown and face Michael and say, 'I know you killed him. I know you're not gonna tell me you killed him, but just so you know, I know you did it. And I'd really like to know if Chris knew that you betrayed him before he died.'"

She sat silently for a long moment. "Of course he would never tell me.

"But I know."

CHAPTER 58

United States Courthouse, Boston, November 30, 1993

So, who killed Chris Moscatiello? Feelings and suspicions aside, all the fingers pointed directly to the man with a motive, an opportunity, and a very, very poor alibi. Although Michael Murray's lawyer would later call the charge "nonsense," everybody else took it much more seriously.

Marquardt got the news a day or two later. "I'm told he was assassinated. This didn't come as a huge surprise. I was told about it when I was taking a shower down at the county jail. A fellow came by, he said, 'You have a partner in Boston?'

"Hmm, how'd you know?

"He laughed and says, 'Well, he's in the newspapers. He's dead.'"

Marquardt had seen something like this coming. "I think that organization got rid of him because they felt that he would be a future danger to them, the people that had financed him, and that he would be a serious risk when he realized that they had used treachery and set him up—that he might retaliate by supplying information that would allow the federal people to file further indictments. And they decided to terminate the problem and any association they might have with the fentanyl operation."

Moscatiello had occupied a very delicate position, placed there deliberately by Murray, who'd never interacted directly with either Marquardt or Martier. By keeping that layer of protection between him and the other fentanyl conspirators, Murray left only one person in a position to testify against him. Killing Chris permanently severed that connection.

That's what Marquardt thought. "Putting him out of the way because he was the obvious link. Martier, in fact, did not talk to these people, but Chris did. Chris knew them. I don't know about Bulger, but he certainly would've been linked to Murray," he said.

Another problem grew from Charlestown's infamous "Code of Silence" and the townies' almost pathological loathing for "rats." The *Charlestown Patriot-Bridge* described the code: "Charlestown was famous for generations for what came to be known as the code of silence. Ten people could witness a homicide here only to be questioned by police with everyone who witnessed the murder to a person saying they had seen nothing, knew nothing about it (sic) and had nothing whatsoever to say about it."

Maryann knew about Charlestown and its Code. "You know everybody that was born and raised in Charlestown, they never talk about each other. No ratting. I remember with everything that hit the papers and the news, a lot came out about Mike later about him being an informant. I'm sure that probably surprised a lot of people in Charlestown because he's one of their own. Back then, who was he? I mean, I call it 'an informant.' But the Charlestown people would call it a 'rat.'"

Alive and in jail, Chris would find out that he was facing thirty or more years in prison because Murray had introduced him to an undercover DEA agent to save his own skin in a marijuana case. Chris would know with certainty that Murray had "used treachery and set him up." Alive, Chris would know that Murray had ratted, had broken the Code. If the DEA busted Chris alive and talking, everybody in Charlestown would know it, too.

And alive, with both Marquardt and Martier already cooperating with DEA, he would have only one person to "roll up" on; he'd have to give up the man he called his best friend.

It got worse. The agents interviewing Marquardt and Martier in Wichita and Pittsburgh learned that Murray's turnover of the thirty-seven pounds of 3-methylfentanyl had been an elaborate charade, cooked up by Murray with Moscatiello's willing, even eager assistance.

Martier, testifying about the scam later, said, "Murray, who was still under house arrest, asked Moscatiello if he could have it. It was his story that he was going to turn it over to the DEA. He was facing ten years for this marijuana thing. And he convinced Chris somehow this was helping him out. And Chris asked me, "can I give it to him?' And I said that's not the greatest idea in the world, but I knew there was nothing in the world I could do to stop him. So, I said, go ahead.

"I learned later that he took these fifteen grams and cut them into fifteen kilos and gave them to Murray, and Murray turned them over to the Boston DEA.

"It turned out that Murray was setting us up. He was buying his way out of the drug bust by setting us up on the fentanyl thing."

Marquardt heard about it later, calling it "the stupidest thing I ever heard," with the predictable result. He also wondered why Martier said he only gave Moscatiello fifteen grams of 3-methyfentanyl, "Since I gave Joe thirty. Both of them, playing games with the DEA, which doesn't generally play games," he said, shaking his head.

Ironically, the "stupidest" scheme actually worked. The DEA got the fifteen kilos through Murray but couldn't connect them to anyone else except through Moscatiello, who was dead. Jerry Graves said, "Michael Murray was never linked—formally, that is—to the fentanyl investigation. His sole linkage was through Moscatiello's activities, and his conversations with Moscatiello about those activities. He had knowledge of it, based upon those [recorded] conversations. Through these conversations, and through us introducing the undercover agent, Michael Murray knew that at some point that Moscatiello could potentially be arrested. Then the evaluation would be on Murray's survival; Moscatiello could be a particular problem to a lot of people, so that made him an ideal subject to be eliminated."

The detectives didn't have any physical evidence linking Murray to the scene, although Graves noticed another interesting coincidence. "The footprints leading up to Moscatiello's body were made by a particular sneaker. The Saucony brand of sneakers I happen to know Michael Murray wore all the time. But the crime scene was badly muddied, and it was polluted with a lot of extraneous footprints. It could have been made by anyone; it wasn't preserved. Also, the fact that it was snow which melts, you can't do your traditional evidence collection on snowy surfaces."

On December 1, the *Boston Globe* reported on an unusual hearing in federal court, where Michael Murray sought to have his agreement with the government enforced, and the potential sentence in his marijuana case reduced from twenty years to five.

"Defense attorney Daniel J. O'Connell had called Vien as a witness in an effort to prove that the government was reneging on the deal, despite extensive cooperation," the *Globe* reported, and Assistant U.S. Attorney Vien, testifying under oath, made it clear that he, too, considered Murray a suspect. Vien said Murray failed to live up to his end of a November 1992 agreement with the government, which called for him to cooperate fully, plead guilty to marijuana charges, and serve less than five years in prison.

"I don't know who killed Mr. Moscatiello. I think it's very suspicious of Mr. Murray's involvement in it, and I can't prove he killed him. I think he killed him," Vien testified, adding, "It was implicit [in the agreement] he wouldn't kill anyone."

Vien's testimony also called attention to Murray's extremely shaky alibi for his whereabouts at the time of the killing. Murray admitted that he'd been "with Moscatiello early on the day he was murdered," but told law enforcement he was "with [Robert] Smith at the time of the murder."

The Boston press described Robert "Bobby" Smith as a "notorious gangster," "notorious reputed member of the Irish mob," and "head of underworld crime in Charlestown." Smith was, the papers said, "to Charlestown what James (Whitey) Bulger is to South Boston." One news story said, "It is widely believed, law enforcement sources say, that Bobby Smith gets a cut of everything illicit in Charlestown. And people who cross Smith have the curious habit of turning up dead."

Barely a month before, Vien had charged Smith and twenty-four others in a conspiracy to distribute "angel dust and cocaine." Michael Murray's alibi for Moscatiello's murder hinged on a close associate of his late brother Joe and the suspect in several unsolved Charlestown murders.

Jerry Graves attended the hearing. "George Vien, who was prosecuting the marijuana case on the Murray brothers, did not believe that he fully cooperated. And George had to take the stand in Boston Federal Courthouse as a witness, and was asked point-blank the same question. George was certainly privy to far more information regarding Murray and the family, and the criminal activity that they were involved in, and the other aspects of debriefings from other individuals connected to the case, than I was. And he concluded, and he stated it on the stand, he believed Michael Murray shot Moscatiello, and I kind of second that."

Ultimately, U.S. District Judge William G. Young had to decide whether Murray had lived up to his November 1992 agreement to fully cooperate with DEA. There was no doubt that Murray's information, his introduction of DEA

Agent German Blanco to Moscatiello, and his turnover of the 30-plus pounds of heavily diluted but very lethal 3-methylfentanyl had been invaluable in getting the DEA all the way to Martier, Marquardt, and the Kansas labs.

There was also no question that when he'd been asked to provide similar information and cooperation against Bulger, Bobby Smith, and others involved in Boston crime, Murray had fallen back on the Code of Silence, refusing to answer questions or testify before a Federal grand jury.

So, on April 25, 1994, Judge Young gave Michael Murray the bad news. Before passing sentence, the judge told the court that "Murray has not performed the agreement he sought to strike with the government. His actions have been, throughout, calculated entirely by his own self-interest."

Murray breached the Code, betrayed his fellow townie Chris Moscatiello, and attempted to use thirty-seven pounds of 3-methylfentanyl as his "Get Out of Jail Free" Card.

It all went for nothing. Judge Young ordered him to serve 30 years and pay a $10 million fine.

Michael Murray was never charged for Moscatiello's murder. Chris Moscatiello's best friend was released from federal prison on October 30, 2015, after serving approximately twenty-one years.

Moscatiello's murder is still considered open and unsolved.

CHAPTER 59

Moscatiello's murder didn't end the DEA's investigation. Even in Boston, agents continued to follow the leads that Marquardt and Martier were providing. They could see, however, that this organization had been utterly destroyed, and all that remained was tidying up some of the rubble. Although none of the top three people in the conspiracy would be going to trial, the case agents in Wichita, Pittsburgh, and Boston had to assume that someone would ask for a jury. The evidence gathering went on, now mostly corroborating the lengthy statements made by Marquardt and Martier.

The day after his arrest, Marquardt made his initial appearance before a federal magistrate, normally a pro forma event to arrange for an attorney and address the issue of bail for the defendant.

Not this time. Asked how he pleaded, guilty or not guilty, Marquardt said, "Guilty."

The judge told him he couldn't plead guilty at the initial appearance, and Marquardt said, "Well, why did you ask me then?"

Barry Jamison, in the courtroom with his agents, remembered the event. "George said that he wanted to plead guilty, and the judge said, 'Well, you can't plead guilty. These are very serious charges. You could possibly be facing the death penalty.'

"George says, 'Well, I want to represent myself.' And the judge says, 'You can't do that, I've got to appoint you an attorney.'

"So, they went through the whole process of how much money George had and whether he could afford a lawyer.

"Finally, the judge ruled that George didn't have the money to pay for a lawyer and appointed a lawyer for him right then and there," Jamison said, but Marquardt wasn't having it, telling the judge, "'I don't want a lawyer.'

"The judge looked at George and said, 'Mr. Marquardt, I'm tired of hearing this. You sit there and you be quiet, or I'll have the marshals remove you from this courtroom. I don't want to hear another word from you.'

"And the judge went on with the proceedings. And all of a sudden, George, big 350-pound man, is sitting there raising his hand over his head going, 'Ooh, ooh, ooh,' in federal court. And the judge is doing his best to ignore him.

"Finally, the judge looks over and says, 'What is it?' And George says, 'Judge, I just want to know, is this man here going to represent me? Is he going to be my lawyer and he's going to do what I want him to do?'

"The judge says, 'Yes, Mr. Marquardt, he's your lawyer. He's going to do what you want him to.'

"George says, 'I'm going to be able to tell him what to do and he's going to listen to me, right?'

"And the judge says, 'Right.' And George looks at his lawyer and goes, 'You're fired.'

"And the judge just about lost it," Jamison said, still laughing about it thirty years later. Finding him to be a flight risk and a danger to the community, the judge set no bail and sent Marquardt back to the Sedgewick County Jail.

When he wasn't in jail, Marquardt was at the DEA offices, making statements and placing recorded phone calls. With Martier incriminated on tape and also in custody, Derby turned to the others in the case. Marquardt couldn't "roll up," providing information about people above him on the ladder; he was at the top of this one. He could implicate others, and Benito Febre was first up.

Febre was supposed to receive the fentanyl in the three videocassettes and on February 4th, Martier, also now cooperating in Pittsburgh, phoned Febre and told him the package had been mailed. In the recorded call, Febre enthusiastically indicated he was ready to get it, saying he was heading up to New York, and complaining that the previous shipment had been too weak.

Martier told him that "this is better than the last time, it'll be OK."

With Febre on record for receiving fentanyl previously and anticipating more that day, the DEA in Los Angeles made up a "sham package" that looked like fentanyl and contained an electronic tracking device and delivered it to an address Febre had provided in Los Angeles on the evening of February 4th. On the following morning, Febre arrived at the address and collected the package. Agents arrested him on the spot.

Because he was primarily connected to Joe Martier, the government opted to indict Febre for conspiracy in Pittsburgh, and it was there, on April 7, 1994, his jury trial began. Martier and Marquardt would be the prosecution's star witnesses and Febre's defense would attack Martier and Marquardt's credibility. Attorney W. Penn Hackney told the jurors, "They are facing life imprisonment. What can they do? They have been through this before. They have been arrested and incarcerated before. The only thing they can do is agree to help the government to convict somebody else." And since Moscatiello was dead, the only person they could testify against was Benny Febre.

Don't believe the liars, Hackney suggested.

Hackney did the best he could with a bad hand, thoroughly challenging both Martier and Marquardt, who was brought to Pittsburgh to testify, on their honesty and their memory. Marquardt, as usual, wasn't shy about admitting all of his past illegal activities, telling the jury under oath, "I'm a drug manufacturer of the clandestine sort."

Hackney, probably recognizing that he had a losing case, concentrated on keeping out any evidence linking Febre to the first deadly weekend in New York City in February 1991. Jack Fasanello and DEA chemists from the Special Testing and Research Laboratory could testify that the fentanyl in those Tango & Cash packets had come from the same lab that manufactured the fentanyl destined for Febre and found in Sam Houston's house. But the government ultimately didn't try to make that connection.

The jury went out on April 20th, coming back with a guilty verdict after an hour and a half of deliberation that included lunch. On June 15th, Febre received a twenty-two-year sentence. Assistant U.S. Attorney Mark Rush said, "in his circumstances, a life sentence because he died in federal custody."

Marquardt also sank his old friend Keith Hollenbeak. He provided information linking him to both the fentanyl manufacturing and Hollenbeak's production of the methaqualone. He also said he got chemicals for PrairieLab from the Halliburton stockroom, and that Hollenbeak used Halliburton's mass spectrometer to analyze samples of fentanyl from each batch before they were shipped. Charged with one count of conspiring to distribute fentanyl, Hollenbeak pleaded guilty. He was released from federal custody in January 1996.

The DEA arrested Sam Houston after finding the fentanyl-laden videocassettes at Houston's house. Marquardt testified that he had supervised Houston as he packed those cassettes, making sure he didn't leave any fingerprints. But Houston's fingerprints were all over the rest of the case; he'd rented PrairieLab, purchased chemicals, and made a delivery of fentanyl to Martier in Pittsburgh.

Released on bail before his November trial date, Houston changed his plea on October 8, admitting that he had possessed fentanyl with intent to distribute it. Like Marquardt, he was cooperating with the DEA's investigation, and it helped. He was rewarded on February 11, 1994, with a four-year sentence he would serve at Leavenworth's camp and then back home in Wichita.

That left Laurence Blakeslee, Marquardt's old acquaintance from Leavenworth who'd gotten a shipment of fentanyl that almost killed him and did kill his roommate. With the DEA listening, Marquardt called Blakeslee in California, where he clearly hadn't been reading the newspapers. Yes, he would like to get some more fentanyl and some methamphetamine, too. Blakeslee flew out to Wichita on October 18. Troy Derby, working undercover, met him at the Sands Motel where Martier stayed when he was in town, showing him a sample of methamphetamine, and then arrested the Californian.

Blakeslee pleaded guilty in April 1994 to possessing two ounces of fentanyl with intent to distribute and was sentenced to five years on June 22, 1994. He died a year later in prison.

* * *

On March 23, 1993, Marquardt made his first appearance before U.S. District Court Judge Patrick Kelly in Wichita. It was another memorable day in court, Marquardt telling the judge he understood he was facing many years in prison but he "did not intend to fight the case." He was going to plead guilty and said he didn't need an attorney. Judge Kelly told him he would be appointing one for him anyway and asked about Marquardt's employment and sources of income.

THE COURT: What is your occupation, sir?

DEFENDANT MARQUARDT: Drug manufacturing.

THE COURT: What kind of drug manufacturing?

DEFENDANT MARQUARDT: Clandestine.

THE COURT: Sir?

DEFENDANT MARQUARDT: Clandestine… I don't know that I've had an occupation outside of being a career drug manufacturer.

A stunned Judge Kelly, who said later he'd never heard anything like that from a defendant before, didn't accept the offered guilty plea but said he'd consider it later in the same way every other criminal case was handled.

On August 4th, Marquardt finally got his chance to plead guilty, telling the judge again that he'd done everything the government alleged in its indictment, and he'd do it again if he got a chance. Judge Kelly found him guilty and would see him again on December 3, 1993, for sentencing.

Taking into account Marquardt's cooperation against Houston, Hollenbeak, Blakeslee, and Febre, the judge gave him 300 months or 25 years—pausing before bringing the final gavel down.

Barry Jamison made it to this hearing, too, another entertaining one. "And all of a sudden the judge stopped, and he looked at George and he says, 'Mr. Marquardt, while you're in prison, if you got access to chemistry books or magazines or chemistry periodicals, would you in any way be tempted to do something illegal or nefarious?'

"And George, without missing a beat, immediately took his big hand and he rapped like three times on the table. Well, there's a microphone on the table to record everything, and as George is banging his hand on the table, it's reverberating through the whole courtroom. And he lifts his hands and looks at the judge and goes, 'Hello. Hello. Like, that's what I do.'

"And the judge put his hands up and went, 'Thank you, Mr. Marquardt. Thank you. And I hereby order that the Bureau of Prisons prohibit Mr. Marquardt from ever being alone in the prison library or receiving any periodicals or chemistry books during his time of imprisonment,'" Jamison laughed. "Once again, George was stealing the show at another court hearing."

This appearance effectively ended the fentanyl conspiracy, and though he wasn't prepared to go that far just yet, Marquardt's criminal career. The 25-year sentence meant he'd be locked up until at least 2015, when he would be 69 years old. He'd be on ten years of supervised release after he got out, and Judge Kelly ordered that he be barred from possessing any of his beloved analytical instruments or doing any chemistry or chemical analysis during that period.

"My suggestion is that during the interim, he take care to learn a new vocation," the judge said. "Maybe bookkeeping."

* * *

That left only one loose end (besides the unsolved murder of Chris Moscatiello). And it bothers the agents who worked on the case to this day. "Where's the money? We never found it," one said.

In their search of Moscatiello's house, the agents found a paper, "a back of the envelope calculation," that Moscatiello had written out, reckoning that he made $6,000 "on each death of a person. Just subdivided the number of deaths that he knew of publicly and divided it by the amount of money that he had cleared, minus expenses, of course," Jerry Graves said. "I thought that was pretty callous. Cold."

That money is still missing. Maybe its secret died with Moscatiello. Jerry Graves said, "We know he made millions of dollars in cash on other deals and other marijuana ventures along with Murray."

Based on debriefings of Michael Murray and others, DEA believes the money is "buried on his various pieces of property that he controlled." Graves said, "Somewhere in Massachusetts on some of these properties, somebody's going to find millions of dollars of cash, and probably in PVC pipes, which was the preferred method of hiding the money, buried on their property somewhere."

Marquardt heard about the $6,000 calculation and did one of his own, based on his smaller cut, the DEA's estimate of the number of addict deaths it attributed to fentanyl for the Febre trial, and his own estimate. "$1,300 per dead junkie," he said.

We do know what happened to Marquardt's money; he spent all of it. Some of it went to the purchase of a plot of land. There are buildings and a barn, and the land is good for grazing or just for lying on with a dog and gazing up at the stars. The rest of the money went for the purchase of equipment, all carefully hidden away. And he bought enough glassware, chemicals, and laboratory supplies, everything he needed to get back in business when or if he ever got out of prison.

The DEA never found the hidden lab. It's somewhere on the prairie, its ownership concealed, protected, he claimed, by booby traps, a web of documents, and an identity he never shared with anyone.

Is it still out there? When he was released from prison in May 2015, he vanished for two days to check on it before reporting to his halfway house in Topeka.

He returned, pronouncing himself satisfied.

AFTERWORD

And just like that, it was all over. On February 3, 1993, fentanyl all but vanished from American streets. Addiction and overdoses from other drugs continued, of course, but across the country, medical examiners and emergency rooms reported declining numbers of fentanyl incidents.

"This is unheard of in drug enforcement," a retired agent said. "The way it always works is you bust one group and shut off that line and another group steps right up with their line. It *never* just ends."

Not this time. Marquardt's arrest closed the fentanyl pipeline at the source and stopped the killing. And so things stayed for almost twelve years. The DEA reported no fentanyl lab seizures anywhere in the United States between 1993 and December 4, 2000, when San Bernadino County Sheriff's detectives raided a house in Big Bear, California, arresting Jason Williamson, 32.

Finding the marijuana plants they expected, they also got a surprise, a working laboratory and 8.8 pounds of heavily diluted fentanyl powder. They also found sixteen ounces of liquid fentanyl: 87 percent pure. Although Williamson had apparently succeeded in making fentanyl on his first try, detectives thought they'd got lucky and stumbled onto his lab before any of his product reached the street.

Rookie Jason Williamson had none of Marquardt's background or talent. Apart from "a couple of college chemistry classes," he had no training or experience. He lacked the knowledge necessary to set up or run a lab or to do any of the reactions needed to produce the fentanyl that utterly defeated Bobby Rubino and Joe Martier back in 1990.

Further, like other would-be fentanyl makers before him, Williamson had no connections to get his product into the marketplace, an insurmountable and ultimately fatal problem for Michael Hovey. By all available precedent, Williamson never should have reached first base.

But at the dawn of the twenty-first century, this amateur had two big advantages over his predecessors. He had Marquardt's process, a quicker, safer, easier route to fentanyl that even a novice like Williamson could manage. He got it from his game-changing second big edge, a revolutionary new development that truly transformed fentanyl into the "nation wrecking," "Darth Vader shit" that Marquardt ominously forecast years before and that we are seeing today.

Jason Williamson had the Internet.

As this is written 2024, there are more than 1.09 billion websites on the World Wide Web, with 250,000 added every day.

In 2000, there were just over 17 million. When Marquardt went to prison in 1993, there were about a dozen.

In 2000, the Internet gave Williamson access to websites that described in meticulous detail exactly how to synthesize fentanyl. Other sites gave him helpful "instructions on how to cut the fentanyl to reduce its purity," avoiding the problem of dead junkies that Marquardt warned his co-conspirators about. But the Internet's gifts were only beginning.

Marquardt and other clandestine chemists obsessed on safely obtaining precursors. He knew which ones the DEA tracked and how to make them from less regulated chemicals. That process, while carrying much lower risks, also took time, energy, and talent.

In 2000, the Internet provided. Now, Williamson and other chemists could go online to purchase precursors from chemical companies overseas in places the DEA couldn't monitor. China has over 25,000 chemical companies and India, more than 80,000, just to name two countries. If the World Wide Web didn't have it, someone on the "Dark Web," would, and those people would sell precursors—or even fentanyl itself—to you even knowing exactly what you planned to make with them.

And the Internet proved equally helpful in solving Williamson's final problem. Like Michael Hovey, Williamson didn't have any customers. Unlike Marquardt, who "had to go to prison to meet gangsters," he could avoid that whole unpleasant experience by simply going online. As one newspaper story said, "Investigators suspect Williamson used Internet chat rooms to contact people looking to buy the drug."

So, fentanyl was back, and supercharged by the Internet, agencies like the DEA and OBN might have expected fentanyl labs to spring up all over America. This didn't happen, and the California lab would be one of the last found in the United States. The reason for that also comes back to Jason Williamson's case, which didn't have a happy ending for the clandestine chemist. Convicted in federal court in Riverside, California, he spent the next nine years in federal prison, released in February 2010.

The message seemed plain; making fentanyl in the United States might be easier, but it still carried high risks, something Marquardt, seven years into a twenty-five-year sentence could have testified to.

Then, in the early 2000s, fentanyl became part of a broader "opioid crisis" that saw an abusive wave of narcotics like oxycodone, which was often overprescribed by medical professionals. The federal government also approved the use of fentanyl for chronic and acute pain, so drug companies produced timed-release delivery systems like transdermal patches and fentanyl lollipops to administer the drug.

Although addicts did abuse these medications, fentanyl deaths remained relatively low until 2005, when the Centers for Disease Control reported an increasing number attributed to illicitly manufactured "nonpharmaceutical fentanyl" (NPF).

Clandestine labs were back...

But not in the United States.

In May 2006, Mexican law enforcement authorities, with help from the DEA, seized a fentanyl laboratory in Toluca, Mexico, which the DEA believed was responsible for the increase in NPF deaths. Jack Fasanello visited this lab after the seizure, and witnessed the beginning of a trend to site laboratories outside the United States.

A DEA *2016 National Drug Threat Assessment* reported that although some shipments of fentanyl precursors had been seized entering the United States in 2015, "Nonpharmaceutical fentanyl is mainly produced in China and likely Mexico. Fentanyl-related compounds such as acetylfentanyl are also manufactured in China."

Today, labs in China, India, and Mexico account for virtually all of the fentanyl consumed in the United States, where it killed most of the 112,000 who died of drug overdoses in 2023.

Marquardt's lab in Kansas was the first to get significant quantities of fentanyl onto American streets. If present trends continue, it will be one of very few domestic clandestine laboratories to do so.

The Drug Enforcement Administration recognized Marquardt and fentanyl's significance. In March 1994, it profiled him with four other "major violators whose illegal activities have damaged American society," and who were stopped by the DEA in the agency's first twenty years. Twenty years later it named the Marquardt fentanyl investigation one of its top ten cases in the DEA's first forty years and commented that Marquardt was the "best and most dangerous clandestine chemist" the agency had ever encountered.

The agents who worked the case also received recognition for their work. In Wichita, Troy Derby received an award from the DEA and in October 1993, the Wichita Crime Commission presented him with its Law Enforcement Officer of the Year Award.

Detective Joanne Leoni received an award for outstanding contributions to law enforcement from the DEA, recognition of her pivotal role in the case.

In Boston, James O'Hara and Jerry Graves received DEA's highest honor, the Administrator's Award of Honor, their citation read in part:

Without S/A's O'Hara's and Graves' dedication to this investigation and their demonstrated professionalism the clandestine laboratories in Kansas would not have been identified and this laboratory could possibly still be producing the fentanyl that would be killing people in the eastern part of the United States.

Sometimes an agent may ask himself what impact did any particular case have on the overall availability of a specific drug. In this investigation, S/A's O'Hara and Graves can say that their investigation played a dramatic part in substantially eliminating the majority of Fentanyl (sic) being produced in the United States and their actions were responsible for saving the lives of a large number of individuals.

DEA Administrator Robert Bonner, commenting on the case, said, "Fentanyl is by far the most potent and deadly designer drug we've ever seen. It is responsible for a large number of overdose deaths in the last two years. We consider it the serial killer of the drug world... This is the only known organization manufacturing fentanyl in the

United States. These deadly laboratories are shut down and out of business."

After a two-year investigation, the DEA ended the nation's first fentanyl crisis and stopped the "goddamn killers" who started it.

Stopping the current crisis is going to be rather more difficult.

POSTLUDE

Sympathy for the Devil

"Knowledge cannot be pursued without morality."

~ **J. Robert Oppenheimer**

Mixed Feelings, Waukesha, Wisconsin, November 2016

I'm sitting with Squeak again, talking about crimes and punishment. Mostly his. It's usually just the two of us, but today we're joined by Patty Savasta, his probation officer. This pleasant and professional woman has the challenging task of keeping this career criminal and fiercest of individualists on a narrow and confined path for the ten years of his supervised release after two decades in federal prison.

She's told me in an earlier conversation that she's never had another client quite like him, and I said I believed it. "Unique," was the word we agreed upon.

They're talking about his supervised release and the possibility of having the term shortened, something Squeak desperately wants. Although he's never sought parole before, he's had short periods of court-ordered supervision going back fifty years. None bode well for this one.

Wisconsin put him on probation after his first equipment caper at the University of Wisconsin in 1965. He promptly violated that by ripping off the nuns at Alverno College, impersonating a federal official, and going to Virginia (a violation of his probation) and getting arrested on suspicion of espionage.

When OBN Agent Jimmy Birdsong helped him out after his theft conviction in 1975, he set up as many as thirty methamphetamine labs from Tulsa to Seattle to Minnesota, most while working with OBN as an informant and witness.

He mentioned this to Patty, saying "I functioned in that capacity for the Oklahoma Bureau of Narcotics. Half the time I was their technical consultant and the other half of the time I was running a drug lab someplace." (I didn't think this confession improved his argument much.)

"We were going to run a trick store, but somebody pulled the rug out from under that thing for some reason or another." (He got arrested in a meth lab in Beggs, Oklahoma; that was the reason, but I thought saying so wouldn't be much help either.)

Most recently, he'd been on supervised release after his federal gun case in Oklahoma in 1988-89. I knew, and I'm sure Patty did, too, that he'd handled that one by reporting a false residence to her counterpart in Oklahoma to keep that officer from finding out he was really running a fentanyl lab in Kansas.

It's not a track record that inspires a lot of confidence in his ability (or even his desire) to follow Patty's path.

Despite all this, she thinks it might be possible for him to apply to a federal judge in Milwaukee for an early discharge. He doesn't sound too hopeful, and again it comes down to the uncompromising philosophy that has guided him since he was a boy.

"We've discussed the possibility of when I might get off this and she has told me that early release from these things is usually dependent – I may be stating this improperly – on some kind of declaration of remorse or something like that," Squeak says.

"That's always good, when you say you're sorry," I said, though I knew his response before he spoke.

"That is not likely to happen," he says firmly.

Patty asks him to think about it and says she's got a survey for him. "I know you love filling out those eighty questions."

"Oh, they want to find out if I'm a psychopath again, huh?" he says.

"Yeah," she says.

"Can I just stipulate that I am?"

"Yes," she laughs. "No, that's the risk assessment."

"Yeah. I don't understand these things. I'll answer the questions honestly and this guy's going to wonder *Who the hell is this man?*"

"It comes up with a risk level based upon your answers, more of your thinking styles," Patty says.

"My thinking style is so strange." He flips through the survey. It looks lengthy, but he's had practice. He's been taking these tests, helping people figure out his thinking style—or hiding it from them—since he lit a school trash can on fire in fifth grade.

"I know. You grid off the charts when I get these results back," she said, standing for her goodbyes.

He *was* thinking about it, I could tell. Trying to figure out how to phrase his responses to appear abject and penitent without actually saying so. To give answers that will present Erik the benign, the non-threat, non-psychopath who deserves a reprieve from supervised release. Not Squeak, the scheming conman and lifelong thief and drug manufacturer, the utterly unrepentant killer of 126 or 300 or more. To lie, basically.

For the next eight and a half years, his life rests completely in the hands of others, those of the personable Patty, an anonymous reader of questionnaires, a federal judge in Milwaukee. The knowledge that these people have control over his destiny weighs heavily on him, more burdensome than even the cancer diagnosis.

He's dying. Keenly aware that he doesn't have eight and a half years, he wants more than anything, to die free.

Not free so that he can go back to the old life that got him here in the first place. "No," he says. "I'm too old to be running around doing that kind of thing. The game has changed too much," he told Patty, who nodded in agreement.

Living on the run from Patty, setting up one last clandestine laboratory, that's not happening now. Those days are gone, buried along with twenty-two years of his life behind steel doors and a razor-wire fence. He knows he can't go back. Maybe somewhat to his own surprise, for the first time in sixty years, he doesn't want to.

But he craves the freedom to make the choice, so he reads through a couple of the questions, thinking about the value of the reward and its cost.

I thought I could predict the outcome; he would, as always, "answer the questions honestly," and the faceless person scoring them would get the measure of the man she's never met and decide she knows him well enough to decree his fate and future at least until next year's survey.

As Patty said her goodbyes, it occurred to me that I had known Squeak in almost all of his various guises: career criminal, informant, teacher, clandestine chemist, defendant, federal prisoner, as an enemy and an ally, and now, collaborator on a book about his life and crimes. I knew him as well as anybody did, and still, his remark about the surveyor's question nags at me.

Who the hell is this man?

I've been trying to figure that out for four decades.

This meeting was an anniversary of sorts for us. It's been forty years to the month since we first met, when I walked out of an interview room at the Oklahoma Bureau of Narcotics, found Jimmy Birdsong, and told him he needed a new undercover because "I just sat in there for three hours and I didn't understand a freakin' word that guy said."

Then, he was Squeak, an impatient instructor, trying to teach clandestine chemistry to the undercover agent assigned to operate OBN's "trick store," and after Jimmy told him not to waste time trying to turn me into an organic chemist, we went back to it.

He turned out to be a pretty good teacher and taught me what I would have needed to know about clandestine chemistry if our store ever went operational. But I still didn't know him, and in our last meeting before he left for Leavenworth in 1978, I raised the issue.

"How can you do this?" I asked him. "You cook stuff that makes people addicts or keeps them addicted, wrecks their lives, maybe kills them." (And this was long before fentanyl.) How did he rationalize that? How did he live with himself?

"They pay their nickels, and they take their chances, just as I do," he said. He and drug users were "like two kids on a teeter-totter," an expression I heard him use on other occasions. Both climb onto the board knowing the risks and the rewards and it takes both of them to make the thing move. Neither would exist if the other didn't.

"I wouldn't have any reason to make these things if nobody was there to buy them. And they're going to buy it from someone, whether it's me or someone like Bob Harris."

Drug users made voluntary choices; nobody forced them to use his meth. And these are always informed decisions. "We're bombarded with messages about how bad these substances are. Everyone's eyes are wide open."

He quoted science fiction writer Robert Heinlein, expressed in *The Moon is a Harsh Mistress*, which he said summed up his approach to life.

"I will accept any rules that you feel necessary to your freedom. I am free, no matter what rules surround me. If I find them tolerable, I tolerate them; if I find them too

obnoxious, I break them. I am free because I know that I alone am morally responsible for everything I do."

Given my position, I couldn't really subscribe to this philosophy, or even approve of it, and said so, saying it put him in direct and apparently permanent conflict with me, OBN, and all of the law-abiding citizens of his country, the conformists he disdained. Society depended on its members following the laws and rules that benefited everyone and protected the weaker among us, I said.

He shrugged it off. "I'm an outlaw. I long ago set myself outside the law. I do not expect any of the law's protections and will not accept any of the law's benefits. I know the potential consequences of my choice. You represent the law and it's your job to impose those consequences on me. But first, you have to catch me, and that is the great game we play."

He and I were also two kids on a teeter-totter, he said, and neither of us could play if the other did not. "I wouldn't have it any other way."

I remember saying it sounded like a lonely life, but he said it was the one he'd chosen. Eyes wide open, he was prepared to accept whatever consequences people like me decided he had coming to him.

Now forty years later, after his fentanyl and all the fentanyl since, after all the misery and deaths, I remind him of our first meeting and the Heinlein quote, saying, "I am free because I know that I alone am morally responsible for everything I do."

"Amen," he said.

In his philosophy, he is morally responsible for his own decisions just as everyone else is responsible for theirs, and in truth, he adhered to his code uncompromisingly for his whole life. You and I enjoy the law's protections. For almost his entire criminal career, Squeak refused them. The Fifth Amendment to the Constitution protects our rights to due process of law, from coerced confessions and self-incrimination. The Sixth Amendment guarantees the rights of criminal defendants to a public and speedy trial, the right to an attorney (paid for by the government, if necessary) and the right to confront accusers. The Eighth Amendment prohibits excessive bail and cruel or unusual punishments.

In his view, as an outlaw, none of these applied to him. He had no right to remain silent, and once he started talking, the OBN and DEA agents couldn't shut him up. He refused to accept an attorney until a court forced one on him, and sometimes not even then. He never took a case to trial, pleading guilty at the first opportunity. He did this in 1993, even when the judge warned him that he could face the death penalty. He never asked for bail, didn't complain about his sentences, and never filed an appeal on any grounds in his whole life. Although others around him cooperated with the government hoping for a reduction in their sentences, he didn't ask for similar treatment from the court.

In the 1978 Beggs case, he told the sentencing judge, "If I did not believe in manufacturing drugs, I would not have manufactured them. I assume responsibility for my act, and I ask for no consideration from this court in sentencing." Fifteen years later in Wichita, facing a possible life sentence, he told that federal judge almost exactly the same thing.

Barry Jamison said, "George had a moral compass; it just didn't point due north. I'm not sure what direction it pointed in, but it wasn't anywhere close to north."

Larry Harris, who also enjoyed many hours of philosophical discussions with his cellmate, agreed, saying of the Squeak he knew, "You may not agree with his principles, but he had them and he was a man who lived up to them no matter what you thought about whether or not they were legal, illegal, Christian, whatever, he was an ethical man. He was an ethical man, a moral man."

Squeak wasn't going to apologize for those principles. "No, I'm not one bit sorry about what I did. And do I like it? No. There's many other things that I would've rather done, but I did them [for] independence, lack of formality, that's how I would sum it up. Why? Money's nice. One has to have money, but it's independence, the ability to be able to do what you want to do, and doing what you want to do comes with some risk.

"I have many regrets about what I've done for obvious reasons. But I had an unreasonable amount of fun. If I drop dead in five minutes, I'll go with a smile and laugh.

"I'm an outlaw," Squeak said. "There aren't many of us left."

* * *

Waukesha, Wisconsin, August 30, 2017

In Waukesha, Wisconsin, the end is here—and so is fentanyl. Hospitals give their dying patients all the narcotics they need… those controls and restrictions and regulations waived today for the big man fading now in the hospital bed. His breathing is ragged and other signs of failure are showing, but there's nothing of pain. Morphine, the age-old remedy, took care of that. And when even that wasn't enough—when the pain leaks past Morpheus' narcotic barrier—there's fentanyl, a hundred times more powerful to shepherd him to the Reaper's door.

His fentanyl took more than a few up to that door over the years, though no one will ever know the full toll. Even the most conservative estimates would make him the biggest mass murderer in American history. Jeffrey Dahmer, John Wayne Gacy, Ted Bundy, and Gary Ridgeway—all of them together have nothing on the man his friends call "Squeak." They'll call him that for a few more hours, although he can't hear them through fentanyl's ironic haze.

That man is gone now, killed by a lifetime of his own evil choices, by his decades of exposure to the carcinogens he used to brew poison for others. Left behind in my mixed feelings, part of me grieves.

Not for "Squeak," the clandestine chemist who brought fentanyl to America, the career criminal who showed the way for those now pouring this toxin into the country and killing tens of thousands every year. That man described himself and his fentanyl manufacturing, saying, "I believe this was an evil plot and [I am] an evil person."

Nothing in my memories of him or his lethal works disputes his judgment; Squeak was a wicked man and unrepentant career criminal who correctly called himself "a goddamn killer" and whose actions created death and destruction for people, families, and society. This should not—must not—be forgotten, and it cannot be forgiven. None of us should mourn for Squeak, the man I knew for forty years, who killed more people than any other criminal in American history, and wasn't "one bit sorry" about it.

I grieve instead for Erik, the boy I never met. Erik the "very brilliant boy with a keen insight into science" who impressed Robert Oppenheimer one night before Squeak had been fully formed. The boy whose incredible gift allowed him to make life-saving medications for AIDS patients and cancer-killing drugs as easily as Squeak would produce the fentanyl that killed so many.

His court-ordered psychiatrist who met Erik at the beginning saw the promise early, saying, "Apparently he is an extremely brilliant boy, if not a genius in his field, who with proper supervision and some direction could be an extremely useful individual." Erik never got that supervision and Squeak adamantly refused to take any direction for the rest of his life, though it cost him decades in prison.

Donald Williams, the *Wichita Eagle* reporter who interviewed Squeak after his 1993 arrest, also saw this wasted talent and wondered whether his "rebellious abilities" could still be harnessed for good. "Who knows but what he might synthesize some products of enough value to the world to outweigh the great harm that his products up to now have caused? And who knows? The government might name Marquardt its chemist laureate. The Nobel people might vote to honor him."

Classmate and friend Alan Stalbaum remembered seeing that potential as well, "People said, 'Well, he's either going to be a Nobel Prize laureate or he's going to wind up in prison,' and that's the truth."

We know how that turned out. Erik, the boy whose gift let him see into molecules and brew magic in a laboratory got lost somewhere along the way and became Squeak, the conscienceless killer and outlaw. It's too late now to reclaim those wasted years or return to the point on the path where Erik made the first wrong turn.

He knows that, saying, "I can't undo what's done. If I could start over at the beginning, would I do things the same way? No, I would not."

He pauses, maybe thinking about those crossroads, decades of choices and their consequences, all of it now behind him. "That isn't possible," he says, finally.

Too late to go back and no time left to change; he is who he is. At the end now, and cushioned by fentanyl, he sleeps. Who is it? It's most likely Squeak, cast backward again into a bedroom laboratory surrounded by hand-blown glassware, the quiet hum of a mass spectrometer, and the smells of chemicals reacting. If so, he's dreaming of molecular structures and the law once more defeated in the great game, played on other days on that long, dark, twisting path.

I hope not.

I hope it's Erik, a gangly kid, starting at the beginning, with a lifetime of choices still ahead, lying once more with his dog on the summer grass of the Great Plains, gazing up and marveling through a child's eyes at the universe of stars filling the prairie sky.

.

For More News About John Madinger,
Signup For Our Newsletter:

http://wbp.bz/newsletter

Word-of-mouth is critical to an author's long-term success. If you appreciated this book please leave a review on the Amazon sales page:

http://wbp.bz/lethaldoses

Also Available from John Madinger and WildBlue Press

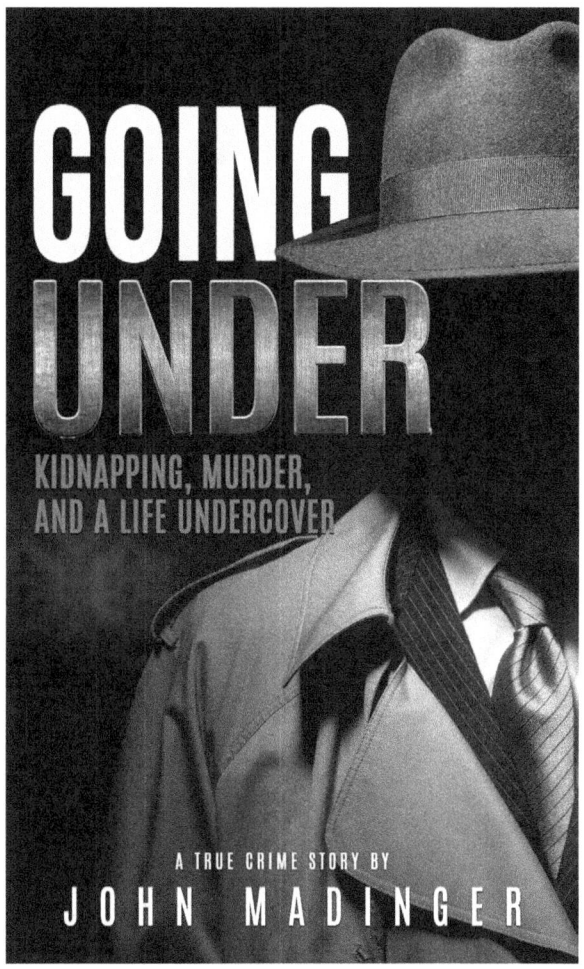

http://wbp.bz/goingunder

2023 Silver Falchion Award Finalist for Best Nonfiction

2022 First-place Winner of Public Safety Writers Association's Writing Competition for Nonfiction

www.ingramcontent.com/pod-product-compliance
Lightning Source LLC
Chambersburg PA
CBHW061131120626
46546CB00005B/1741